Building Power in Reading

Building Power in Reading

HENRY I. CHRIST

Dedicated to serving

AMSCO

our nation's youth

Amsco School Publications, Inc.
315 Hudson Street/New York, N.Y. 10013

Henry I. Christ has had a long and distinguished career as writer, editor, teacher, and supervisor. A specialist in language, literature, and composition, he has written more than a hundred textbooks in the field of English, including many published by Amsco. For nearly ten years, he was the editor of the teachers' magazine *High Points*. He has been active in professional organizations and has held office at the local, state, and national levels. A frequent speaker at English conventions and workshops throughout the United States, he has also lectured on educational television and participated in curriculum development and evaluation.

Marie E. Christ has worked with Henry I. Christ as a partner throughout his writing career. She has provided many practical suggestions and usable materials. As always, her good judgment, common sense, and hard work played a major role in the development and preparation of this book.

When ordering this book, please specify:
either **R 549 W** or Building Power in Reading

ISBN 0-87720-773-9

TO THE STUDENT

Reading is to the mind what exercise
is to the body.

Joseph Addison

A tennis player must learn many skills. There are the all-important strokes: the forehand, the backhand, the overhand, the volley, the dropshot, and many more. There is tennis strategy: knowing what kind of stroke to use in a given situation and determining where to hit the ball. Like tennis, reading is a complex of many skills.

Even professional tennis players seek help in solving nagging problems. "I think I'm letting my racket drop too far when I stroke crosscourt." The tennis coach then points out specific helps. *Building Power in Reading* is like the coach used by an athlete. It reviews the various skills and strengthens those that may be weak. Then it provides opportunities for putting all the skills together.

Building Power in Reading begins with a discussion of the reading process, including the kinds of skills needed, resources, attitudes, and reading speeds. Section 2 provides specific helps in building vocabulary through a knowledge of word elements. Section 3 continues the work on vocabulary, a crucial element in reading. This section helps you guess the meanings of unfamiliar words by examining the context, the word's surroundings.

The next sections zero in on specific reading skills, including getting the main idea, finding the best title, and drawing inferences, or conclusions. The author's role in writing is analyzed in a special section.

A bread-and-butter section familiarizes you with a common reading challenge: reading for information. It discusses the parts of a book, library resources, and other aids to better reading.

Since thinking is an important element in reading comprehension, a section analyzes various obstacles to understanding. It also offers practice in correcting confused thinking.

The concluding section of Part I considers the various literary types you will meet in school and afterward. What, for example, is the difference between fiction and nonfiction? How does an essay differ from an article? Does an autobiography present a true and complete picture of a person's life? These are questions you may have wondered about. The discussion will satisfy your curiosity.

After working with the sections in Part I, you will have the opportunity to review and test what you have learned. Part II is a set of comprehensive review-tests of the key ideas in Part I. It may serve as a review of materials covered. You may also use it as a diagnostic test to discover what your areas of weakness may be. Handy cross-references will help you find the pages you need. Part III contains four practice tests, each containing a number of reading passages that will interest and challenge you.

Building Power in Reading has been designed to improve your reading, increase your reading pleasure, and provide interesting reading materials along the way.

Henry I. Christ

CONTENTS

PART I

Review of Reading Skills

PART II

Multiple-Choice Tests

PART III

Reading Practice Tests

PART I

Review of Reading Skills

1.   Reading Process

What   sses are involved? If you think
about reading   between the printed page and
a reader is noth   k can make you amused, sad,
angry, cheerful,   ding, you don't need a TV
screen, a radio, or   oes off, you can still read—
by sunlight, flashlig.   from civilization, you can
read. The reading sk   t of us take for granted
and tend to underuse.

In this section, you w   reading and analyze
ways in which you can imp.   r elements: reader,
setting, and material. Intera   a suitable setting
makes for successful reading

You, the reader, are of course   important ingredient in the reading
process. You are growing, changing,   ver the same person in two different situations. You are influenced by a great many factors, some of which are outside your
control. Surprisingly, though, you can control a great many elements and thus
improve your reading.

Attitudes and Expectations

If you enter a sport with the expectation of success, you will do better than
a pessimistic athlete of approximately equal skill. In this respect, reading is like
tennis, golf, baseball, or any other sport. Your attitude toward the task is a major
ingredient. If your attitude is positive and your expectations high, you have turned
an important corner. Optimism depends to a degree upon past success, but failure
needn't be a cause for defeatism. Thomas Edison tried hundreds of filaments for
his electric light bulb before he found the one that worked.

Concentration

You are surrounded by distractions: traffic outside, radio and television inside, conversations going on around you. The best solution is to find a quiet place, if possible. The local library, a park bench, a corner of the house—search for a good setting. If you must read with distractions, learn to shut them out. Some people learn to concentrate in the heart of a big city with noisy air conditioning, fire engines, shrieking ambulances, power machinery, honking horns, and nearby airfields conspiring against them. The modern world provides many distractions. A good reader learns to live with them and shut them out.

Flexibility

Not all reading material is the same. The levels of difficulty vary. Learn to appraise your reading material and adjust your speed to the selection. Decide on your purpose. Are you reading for information, relaxation, entertainment? See also pages 4–7.

Resources

Certain types of reading material call for additional help. If you are reading a history book and come upon the name of John C. Fremont, you may be curious to learn more about this colorful explorer. See pages 160–164 for suggested reference sources. Self-enrichment is an important part of intellectual growth.

One resource must be singled out for special mention. A handy desk dictionary helps you fill gaps in your reading, check the spelling of words you're uncertain about, and look up the meanings of key words when context doesn't help. Suppose you have just received a newsy letter from an old friend. Along with other news, your friend makes this comment: ''Jud was unusually loquacious at the party.'' Though context is a great help in many situations (pages 27–33), here is one occasion when the dictionary is your best ally. If you look up *loquacious*, you'll find that Jud was *talkative*. (See pages 164–166.)

For more effective reading, get the dictionary habit.

Reading Skills

You have been developing reading skills since your very early years. You learned that certain words refer to actual objects in the real world. When young Helen Keller, blind and hearing-impaired, discovered that there was a way to refer to actual objects, she and her teacher rejoiced. Though the ''words'' were touch signals, they acted like words to a sighted person. But there is more to communication than a knowledge of words.

A traveler in France can often get by with a French-English dictionary. He or she can carry on with ample use of gestures. But such communication is on the most elementary level. Getting meaning is not just decoding words.

There are many skills involved in reading—for example, getting the main idea, locating details, and making inferences. In the same way, there are many skills in sports. In tennis, for example, the top players excel in serving, volleying, drop shotting, and hitting cross court. Every now and then, however, they take stock of their skills to make sure that one phase is not slipping.

Taking stock in reading is a good idea, too. This book has been designed for that purpose. Sections 3–17 will review your skills, give added practice with those you feel confident in, and introduce you to some new skills that help in the reading process.

Practice 1: Reviewing What You Have Read

Take this practice reading test to check your understanding of the text thus far. Base your answers only on the text. Write the letter of the alternative that best completes each statement.

1. A major advantage of reading as opposed to television is that it
   (*a*) has generally better material (*b*) is available in different kinds of situations (*c*) is easier on the eyes (*d*) can be shared with others.   1. _____

2. Which of the following is NOT listed as one of the three major ingredients of reading?

   (*a*) reader   (*b*) setting
   (*c*) quality of printing   (*d*) material   2. _____

3. Which of the following is mentioned as a major obstacle to success in reading?

   (*a*) poor eyesight   (*b*) ill health
   (*c*) pessimism   (*d*) laziness   3. _____

4. All the following are mentioned as distractions in the city EXCEPT
   (*a*) ambulances (*b*) auto horns (*c*) fire engines (*d*) garbage trucks.   4. _____

5. Which is a reasonable conclusion to draw from the comments in this chapter?

   (*a*) Reading skills can be learned.
   (*b*) It's impossible to concentrate in the average home.
   (*c*) If at first you don't succeed, drop the reading challenge.
   (*d*) For communicating, gestures are better than reading.   5. _____

The Setting

The importance of setting has already been mentioned in the section on concentration. Some settings seem to lend themselves to concentration. If you have a favorite spot for reading, take advantage of the possibilities. You will probably find challenging material easier to read in certain spots than in others. You will do some of your reading and probably take all your tests in school. Learn to give reading your complete attention.

One of the deadliest of all distractions is the radio or television. A common mistake is trying to do homework while also listening to a blaring loudspeaker. If the work requires concentration, set the volume as low as possible. A quiet room in the corner of your house or apartment is preferable to a living-room desk near family members listening to the radio or watching TV.

Besides quiet, another important factor is lighting. A glaring page can cause headache, fatigue, and eyestrain. Too little light can also interfere with concentration. If possible, have the light behind, over your shoulder, or in any other position that removes glare.

When strain is absent, reading can be fun (pages 6–7).

The Material

When you face the printed page, decide on the context (pages 27–33) and the purpose of your reading. Is the material a section of a biology text, a chapter of a modern novel, a short detective story? Each requires a different approach. Are you reading for fun or for study?

Reading Speeds

Different materials call for different reading speeds. You should read this section on the reading process somewhat more carefully than you would the report of a football game. It presents a medium challenge: more demanding than a sports story, less demanding than an explanation of the optics used in telescopes. Adjust your reading speed to the reading selection.

Skimming

At times, you will need to look hastily at a page in search of needed information. This skill, called *skimming*, helps you to find a word in a dictionary, a telephone number in the phone book, or a special want ad in the classified section of a newspaper. In a preceding paragraph, you were referred to pages 27–33 in this book. To find the meaning of *context*, skim the pages till you find the definition.

Practice 2: Comparing Reading Speeds

Read the following three selections. Then decide which selection is least difficult, suggesting a faster reading speed. Which is next in order of difficulty? Which seems most difficult?

A

Ben and Phil were talking about their favorite subject—food and the pleasures of eating.

"Do you like eggs?" asked Phil.

"I love them," replied Ben.

"How many do you think you could eat on an empty stomach?" asked Phil.

"Only one."

"Only one!" exclaimed Phil. "Don't you like them? I thought you said you love them."

"I do, but after I eat the first one, my stomach isn't empty."

B

What is important, then, is not that the critic should possess a correct abstract definition of beauty for the intellect, but a certain kind of temperament, the power of being deeply moved by the presence of beautiful objects. He will remember always that beauty exists in many forms. To him all periods, types, schools of taste, are in themselves equal. In all ages there have been some excellent workmen, and some excellent work done. The question he asks is always—In whom did the stir, the genius, the sentiment of the period find itself? Who was the receptacle of its refinement, its elevation, its taste? "The ages are all equal," says William Blake, "but genius is always above its age."

C

People sometimes ask, "Why vote? What good is one vote anyway?" Throughout history, single votes have often made a difference. In 1649, one vote cost Charles I of England his head. In 1845, one vote brought Texas into the Union. In 1868, one vote saved President Andrew Johnson from being impeached. In 1876, one vote gave Rutherford B. Hayes the Presidency of the United States. Unluckily for the world, in 1923 one vote gave Adolf Hitler leadership of the Nazi Party.

Your answer: _____

Answer

The increasing order of difficulty is A, C, B. Selection B is most difficult because sentences tend to be longer and more involved than those in A and C. There are a number of abstract words: *beauty, temperament, schools of taste*. It uses a colorful figure of speech (pages 108–118): "the receptacle of its refinement." The words themselves are not especially difficult, but the thought is subtly presented.

Selection A is the easiest. Sentences are short. Quotations quickly identify the speakers. The point is quickly and easily made.

Selection C is in-between. It is not quite so easy as A and not quite so challenging as B. Selection A can be read quickly. Selection C takes a bit more time. Selection B bears re-reading.

Did you adjust your reading speed to the challenges of the three selections?

The answers to On Your Own exercises are not in this book. Your teacher will help you correct your work.

On Your Own 1: Checking Your Reading Skill

How well can you meet the reading challenges of the three selections in Practice 2? Take the following test to check your skill.

1. In Selection A, the point of the joke is (*a*) misunderstanding of the word *empty*. (*b*) a lack of friendliness between Ben and Phil (*c*) a pun on the word *egg* (*d*) boastfulness on the part of Ben.   1. _   _

2. In Selection C, the date associated with Andrew Johnson is (*a*) 1649 (*b*) 1845 (*c*) 1868 (*d*) 1876.   2.

3. The word *unluckily* in Selection C suggests that Adolf Hitler was (*a*) unfortunate (*b*) ahead of his time (*c*) evil (*d*) blessed.   3. _

4. In Selection B, the main point is (*a*) a clearcut definition of beauty (*b*) a tribute to William Blake (*c*) an analysis of beautiful objects (*d*) a description of the ideal critic.   4. _

5. Selection B suggests that (*a*) some ages seem to lack a sense of beauty (*b*) there are excellent workmen in all periods (*c*) some schools of taste are better than others (*d*) genius is created by the age.   5. _

Reading for Pleasure

My early and invincible love of reading,
I would not exchange for the treasures of India.
Edward Gibbon

Reading to gain information or to solve problems is important, but there is another kind of reading that should not be overlooked: reading for the sheer joy of it. There is reading for every mood. Humor is an important ingredient in reading for pleasure, but there are other satisfactions. A novel can so capture a reader that he or she will stay up late to finish it.

In Charlotte Brönte's novel *Jane Eyre*, the narrator dwells lovingly on a reading experience that suggests the importance of an appropriate setting.

> A small breakfast-room adjoined the drawing-room. I slipped in there. It contained a book-case: I soon possessed myself of a volume, taking care that it should be one stored with pictures. I mounted into the window-seat: gathering up my feet, I sat cross-legged, like a Turk; and, having drawn the red moreen curtain nearly close, I was shrined in double retirement.

Think back to your own reading experiences. When you were younger, you probably enjoyed being read to. The pleasant setting, the security of being with family, made the reading especially enjoyable. Perhaps you can recall trying to read a book by flashlight after the call for "Lights out!" If you have experienced the joy of reading, keep the interest alive. If you have not been a frequent reader, try to kindle the pleasure of reading. Try to find books that might interest you. Friends, family members, teachers, and librarians can help you.

The novels of the British author Charles Dickens were written serially, much as a modern soap opera might be written. When Dickens started a book, he had no clear idea of where he would take his characters. His novels were published in America serially. Readers got so excited by them that they could scarcely wait for each new installment. When the ship carrying an installment of *The Old Curiosity Shop* docked in the United States, a crowd lined the pier, shouting, "Did Little Nell die?" (She did!) You can develop the same keen interest in reading without waiting for a ship to dock.

On Your Own 2: Reviewing What You Have Read

Check your understanding of this section. Base your answers only on the text.

1. The resource singled out as a major help in reading is (*a*) television (*b*) the desk dictionary (*c*) radio (*d*) maps.   1. ___

2. Which of the following is NOT listed as the result of poor lighting?

    (*a*) headache   (*b*) eyestrain
    (*c*) nausea   (*d*) fatigue   2. ___

3. *The Old Curiosity Shop* is a novel by (*a*) Edward Gibbon (*b*) Charlotte Brönte (*c*) Charles Dickens (*d*) none of these.   3. ___

4. Little Nell is (*a*) a child author (*b*) a young actress (*c*) the name of a boat (*d*) a character in a novel.   4. ___

5. The crowd waiting at the pier for the ship to dock consisted of (*a*) enthusiastic readers (*b*) would-be authors (*c*) book publishers (*d*) bookstore owners.   5. ___

2. Building Vocabulary

Would you be interested in a key that unlocks the meanings of thousands of words? The possibility seems absurd, but it is true. Because of the way that the English language has grown, you can often guess at the meaning of a word just by knowing its parts.

Many words consist of three parts:

Prefix: beginning word part
    *un*kind, *de*fend, *post*pone

Root: main word part
    un*kind*, de*fend*, post*pone*

Suffix: ending word part
    unkind*ness*, defend*er*, postpone*ment*

Some words, like *unkind* and *defend*, have prefixes and roots. Other words, like *kindness* and *fender*, contain roots and suffixes. Still other words contain all three: prefixes, roots, and suffixes—for example, *unkindness* and *postponement*. Some words, like *kind* and *course*, contain only roots.

Three Rivers Into One

Our language has three major sources: Anglo-Saxon, Latin, and Greek. All three language rivers have flowed into one, to create our rich English tongue, the most widely used in the world. If we go far enough back in time, we find that all three rivers come from the same source: Sanskrit, a parent Indo-European language. For a helpful analysis, however, three main divisions illuminate the source of English.

In addition to the major rivers, there have been important smaller streams like Celtic and Danish. English isn't fussy; it borrows from all languages, new and old. If a helpful new word arises in German, French, or Spanish, English quickly borrows it.

Anglo-Saxon

Anglo-Saxon is the backbone of English. Most of the common words we use are of Anglo-Saxon origin. Often-used words like *house, home, mother, father, son, daughter, do,* and *laugh* come to English through the Anglo-Saxon branch.

Since Anglo-Saxon includes the most common words, its suffixes, prefixes, and roots present few problems. You can quickly decide that *hopeful* means *full of hope.* Words like *unfriendly, parenthood, childish, foresee,* and *careless* present no problems. Anglo-Saxon words are quickly learned at the mother's knee.

Throughout this book, question-and-answer activities will check your understanding of the text and expand your reading activities.

Question 1: How Do Anglo-Saxon Prefixes and Suffixes Contribute to Word Meanings?

For each blank in the following sentences, choose from the list the appropriate Anglo-Saxon word. For each, point out the prefix or suffix.

foretell	hardship	mishandle	outreach	unbend
friendless	laziness	nationhood	prankster	underpay

Prefixes

1. In Greek mythology, Cassandra could _____ the future, but no one believed her.

2. The shortsighted store owner thought he could _____ his help and thus increase his profits.

3. It is all too easy to _____ a young horse unused to the saddle.

4. Did Denny _____ himself and get tangled in his own plot?

5. Doreen is too serious; she just cannot _____ .

Suffixes

6. What sometimes seems to be _____ may actually be a form of illness.

7. The 13 colonies fought to break away from Great Britain and attain independent _____ .

8. By the end of *A Christmas Carol*, the reformed miser Scrooge was no longer _____ .

9. To a true mountain climber, every _____ is just an interesting challenge.

10. Carl is a(n) _____ who believes everyone should enjoy a practical joke.

Anglo-Saxon Words and the Emotions

The first words we learn as children are mostly Anglo-Saxon words: *dog, cat, horse, love, like, good, see, home*. Because such words are associated with things we knew as children, they tend to arouse emotional responses in us. Under the stress of great emotion—of happiness, grief, anger—people tend to use simple Anglo-Saxon words.

On Your Own 1: Investigating Words Expressing Emotions

Nearly every word in the following statements is of Anglo-Saxon origin. What does this information tell us of the importance of Anglo-Saxon words in everyday life?

1. I was deeply grieved to learn of the death of your brother.

2. Stay away from the stove; it's hot!

3. I just made a hundred on my spelling test!

4. Don't ever ask me to go there again!

5. Where did you leave the tickets for tonight's meeting? We'll be late!

Latin

Latin has the distinction of entering the English language at many different times. The Romans were everywhere during the classical period. They not only left magnificent roads, theaters, and aqueducts behind; wherever they went, they also left remnants of the Latin language. Roman campaigns into central and northern Europe brought words like *mile, street*, and *pound* to Germanic tribes that would later invade Britain. The Roman occupation of Britain from Julius Caesar's time onward brought place names like *Lancaster* (from *castra, camp*), *Greenwich* (from *vicus, village*), and *Lincoln* (from *colonus, colony*). The introduction of Christianity into Britain at the end of the sixth century brought Latin church words like *temple* and *candle* as well as other words like *lentil, spend*, and *consul*.

A key merger of Latin and the native Anglo-Saxon language of Britain came with the Norman invasion in 1066 and the victory of William the Conqueror. Norman was a French, or Romance, language. Its basic composition was Latin. Anglo-Saxon was a Germanic language. Two major streams of language thus came together to make English one of the richest languages ever spoken, with the largest vocabulary of any language. Hundreds of French (and thus Latin) words came into the language with words like *demand, sermon*, and *pork*.

In general, Anglo-Saxon words are short, simple, informal. Their Latin synonyms tend to be longer, more complex, and more formal. For example, look at the following pairs of synonyms:

Anglo Saxon	*Latin*
birth	nativity
chew	masticate
dead	deceased
end	terminate
walk	ambulate

To speak straight from the heart, an author will use words from the Anglo-Saxon. For more intellectual discourse, he or she will employ words of Latin origin. A witty British politician once used such words to demolish a rival by describing him as ''a sophisticated rhetorician, inebriated with the exuberance of his own verbosity.''

As a result of the intermingling of languages, English has a tremendous range of synonyms. Sometimes a pair of synonyms provide interesting differences. *Storm* (from Anglo-Saxon) and *tempest* (from Latin) are synonyms, but there is a shade of difference between them. *Storm* is a general word applying to a brief thunderstorm or a prolonged disturbance. *Tempest* is short but violent. We might say the *storm* lasted only a few minutes, but we couldn't say the *tempest* lasted only a few minutes.

Question 2: How Do Latin and Anglo-Saxon Synonyms Enrich the Language?

In each of the following sentences, there is a blank to be filled by one of the synonyms in parentheses. The first word in each pair is from Anglo-Saxon. The second is from Latin. Which seems better to complete each sentence?

1. Helen suffered from a slight _____ and was back to work after a day's absence. (illness, disease)

2. I wasn't hungry but I _____ a little to keep my strength up. (ate, devoured)

3. When we heard the loud noises and angry voices, we all rushed into the lobby to see what the _____ was. (stir, commotion)

4. When sterling silver is kept in the open air, the surface will _____. (tarnish, stain)

5. Our dog is a fast _____. He quickly was able to put out his paw, roll over, and bark for a bone. (learner, student)

Answers

1. illness   *Disease* suggests a more serious condition.
2. ate   *Devoured* suggests a ravenous appetite.
3. commotion   Though both *stir* and *commotion* suggest agitation and excitement, *commotion* is a stronger word.

4. tarnish   *Tarnish* suggests a discoloration because of chemical interaction of
                and air. *Stain* suggests the discoloration because of another subst
5. learner   *Student* involves *study*, an intellectual pursuit alien to a dog.

At the time of William Shakespeare, Latin came pouring into the language as hundreds of new words were coined, many by Shakespeare himself. Throughout the Renaissance, the borrowing continued unabated, as words like *exterior, adapt*, and *exist* achieved respectability. The borrowing goes on as modern scientists (itself a Latin word) call upon Latin for new ideas, new products: *video camera, Lux detergent.*

Latin Prefixes

These prefixes occur over and over again. If you learn them now, you'll save yourself trouble in mastering new words. Look up the meaning of all unfamiliar examples so that the way each word is put together is clear to you.

Prefix	*Meaning*	*Example*
a-, ab-	away, from	apart, abnormal
ad-	to, toward	admit
ambi-	both	ambidextrous
ante-	before	antecedent
circum-	around	circumference
com-	with	compare
contra-	against	contradict
de-	down from, away	depose
dis-, di-	not, apart from	disagree, digress
e-, ex-	out of	eject, exit
extra-	beyond, additional	extraordinary
in-	into	insert
in-	not	infertile
inter-	between, among	intervene
intra-, intro-	within	intramural, introduce
non-	not	nonproductive
ob-	against, toward	obstruct
per-	thoroughly, through	pernicious, permit
post-	after	postpone
pre-	before	prearrange
pro-	forward, for	proclamation, proportion
re-	back, again	remit, reread
retro-	backward	retrograde
se-	aside, apart	secede
sub-	under	submarine
super-, supra-	above	superhuman, supranational
trans-	across	transmigrate
ultra-	beyond, extremely	ultramodern
vice-	in place of	vice-president

Prefixes Denoting Number

Prefix	Meaning	Example
semi-	half	semicircle
uni-	one	unilateral
bi-	two	biennial
tri-	three	triple
quadr-	four	quadrilateral
quinque-, quint-	five	quinquennial
sex-	six	sextet, sextant
sept-	seven	September
oct-	eight	October, octave
nona-	nine	nonagenarian
novem-	nine	November
dec-	ten	decimal
duodec-	twelve	duodecimal
cent-	hundred	centimeter
mill-	thousand	millennium
multi-	many	multitude

Question 3: How Do Latin Prefixes Provide Clues to Meanings?

For each blank in the following sentences, choose from the list the appropriate word of Latin origin. For each, point out the prefix and tell what the prefix and root mean. Sometimes Anglo-Saxon and Latin word elements are combined, as in *anteroom*.

anteroom	incompetent	retrorockets
circumnavigate	postgraduate	superpowers
contrary	prepay	translate
extravagant		

1. Ferdinand Magellan tried to _____ the globe, but his around-the-world journey ended with his death in the Philippines.

   _____

2. Before Jack met the personnel director, he had to wait outside in the _____ .

   _____

3. The Soviet Union and the United States were often referred to as _____ .

   _____

4. Annette will stay an extra year in college to take a(n) _____ course.

   _____

5. The astronauts fired the _____ to reverse the thrust of the spaceship.

   _____

6. I admire anyone who can cross from one language to another, and _____ rapidly even while a person is speaking.

   _____

7. If you _____ the charges on the mail-order item, you'll avoid c.o.d. charges.

   _____

8. Les is _____; in his spending habits he goes far beyond any reasonable need.

   _____

9. In any disagreement, Sheila is _____, always taking an opposing viewpoint.

   _____

10. Most businesses will fire a(n) _____ employee who can't work and doesn't care.

    _____

Answers

1. circumnavigate—circum—"sail around"
2. anteroom—ante—"room before another"
3. superpowers—super—"powers above the average"
4. postgraduate—post—"after graduation"
5. retrorockets—retro—"rockets that thrust backward"
6. translate—trans—"cross from one language to another"
7. prepay—pre—"pay in advance"
8. extravagant—extra—"going beyond reason"
9. contrary—contra—"opposite"
10. incompetent—in—"not competent"

On Your Own 2: Studying Number Prefixes

Study the list of number prefixes on page 13. Then, without looking back, answer each of the following questions.

1. Of course it's an exaggeration, but according to the word meaning how many legs should a millipede have?   1. _____

2. How many centimes are there in a franc?   2. _____

3. About how old would an octogenarian be?   3. _____

4. How many singers constitute a septet?   4. _____

5. Into how many parts do you cut an object if you bisect it?   5. _____

6. How many times a year does a semimonthly club meet?   6. _____

7. How many decimeters are there in a meter?   7. _____

8. How many wheels does a unicycle have?   8. _____

9. Is a person engaged in multifarious activities involved in one, two, or more?   9. _____

10. How many quadrants make up a circle?   10. _____

Latin Roots

The root carries the essential meaning of a word. Study the following list and look up the meaning of all unfamiliar words.

Root	Meaning	Example
ag, act, ig	do, act, drive	agile, action, exigency
ali	other	alien
am	love	amiable
anim	life, mind	animated, unanimous
ann	year	annual
aqu, aqua	water	aqueduct, aquarium
aud	hear	audience
ben, bon	well, good	benefit, bonus
brev	short	brevity
cad, cas	fall	cadence, casualty
cid, cis	kill, cut	homicide, incision
cant, chant	sing	incantation, enchant
cap, capt, cip	take	capable, capture, incipient
ced, cess, cede, ceed	go	procedure, excess, recede, succeed
clud, claus, clus	shut	include, clause, conclusive
cogn	know	recognize
cor	heart	cordial
corp	body	corporal
cred	believe	credit
curr, curs	run	current, cursory
dat, don	give	data, donate
dic, dict	say	dictate, diction
dign	worthy	dignify
doc	teach	doctrine
dom	house	domicile
domin	master	dominate
dorm	sleep	dormant
duc, duct	lead	reduce, deduct
fac, fec, fic, fy	do, make	manufacture, infect, sufficient, satisfy
fer, lat	carry	refer, translate

fin	end	final
flect, flex	bend	reflect, flexible
flu, flux	flow	influence, influx
fort	strong	fortify
frang, fract, frag, fring	break	frangible, infraction, fragile, infringement
fug	flee	fugitive
fund, fus	pour	refund, confuse
ger, gest	carry	belligerent, digest
grad, gress	walk	gradual, progress
greg	flock	congregation
hab	hold	habit
ject, jac	throw, lie next to	projectile, adjacent
junct, jug	join	junction, conjugate
labor	work	laboratory
leg, lect	read, law, gather	legible, legal, collect
loqu, locut	speak	loquacious, elocution
luc, lum	light	translucent, illuminate
magn	great	magnify
mal	evil	malice
man	hand	manual
ment	mind	mental
mit, miss	send	transmit, commission
mob, mov, mot	move	automobile, movable, motor
mort	death	immortal
mut	change	mutable
nov	new	novel
pat, pass	suffer	patient, passive
ped	foot	pedal
pell, puls	drive	propeller, propulsion
pend, pens	hang	impending, suspense
pet	seek	centripetal
plaud, plaus, plod, plos	clap	plaudit, applause, explode, explosive
pon, pos	place, put	exponent, depose
port	carry	import
prehend, prehens, pris	seize	comprehend, apprehensive, comprise
prob	prove	probate
pugn	fight	pugnacity
quir, ques, quis	seek	inquire, question, inquisitive
rid, ris	laugh	ridiculous, derision
rog	ask	abrogate
rupt	break	corruption

sail, sal, sult	leap	assail, salient, insult
sci	know	science
scrib, script	write	describe, scripture
sec, sect	cut	secant, section
sed, sess	sit	sedentary, session
sequ, secu	follow	sequence, consecutive
sol	alone	solitary
solv, solut	loosen	solvent, solution
son	sound	resonance
spec, spect, spic	look	speculate, inspect, conspicuous
sta, sist	stand	distant, consistent
string, strict	bind	stringent, restrict
stru, struct	build	construe, construct
sum, sumpt	use up, spend	consume, consumption
tang, tact	touch	tangent, intact
temp	time	temporary
ten, tend, tent, tain	hold	tenant, attend, attentive, retain
torqu, tort	twist	torque, contortion
tract	draw	attract
vad, vas	go	invade, pervasive
vag	wander	vagrant
ven, vent	come	convenient, adventure
vert, vers	turn	convert, reverse
via	way	trivial
vid, vis	see	provide, vision
vinc, vict	conquer	invincible, victory
viv, vict	live	revive, victuals
voc, voke	call	vocation, provoke
vol	wish, will	volunteer
volv, volut	turn	revolve, revolution

On Your Own 3: Supplying Latin Roots

Complete each blank by supplying the missing letters. Use the preceding list of roots. The number of dashes is the clue to the number of letters needed. The key to the correct root is printed in the sentence in *italic* type.

EXAMPLE: The color of sea *water* is often called _ _ _ _ marine.

ANSWER: We need four letters here. Since water is *aqua*, the complete word is *aquamarine*.

1. That which cannot be *heard* is in _ _ _ ible.

2. To *say* in advance is to pre _ _ _ _ .

3. To *shorten* is to ab _ _ _ _ iate.

4. One who is *evil* is called _ _ _ _ ignant.

5. One not in his right *mind* is de _ _ _ _ _ ed.

6. That which is *sent* back is a re _ _ _ _ _ ance.

7. If we *believe* a report, we put _ _ _ _ _ ence in it.

8. That which has no *life* is called in _ _ _ _ _ ate.

9. A name *other* than your own is called a(n) _ _ _ _ as.

10. Those who *work* together are said to col _ _ _ _ _ _ ate.

11. That which *flees* the center is called centri _ _ _ _ al.

12. People who like to *flock* together are called _ _ _ _ _ arious.

13. When things are *poured* together, _ _ _ _ ion takes place.

14. A man of *great* spirit and generosity is called _ _ _ _ _ animous.

15. That which shines with *light* is said to be _ _ _ _ inous.

16. A *new* idea or plan is called an in _ _ _ _ ation.

17. To prevent someone from *knowing* you, you might travel in _ _ _ _ _ ito.

18. People *come* together at a con _ _ _ _ _ ion.

19. To *drive* back is to re _ _ _ _ .

20. A group that *goes* away from another group se _ _ _ _ _ _ s.

21. A snake that *binds* and crushes its foe is called a con _ _ _ _ _ _ _ or.

22. If we *write* our names in a book, we in _ _ _ _ _ _ e it.

23. Actions which *follow* as the result of other actions are con _ _ _ _ _ ent upon them.

24. A congressman *stands* in the legislature for his con _ _ _ _ _ uents.

25. Those who *see* a game are called _ _ _ _ _ _ ators. Those who *hear* a concert constitute the _ _ _ _ ience.

Word Derivations and Figurative Language

Because most words from Latin roots have been in the English language for a long time, they sometimes acquire figurative meanings. (See pages 108–118.) Here are a few examples to show how the present meaning may wander from the original meaning as suggested by the roots and prefixes.

Eliminate now means *remove, eradicate*. The basic root of the word is *limen*, or *threshold*. Thus, to *eliminate* something is to *throw it over the threshold*, discard it. The synonym *eradicate* has broadened its meaning, too. The root is *rad*, which itself means *root*. Thus, to *eradicate* is to *root out*. When a gardener *eradicates* weeds, he or she demonstrates the original meaning of the word.

Dilapidated means *utterly broken down and ruined*. The root is *lapis*, meaning *stone*. Strictly speaking, *dilapidated* should apply only to run-down *stone* structures, but the word is now generally used to mean *broken down*, whether it refers to a wooden building or an automobile.

Now try your skill on a more difficult exercise. The Bonus is designed to introduce you to harder words and more challenging ideas. The answers to Bonus exercises are not in this book. Your teacher will help you correct your work.

Bonus 1: Studying Word Derivations

In an unabridged dictionary, look up the meaning and origin of each of the following words. On a separate sheet of paper, show how the word took on its present meaning.

EXAMPLE: *proceed*

ANSWER: *Proceed* means *to go forth*, from *pro*, meaning *forward*, and *ceed*, meaning *go*.

accord	credulous	infusion	recur
advocate	defer	invincible	repugnant
anniversary	deride	missile	retract
aquatics	disruption	mobilize	sedentary
avert	dissect	pervasive	tenable
avocation	divert	precursor	tenacious
compose	eject	prevent	transaction
conductor	extravagant	profuse	transfusion
convivial	fluctuate	provident	transmute
corpulent	incursion	recipient	transport

Latin Suffixes

By using suffixes, you can create two or more words where only one existed before. By adding suffixes to *act*, you can create the nouns *action* and *actor*, and the adjective *active*. If you know one, you can figure out others. Notice how suffixes are used in the following list.

Noun	*Verb*	*Adjective*
expansion	expand	expansive
explanation	explain	explanatory
infection	infect	infectious
orator	orate	oratorical
permission	permit	permissible

Question 4: How Do Suffixes Help to Form Words?

Complete the following chart by supplying the missing forms.

Noun	Verb	Adjective
1. _____	familiarize	_____
2. acquisition	_____	_____
3. _____	_____	altered
4. _____	_____	preferable
5. _____	submit	_____
6. oppression	_____	_____
7. _____	favor	_____
8. _____	_____	informative
9. _____	_____	identifiable
10. injury	_____	_____

Answers

Noun	Verb
1. familiarity	familiari:
2. acquisition	acquire
3. alteration	alter
4. preference	prefer
5. submission	submit
6. oppression	oppress
7. favorite	favor
8. information	inform
9. identification	identify
10. injury	injure

Greek

The Greek tributary has been pouring into the great English river since ancient times. Because Greek had such an important influence on Latin, Greek words came to English through the Latin. When Christianity took hold in Britain, Greek words came with the Latin. This is the period when Greek church words entered—for example, *angel, apostle, deacon, disciple, epistle, hymn, martyr, organ,* and *psalm.*

During the Renaissance, when Latin words entered English in a torrent, Greek words were added, too, by scholars and writers. Words like *academy* and *acme* can be traced to this period.

The borrowing goes on today. Because Greek roots combine easily, they are favored by scientists for creating new words. Think of all the words ending in *logy*, "the study of." *Geology* is the *study* of the earth. *Psychology* is the *study* of the mind. *Metr* meaning *measure* appears in *thermometer*, a *measure* of heat; *telemetry, measuring* at a distance; *perimeter*, a *measure* around. New words are constantly being coined for new inventions, new products, new ways of thinking.

Greek Prefixes

Like Latin prefixes, these Greek prefixes keep occurring over and over again. Study the following list and look up the meaning of all unfamiliar examples.

Prefix	Meaning	Example
a-, an-	no, not	atypical, anarchy
amphi-	around, both	amphitheater
ana-	up, again	analysis
anti-	against	anticlimax
apo-	off, away from	apology
cata-	down	catastrophe
dia-	across, through	diagonal
ec-, ex-	out of	eccentric, exodus
en-	in	energy
epi-	upon	epigram
eu-	well	euphemism
hyper-	above	hyperbole
hypo-	under	hypocrite
meta-	after	metamorphosis
mis-, miso-	hatred of	misanthropic, misogynist
para-	beside	paraphrase
peri-	around	periphery
poly-	many	polysyllable
pro-	before	program
sym-, syn-	with	symphony, synopsis

Greek Number Prefixes

Prefix	Meaning	Example
hemi-	half	hemisphere
mono-	one	monotonous
di-	two	diphthong
tri-	three	tricycle
tetra-	four	tetrameter
penta-	five	pentagon
hexa-	six	hexagonal
hepta-	seven	heptameter
octa-	eight	octagon
deca-	ten	decade
kilo-	thousand	kilowatt

On Your Own 4: Using Greek Prefixes

Complete each blank by supplying the missing prefix. Use the preceding list of prefixes as your guide. The number of dashes is the clue to the number of letters needed. The key to the correct prefix is printed in the sentence in *italic* type.

EXAMPLE: The line *across* a circle is called the _ _ _ meter.

ANSWER: We need three letters here. Since *dia* means *across*, the complete word is *diameter*.

1. The *Ten* Commandments are often called the _ _ _ _ logue.

2. A support with *three* feet is a(n) _ _ _ pod.

3. A *thousand* meters is called a(n) _ _ _ _ meter.

4. A(n) _ _ logy speaks *well* of a person.

5. A guardian *against* infection is a(n) _ _ _ _ septic.

6. A figure with *many* sides is called a(n) _ _ _ _ gon.

7. A flood that washes *down* all before it is called a(n) _ _ _ _ clysm.

8. A needle for piercing *under* the skin is a(n) _ _ _ _ dermic.

9. That which goes *before* the rest of the story is the _ _ _ logue.

10. When we suffer *with* someone we extend him or her our _ _ _ pathy.

Greek Roots

Think of all the common words that use Greek roots: *telephone, telegraph, autograph, cyclist, synonym, democrat, dynamite*. The list stretches on and on. In this section, you will meet some of the most helpful Greek roots and open the way to many new words for your vocabulary.

Question 5: How Can a Reader Guess at the Meanings of Roots?

In each of the following ten groups, one root is common to all four words. At least three of the four words will be familiar to you in every group. Judging by the meanings of the words you know, what do you guess the meaning of the root to be? The answer will be found among the words following the root.

EXAMPLE: phonograph, telephone, radiophone, euphony

ANSWER: The root *phon* probably has something to do with light, heat, sound, or water. Since the first three words are familiar to you and have something to do with sound, you would answer *sound*. If the fourth word is unfamiliar to you, look up its meaning in a good dictionary. Does *euphony* have something to do with sound?

1. telegraph, autograph, biography, graphic
   graph: distance, writing, friends, or pictures   1. _____

2. automatic, autograph, automobile, autocrat
   auto: ruler, self, only, or written   2. _____

3. monotone, monopoly, monarchy, monogram
   mono: busy, loud, two, or one   3. _____

4. democrat, aristocrat, autocrat, bureaucrat
   crat: person, rule, wealth, or nature   4. _____

5. synonym, antonym, homonym, patronymic
   onym: name, opposite, father, or same   5. _____

6. bicycle, cyclone, cycle, encyclopedia
   cycl: storm, circle, play, or two   6. _____

7. centimeter, meter, metric, perimeter
   meter: coin, instrument, 100, or measure   7. _____

8. biology, biography, autobiography, amphibian
   bio: book, life, science, or water   8. _____

9. antislavery, antitoxin, antidote, antipathy
   anti: related, before, against, or afterward   9. _____

10. microscope, microphotograph, microbe, microcosm
    micro: small, picture, germ, or telescope   10. _____

On Your Own 5: Guessing at the Meanings of Greek Prefixes and Roots

Each word in the following pairs has one root (italicized) in common with the other. From the word pool below, select the word that you feel best expresses the root meaning. Look up each unfamiliar word in the dictionary.

EXAMPLE: tele*scope*, micro*scope*

ANSWER: *Scope*, which is common to both words, probably means *to look* or
           to see, since a telescope is used to look at very distant things and a
           microscope is used to look at very small things.

book	nature
breath	power
city	sight
concealed	skin
false	star

1. *Bib*le, *bibl*iography   1. _____   6. *opt*ometrist, *opt*ician   6. _____

2. *crypt*ic, *crypt*ogram   2. _____   7. *pol*ice, *pol*itics   7. _____

3. *dynam*ite, *dynam*ic   3. _____   8. *pneu*matic, *pneu*monia   8. _____

4. epi*dermis*, taxi*dermist*   4. _____   9. *pseudo*nym, *pseudo*pod   9. _____

5. *astro*nomy, *astro*logy   5. _____   10. *phys*ics, *physi*ology   10. _____

Other Greek Roots

Root	Meaning	Example
andro, anthrop	man	android, anthropoid
arch, archi	chief, first	archbishop, architect
baro	heavy	barometer
chiro	hand	chiropodist
chrom	color	chromatic
chron	time	synchronize
dem	people	demagogue
dos	give	dose
erg	work	energy
gam	marriage	bigamist
gen	birth	eugenics
heli, helio	sun	helium, heliotrope
hetero	different, other	heterogeneous
hom, homo	same	homeostasis, homogeneous
hydr	water	hydraulics
lith, litho	stone	neolithic, lithograph
morph	form	metamorphic
neo	new	neolithic
nom, nomy	law	economics, taxonomy
ortho	straight, correct	orthodox
pan	all	pan-American
phan, phen	show	phantom, phenomenon
phil	loving	Philadelphia
phos, phot	light	phosphorus, photograph
pod	foot	podiatrist
proto	first	protoplasm
psych	mind	psychology
pyr	fire	pyre
soph	wise	sophomore
techn	art	technical
tele	far, far off	teletype
tom	cut	anatomy
trop	turn	tropic
typ	print	typography
zo	animal	protozoa

On Your Own 6: Using Greek Roots

Complete each blank by supplying the missing root. Use the preceding list of roots as your guide. The number of dashes is the clue to the number of letters needed. The key to the correct root is printed in the sentence in *italic* type.

EXAMPLE: A flower that turns toward the *sun* is called the _ _ _ _ _ trope.

ANSWER: We need five letters here. Since *helio* means *sun*, the complete word is *heliotrope*.

1. An opinion that *differs* from other opinions is labeled _ _ _ _ _ _ _ dox.

2. One who *loves* wisdom is called a(n) _ _ _ _ _ osopher.

3. That which is without *form* is a _ _ _ _ _ _ ous.

4. A *chief* angel is a(n) _ _ _ _ _ angel.

5. One who makes many *marriages* is a poly _ _ _ _ ist.

6. One who loves *mankind* enough to give money away is a phil _ _ _-_ _ _ _ _ ist.

7. A single block of *stone* is a mono _ _ _ _ _ .

8. Something that appears out of its proper *time* is an ana _ _ _ _ _ _ ism.

9. The *art* of making woodcuts is a special _ _ _ _ _ _ ique.

10. The *first* animals are called _ _ _ _ _ _ zoa.

11. A speech of praise, formerly given before *all* the people of a town, is called a(n) _ _ _ _ egyric.

12. An airplane made to land on *water* is called a(n) _ _ _ _ _ oplane.

13. A substance that glows with *light* in the dark is called _ _ _ _ _ phorescent.

14. A disease that is visited upon the *people* is called an epi _ _ _ _ ic.

15. One who *straightens* teeth is called a(n) _ _ _ _ _ _ dontist.

16. A word that has the *same* spelling and pronunciation as another word is called a(n) _ _ _ _ onym.

17. A wrapping that *shows* us the article through it is called cello _ _ _ _ _ e.

18. *Fire*works are often called _ _ _ _ otechnics.

19. A person who seems to have unusual powers of *mind* is called _ _ _ _-_ _ ic.

20. The study of *animals* is called _ _ _ ology.

Bonus 2: Reviewing What You Have Read

For each blank in the following sentences, choose the appropriate word from the list below. The key to the word is printed in the sentence in *italic* type.

aquifer	millimeter
automatic	multilingual
credulous	photosynthesis
epitaph	quadruplets
invincible	ultraviolet

1. The color just *beyond* the visible spectrum is called _____ .

2. Jeremy is so _____ he'll *believe* anything.

3. Plant foods are created by the presence of *light* in _____ .

4. The *thousandth* part of a meter is a(n) _____ .

5. *Four* children who are born to the same mother at the same time are called

   _____ .

6. A process that is *self*-operating is _____ .

7. A team that goes through a football season without a *defeat* can rightly be considered _____ .

8. The inscription *upon* a tombstone is called a(n) _____ .

9. A person who speaks *many* languages is _____ .

10. A(n) _____ is an underground layer of rock containing *water*.

3. Using Context Clues

''You are known by the company you keep.''

Probably you have heard this saying before. Now let's change it a bit to help you look at words in a new way.

''A word is known by the company it keeps.''

When you meet a word, it is seldom alone. Usually it is surrounded by other words. The meaning of a word can often be known by looking at these other words. Here's an example.

The author used a **pseudonym,** keeping his real name a secret.

Getting the Meanings of Words Through Context

The word *pseudonym* may be new to you. You may not even know how to pronounce it. Keep in mind, though, that a word is known by the company it keeps. All the other words in the sentence help to tell you what *pseudonym* means. The other words provide clues. If the author is ''keeping his real name a secret,'' then a *pseudonym* must be a false name.

There is a word used to describe the words surrounding another word: *context*. The context of *pseudonym* is all the other words surrounding it in the sentence.

The word *context* may be new to you, but you have been using context and context clues since you were a child. Context can be just words, or it can be more than words. Context can also be what is happening in the world around you. For example:

Would you like this cookie?

When your mother gave you a cookie as a child, you soon learned the meaning of the word *cookie.* You learned the names for all the objects in your house the same way. For instance, you never looked up the word *table*, *rug*, or *spoon* in a dictionary.

When you began to read, you learned more words. You didn't look up most of these words in the dictionary either. You learned their meanings through context, just as you discovered the meaning of the word *pseudonym* in the example.

Do the following Question to help you understand context clues.

Question: How Does Context Aid in Guessing at Word Meanings?

Write the letter of the word or expression that has the same meaning as the underlined word in each sentence.

1. My affairs are in such a **muddle,** I can't straighten them out.

    (*a*) mess   (*b*) order   (*c*) surprise
    (*d*) dream   (*e*) file   1. _____

2. Be **neutral** in an argument between friends; don't take sides.

    (*a*) strong   (*b*) silent   (*c*) impartial
    (*d*) interested   (*e*) active   2. _____

3. San Antonio has **diverse** groups of people that are quite different from one another.

    (*a*) many   (*b*) unlike   (*c*) highly educated
    (*d*) few   (*e*) generous   3. _____

4. The recipe called for **cloves,** pepper, ginger, cinnamon, and celery seeds.

    (*a*) a hot oven   (*b*) a dish   (*c*) a kind of spice
    (*d*) a recipe   (*e*) a liquid   4. _____

5. If you build a cabinet, good plans are **essential**.

    (*a*) overlooked   (*b*) confusing   (*c*) difficult
    (*d*) necessary   (*e*) simple   5. _____

Check your answers below. Then read the explanations to be sure you understand the correct answers.

Answers

1. (*a*) If your affairs can't be straightened out, they must be in a *mess*.
2. (*c*) When you don't take sides, you are being *fair* to both sides.
3. (*b*) If the groups are different, they must be *unlike*.
4. (*c*) Since cloves are grouped with other spices, the answer must be *a kind of spice*.
5. (*d*) To build a cabinet, you'll find it *necessary* to have good plans.

Context Clue 1: Words with the Same Meanings

Context clues work in different ways. Sometimes a context clue comes from a single word in the sentence. That one word means almost the same thing as the word being defined.

The mayor's **inquiry** followed the same line of questioning as the judge's.

Since *questioning* seems to mean the same thing as *inquiry* (and you know what *questioning* means), you have a good clue to the correct answer.

In the Question on page 28, the word *different* in sentence #3 provides a clue to the meaning of *diverse*.

Context Clue 2: Related Words and Ideas

Sometimes a word in the sentence doesn't mean exactly the same thing as the word being defined. Instead, it means something similar.

The visitor from Tibet stared with open mouth at the busy traffic in Houston and **gawked** at the flashing advertising signs.

The word *gawked* is paired with *stared.* So you can guess that *gawk* means ''stare in astonishment.''

Context Clue 3: Grouped Words and Ideas

A word may also be grouped with other words in the same general class.

In the truck, she had a hammer, a screwdriver, an electric drill, three kinds of saws, and a **spokeshave.**

You may not know what a *spokeshave* is. By looking at the other words in the group, though, you can safely guess that it is some kind of tool.

In the Question on page 28, you can guess in #4 that *cloves* are a kind of spice.

Context Clue 4: Opposed Words and Ideas

If words or ideas are **opposed** to each other, they are nearly opposite in meaning. Look at the following example.

Sometimes bad luck can **energize** people, not weaken them.

The word *not* shows that *energize* is opposed to *weaken. Energize* means the opposite of *weaken.* Therefore, *energize* means ''to give power to.''

Let's look at another example.

Most fads last only a short time, but great art **endures.**

The word *but* tells you that the two ideas are opposed. Great art is opposed to fads. If fads last a short time, then something that *endures* must last a long time.

Context Clue 5: The Whole Sentence

Now look at the next sentence.

Sue awaited the **outcome** patiently, for she wanted to see what would happen.

Here the clue is in the whole sentence. If Sue wanted to see what would happen, the word *outcome* must mean ''something that happens as a result.'' For instance, when you take pictures with your camera, you're interested in the outcome.

In the Question on page 28, the whole sentence in #5 provides a clue to the meaning of the word *essential*.

Practice: Studying Context Clues

Write the letter of the word or expression that has the same meaning as the underlined word in each sentence.

1. Bert was a **moody** person, cheerful one moment and gloomy the next.

   (*a*) changeable   (*b*) sweet   (*c*) cruel
   (*d*) friendly   (*e*) bitter   1. _____

2. Don't **cram** for a test, but instead study over a long period before taking it.

   (*a*) be late   (*b*) prepare   (*c*) forget your
                                                          book

   (*d*) study in a   (*e*) take too much
          hurry   time   2. _____

3. Myra has the ability to think clearly and the **capacity** to get a job done promptly.

   (*a*) skill   (*b*) courage   (*c*) weakness
   (*d*) sweetness   (*e*) slowness   3. _____

Answers

1. (*a*) If Bert is cheerful one moment and gloomy the next, he is *changeable*. The sentence as a whole provides the clue.
2. (*d*) The use of *not* (in *Don't*) and *but instead* shows that two ideas are opposed—cramming and studying over a long period.
3. (*a*) The word *ability* seems to have almost the same meaning as *capacity*. Both words mean *skill*.

On Your Own: Studying Context Clues

Write the letter of the word or expression that has the same meaning as the underlined word in each sentence. Take your time and work carefully.

1. When my brother completed the course, his high marks surprised me and **astounded** our parents.

   (*a*) annoyed   (*b*) confused   (*c*) astonished
   (*d*) amused   (*e*) depressed   1. _____

2. Max is usually shy, not **rash**.

   (*a*) bold   (*b*) quiet   (*c*) likable
   (*d*) athletic   (*e*) boring   2. _____

3. Their suggestion was the silliest, most **nonsensical** idea I've ever heard.

   (*a*) brilliant   (*b*) sound   (*c*) senseless
   (*d*) cruel   (*e*) proud   3. _____

4. By his foolish use of money, Wesley showed himself to be a **spendthrift**.

   (*a*) leader   (*b*) joker   (*c*) penny-pincher
   (*d*) friend   (*e*) money-waster   4. _____

5. Allison **dissociated** herself from her former friends and joined a group of more serious students.

   (*a*) connected   (*b*) separated   (*c*) invited
   (*d*) called   (*e*) lost   5. _____

6. Although Dorothy's sister was **distinguished** as a scientist, Dorothy remained unknown.

   (*a*) strange   (*b*) easily upset   (*c*) likable
   (*d*) famous   (*e*) clever   6. _____

7. Mel was confident and always felt it was his **destiny** to become a famous writer.

   (*a*) loss   (*b*) fate   (*c*) misfortune
   (*d*) worth   (*e*) coincidence   7. _____

8. The **telltale** mud stains showed that the twins had walked on the new rug with muddy shoes.

   (*a*) ugly   (*b*) dark gray   (*c*) attractive
   (*d*) common   (*e*) revealing   8. _____

9. Dr. Ortega cleaned the wound and then used **antiseptic** powder for extra safety.

   (*a*) soothing   (*b*) time-saving   (*c*) infection-
                                                  fighting
   (*d*) poisonous   (*e*) sweet-smelling   9. _____

10. The winners were chosen not **randomly** but very carefully.

   (*a*) wisely   (*b*) slyly   (*c*) by voting
   (*d*) by chance   (*e*) by judges   10. _____

Bonus: Studying Context Clues

Write the letter of the word or expression that has the same meaning as the underlined word in each sentence.

1. If you wish to encourage someone, **commend** his or her actions. Do not criticize harshly.

   (*a*) belittle   (*b*) report   (*c*) duplicate
   (*d*) praise   (*e*) try   1. _____

2. The wound was **superficial** and barely scratched the surface of the skin.

   (*a*) slightly   (*b*) badly infected (*c*) not deep
        inflamed
   (*d*) not visible   (*e*) unexpected   2. _____

3. The **stress** of working long hours without proper rest exhausted Ben. Therefore, he quit the job.

   (*a*) relaxation   (*b*) confidence   (*c*) complications
   (*d*) disgust   (*e*) strain   3. _____

4. Because the judge was **dubious** about the defendant's sincerity, she refused to set bail for his release.

   (*a*) enthusiastic (*b*) doubtful   (*c*) certain
   (*d*) angry   (*e*) careful   4. _____

5. Many young people seek the **commitment** of marriage, the promise to stay together for the rest of their lives.

   (*a*) pledge   (*b*) hope   (*c*) refusal
   (*d*) attempt   (*e*) deception   5. _____

6. The Norse believed that the world would end in revolts, war, and universal **strife,** with even the gods defeated at last.

    (*a*) agreement   (*b*) conflict   (*c*) indifference
    (*d*) irritation   (*e*) questioning   6. _____

7. For her report, Charlene **delved** into many books and mined a great many nuggets of information.

    (*a*) gazed   (*b*) stared   (*c*) dug
    (*d*) glimpsed   (*e*) cut   7. _____

8. The strikers and their employer were in a **deadlock;** neither side would give an inch.

    (*a*) conference   (*b*) debate   (*c*) solution
    (*d*) rage   (*e*) standstill   8. _____

9. The teacher urged us to be **terse,** not wordy, in our reports.

    (*a*) humorous   (*b*) complete   (*c*) entertaining
    (*d*) brief   (*e*) sincere   9. _____

10. The defense attorney **conceded** that her client had lied and admitted that his lies had surprised her.

    (*a*) agreed   (*b*) denied   (*c*) shouted
    (*d*) whispered   (*e*) proved   10. _____

4. Getting the Main Idea

"You can't see the forest for the trees."

Have you ever heard this saying? It means that you can't see the big picture. You can see the "trees" (the separate details), but you miss the "forest" (the main idea).

The saying makes an important point about reading. Some students can find the details in what they read, but they don't understand the main idea. That can be a problem, because the details don't mean much unless you get the main idea.

The Main Idea and the Details of a Paragraph

The *main idea* of a paragraph is what the entire paragraph is about. For instance, the main idea of a paragraph might be this: "A number of American cities have well-known festivals."

A *detail* is any fact, example, or other statement that supports the main idea. It may be expressed in one or more sentences. In the paragraph about festivals, a detail might be, "The Mardi Gras in New Orleans is famous throughout the world." Other details could include information about the Cherry Blossom Festival in Washington, D.C., and the Tournament of Roses in Pasadena, California.

Question: How Do You Find the Main Idea?

Read the following passage and answer the question at the end.

> What is a television *miniseries*? Is it a weekly comedy show, with the same comedian as the star? Is it a news program that covers parts of the same news story on different nights? Is it a soap opera in which the same characters get into and out of trouble week after week? No, a miniseries is none of those. It is a special kind of program. A miniseries presents a single story that is broken down into parts. These parts are shown on separate nights. Usually, the story is completed within a week. The story may be based on real events or people, such as the Civil War or George Washington. Or it may be entirely make-believe. It may be serious or humorous.

KNOW THIS WORD

special: different; not like others

Write the letter of the statement that best expresses the main idea.

(*a*) Television handles sports programs very well.
(*b*) Television offers many different kinds of programs.
(*c*) A miniseries was made about George Washington.
(*d*) A television miniseries is a special kind of program.

Your answer: _____

Answers

Let's examine the possible answers.

(*a*) This answer is completely off the topic. The passage doesn't mention sports programs.
(*b*) Although this statement is true, it says nothing about a miniseries. Since the passage sets out to define a miniseries, you are almost sure to find the word *miniseries* in the answer.
(*c*) This is a detail within the passage. It is not the main idea. (In fact, the passage gives George Washington only as the possible subject of a miniseries. It does not say that such a miniseries was ever made.)
(*d*) This is the correct answer. It expresses the main idea well. The passage says that a miniseries is a special kind of program. The purpose of the passage is to define *miniseries*.

There are a number of hints that can help you find the main idea of a passage. Study the following Practice activities to learn more about finding main ideas.

Practice 1: Getting the Main Idea

What is the main idea of the following passage?

> The famous inventor Thomas A. Edison owned a house in the country. He liked to show visitors around his property. He had invented many labor-saving devices and enjoyed talking about them. At one place in the garden, he had installed a heavy turnstile. This is a kind of metal gate with arms that a person has to push in order to get through. Every visitor had to move these heavy arms while walking through Edison's garden.
>
> "You have so many clever gadgets around," one visitor commented; "why do you have such a heavy turnstile?"
>
> "Well, you see," Edison replied, "everyone who goes through the turnstile pumps eight gallons of water into the tank on my roof."

Write the letter of the statement that best expresses the main idea.

(*a*) Edison invents a clever labor-saving device.
(*b*) A good invention is rare indeed.
(*c*) Edison's visitors were annoyed by the turnstile.
(*d*) Edison owned a house in the country.

Your answer 1: _____

Answers

You have four choices. One of them has to be correct. If you think carefully about each one of the four, you should get the right answer.

Only (*a*) expresses the main idea of the passage. Edison's turnstile used people power to pump water! Let's see what's wrong with the other three answers.

(*b*) Watch out for statements like this one. It is too general. It is not clear and exact for the passage. Besides, the passage doesn't really say this.
(*c*) There is no suggestion that Edison's visitors were annoyed. The visitor who asked about the turnstile seemed to be simply looking for information.
(*d*) Don't be misled because this is what the first sentence says. In this case, the first sentence does *not* state the topic, or main idea, but only a detail.

Practice 2

What is the main idea of the following passage?

> How do you think people catch colds? If you get your feet wet, will you come down with a cold? If you go outdoors on a chilly day without a sweater, will you catch a cold? Perhaps, but a greater danger lies elsewhere, according to scientists. A recent study says, "Don't shake hands with a person who has a cold. If you do, wash your hands soon and thoroughly. Don't rub your nose and eyes before washing." The study points out that viruses of the common cold remain dangerous for at least three hours on dry hands. Hand contact may be even more dangerous than coughing or sneezing.

KNOW THIS WORD

viruses: tiny germs that may cause disease

Write the letter of the statement that best expresses the main idea.

(*a*) You will surely catch a cold if you have wet feet.
(*b*) Scientists are studying many kinds of diseases.
(*c*) Hand contact can easily spread colds.
(*d*) Scientists have studied the common cold.

Your answer 2: _____

Answers

Only (*c*) expresses the main idea of the passage. Many colds are spread by hand contact. The other answers are faulty.

(*a*) This is not stated as a fact—only as a question—in the passage. If stated, it would be a detail.
(*b*) Although the statement is true, it is much too broad. The passage deals only with colds, not with other diseases.
(*d*) This is a detail, not the main idea.

On Your Own 1: Getting the Main Idea

Read the following passage and answer the question at the end.

> What did Babe Ruth and Benjamin Franklin have in common? They were both left-handed. So were Michelangelo and Johann Sebastian Bach, two of the world's greatest geniuses. If you are a lefty, you are in good company. You also have certain advantages. If you play baseball, you have a slight advantage in hitting, because you stand closer to first base and can run there faster than a right-hander. If you play tennis, you face mostly right-handers. Therefore, you know how to play against righties, but they may have trouble playing against you. As a lefty, you have a slight edge. Once upon a time, left-handedness was frowned upon. Today, however, more than ever, lefties go on to great achievements in sports and other fields.

KNOW THESE WORDS

in common: (that they) shared together
frowned upon: believed to be a fault

Write the letter of the statement that best expresses the main idea.

(*a*) Benjamin Franklin was left-handed.
(*b*) Tennis is more popular with right-handers than with left-handers.
(*c*) Left-handedness was once frowned upon.
(*d*) Left-handedness is not always a disadvantage and can even be an advantage.

Your answer 1: _____

On Your Own 2

Read the following passage and answer the question at the end.

> Caffeine is a popular stimulant found in many products. Perhaps the most obvious product containing caffeine is coffee. But caffeine is also present in tea, cocoa, and chocolate bars. Many soft drinks, especially colas, have caffeine. There may be as much caffeine in a 12-ounce bottle of cola as in four cups of instant coffee. Some people don't realize how much caffeine they're taking. Caffeine provides an instant jolt to the nervous system. It also can cause nervousness and sleeplessness.

KNOW THESE WORDS

stimulant: something that excites or makes more active

obvious: easy to see

Write the letter of the statement that best expresses the main idea.

(a) Caffeine is a stimulant.
(b) Caffeine jolts the nervous system and can cause sleeplessness.
(c) A number of familiar products contain the stimulant caffeine.
(d) Colas have a surprisingly large amount of caffeine.

Your answer 2: _____

Bonus 1: Getting the Main Idea

Read the following passage and answer the question at the end.

> How many Presidents of the United States were related to other Presidents? Most people know that John Adams and John Quincy Adams were father and son. Many know that William Henry Harrison and Benjamin Harrison were grandfather and grandson. Many also know that Theodore Roosevelt and Franklin D. Roosevelt were distant cousins. Few people, however, know that Harry Truman was a distant cousin of John Tyler. Can these surprising relationships be explained by coincidence? Or does the Presidential fever run in the blood of certain families? Whatever the explanation, four pairs of Presidents show surprising relationships.

KNOW THIS WORD

coincidence: happenings that seem connected

Write the letter of the statement that best expresses the main idea.

(a) John Adams and John Quincy Adams were father and son, the first of four pairs of Presidents.

(b) Truman and Tyler became President on the death of the then current President.

(c) There is a blood relationship between the individuals in four Presidential pairs.

(d) Four pairs of American Presidents have the same name.

Your answer 1: _____

Bonus 2

Read the following passage and answer the question at the end.

> The great Greek philosopher Aristotle was famous for his work in physics, astronomy, drama, poetry, politics, ethics, and logic. Yet, according to science writer Isaac Asimov, Aristotle was primarily a biologist. Somehow this important part of his work was generally ignored, while other parts were studied. There were exceptions. Charles Darwin praised Aristotle as one of the most important biologists. Linnaeus, who developed modern scientific classification, owed Aristotle a great debt. Cuvier, a pioneer in comparative anatomy, was greatly influenced by Aristotle. Without Aristotle, the course of biology would have been different.

KNOW THESE WORDS

ethics: study of right and wrong

logic: science of reasoning

comparative: studying similarities and differences

Write the letter of the statement that best expresses the main idea.

(a) Aristotle's work as a biologist is unfairly overshadowed by his work in other fields.

(b) Charles Darwin could not have achieved the worldwide success he earned without Aristotle.

(c) In their studies of biology, Linnaeus and Cuvier owed a tremendous debt to Aristotle.

(d) Aristotle was famous in physics, astronomy, drama, poetry, politics, ethics, and logic.

Your answer 2: _____

5. Finding the Best Title

CONGRESS PASSES NEW TAX BILL

You see dozens of headlines like this one every day in your newspaper. A headline tries to capture the main idea of the story that follows. In some reading tests, you are asked to judge headlines, though in tests the headlines are called *titles*. You are given a number of choices and asked to select the title that best summarizes the main idea. In these test items, main ideas are often not expressed as complete sentences. Like many headlines, they may be sentence fragments, but they must still include the central idea of the passage.

Question: How Can You Find the Best Title?

Read the following passage and answer the question at the end.

> Henry Augustus Rowland was an American physicist who was famous for his modesty. Since experts are often called as witnesses at trials, Rowland once found himself in the witness chair. While he was being cross-examined, the lawyer asked him, "Who is the greatest living American physicist?"
>
> Without hesitation, Rowland answered, "I am."
>
> After the trial, a friend who was shocked at this unexpected answer asked, "How could you give such a conceited answer?"
>
> "I couldn't help myself," Rowland replied, "I was under oath."

KNOW THESE WORDS

physicist: science specialist in physics
conceited: having a high opinion of oneself

Which of the following titles best summarizes the content of the passage?

(*a*) The Dangers of Cross-Examination
(*b*) A Funny Story
(*c*) Honesty Before Modesty
(*d*) The Importance of Telling the Truth

Your answer: _____

Answers

Let's examine the possible answers.

(a) This is a detail in the passage, not the central idea.

(b) This is much too broad. It could apply to thousands of passages.

(c) This captures the point of the paragraph. Though modest, Rowland felt he had to tell the truth as he saw it. This is the correct answer. It also suggests the humor of the passage.

(d) Rowland's insistence on telling the truth is not the main idea but the punch line, the surprise line that gives the point of a joke. The title also leaves out any reference to modesty, an important part of the passage.

Practice 1: Finding the Best Title

Read the following passage and answer the question at the end.

Where is all the world's land ice stored? Almost four million square miles of the earth's land surface are permanently under ice. Antarctica holds 80% of all that ice. Greenland stores about 12%. The remaining 8%, a very small percentage, is stored on mountain peaks and polar islands. These percentages refer to a permanent ice cover, not to the ice that forms around the world during winter and melts during summer. Because the ice at the North Pole covers a sea, not any land surface, this polar ice does not figure in these percentages.

KNOW THIS WORD

polar: concerning the North or South Pole

Which of the following titles best summarizes the content of the passage?

(a) The Extent of Polar Ice
(b) Greenland: The Icebox of the World
(c) A Cold Story
(d) The Earth's Permanent Land Ice Cover

Your answer 1: _____

Answers

You have four choices. One of them has to be correct. Sometimes the best method is to eliminate (get rid of) unsuitable answers first.

(a) Polar ice is mentioned in connection with the North Pole, but this is sea ice, not ice covering a land surface.

(b) This is a detail only. Greenland is mentioned as only one place where some of the world's land ice is stored.

(c) This is much too broad. It does not tie specifically into this passage.

(d) The passage deals with the permanent land ice cover by giving percentages of areas involved and excluding both temporary ice and sea ice. This is the best title.

Practice 2

Read the following passage and answer the question at the end.

Before the tunnel between France and England had been started, many inventors and contractors came up with ideas for constructing this important link. There is a favorite joke about a man who volunteered to dig the tunnel for 5,000 pounds. He said that he and his son could do the job and do it well.

"How will you do it?" he was asked.

"My son will start in France and I'll start in England. We'll dig toward each other and meet in the middle."

"Suppose you miss?" he was asked.

"Then you'll have two tunnels," he replied.

Which of the following titles best summarizes the content of the passage?

(a) Two Tunnels for the Price of One
(b) A Wild Idea
(c) A Plan for Joining France and England Together
(d) Tunnel Technology: The Wave of the Future

Your answer 2: _____

Answers

The tone of this passage is humorous. Therefore, the title should not be serious. It should be in keeping with the light touch of the passage.

(a) This is the best title. It perfectly captures the content and tone of the passage. The "two tunnels for the price of one" is a good title on two levels. First, the passage is indeed about building a tunnel between France and England. Second, the humor is the absurdity of the entire concept, which the suggested title catches.
(b) This is much too general, suitable for all kinds of passages other than this one.
(c) This is much too serious a title for this lighthearted joke.
(d) This is also too serious, taking seriously what is obviously an absurdity.

On Your Own: Finding the Best Title

Read the following passage and answer the question at the end.

One of the strangest stories in the history of metallurgy concerns aluminum. This is the most common metal in the crust of the earth, more common than iron, copper, or any other metal. Yet it is only fairly recently that aluminum has been extracted in useful form. Because it always occurs in combination with other minerals, it must be freed from its partners in order to be useful. It wasn't until 1886 that a good method was discovered for extracting the metal economically. Since that time, aluminum has played a major role wherever metals are used.

KNOW THESE WORDS

metallurgy: science of metals and metalworking

extracted: separated; taken out

economically: cheaply

Which of the following titles best summarizes the content of the passage?

(a) Aluminum and Its Brother Metals: Iron and Copper
(b) The Joys of Metalworking
(c) Aluminum: A Recently Useful Metal
(d) Problems with an Important Metal

Your answer: _____

Bonus: Finding the Best Title

Read the following passage and answer the question at the end.

A visit to an old graveyard reveals some sad information. The number of tombstones for infants and young children is enormous. But in the past, even adults tended to die young. In movies of life in 18th-century America, we are used to seeing pictures of happy, white-haired old people, but these were the exceptions. Few people lived long enough to see their children grown. A handful survived to see their grandchildren married. How short was the average life span in 1790? Dr. Benjamin Rush, a famous doctor, wrote that of a hundred people born in a given year in Philadelphia, more than a third died before the age of six. Only one quarter reached their twenty-sixth birthday. We owe a great debt to modern medicine and sanitation.

Which of the following titles best summarizes the content of the passage?

(a) A Report by Dr. Rush
(b) Life Spans in the Eighteenth Century
(c) How to Prevent Infant and Child Death
(d) The Story the Tombstones Tell

Your answer: _____

6. Finding Details

Details Support the Main Idea

Now that you have worked with getting the main idea, you are ready for the next step—*finding details.* You will not be looking mainly at the big picture. Instead, you will be trying to locate and understand particular items of information that support the main idea. These items are stated in the passage.

Before beginning the Question that follows, you may wish to review the topics of main idea and details on page 34.

Question: How Do You Find Details?

Read the following passage and answer the questions at the end.

> Television programs change as the tastes of viewers change. Westerns are popular for a while. Then they give way to detective stories. Situation comedies seem to be always available, but the number of people viewing them varies over time. Talk shows and variety shows have their ups and downs in popularity, too. But game shows seem to remain popular year after year. Game shows have tempting titles like *Wheel of Fortune* and *The $25,000 Pyramid.* Weekday morning game shows include *The Price Is Right, Tic Tac Dough, Scrabble, Headline Chasers,* and *Joker's Wild.* Some programs, like *Jeopardy,* challenge the knowledge of the contestants. Others are based more on luck. All game shows have their special fans, viewers who tune in day after day. Other television programs come and go, but game shows seem to go on forever.

Write the letter of your answer on the line at the right.

1. The programs that are said to be always available are

   (a) westerns   (b) situation comedies
   (c) detective stories (d) talk shows   1. _____

2. A program that challenges a contestant's knowledge is

   (a) *Jeopardy*   (b) *Headline Chasers*
   (c) *Tic Tac Dough*   (d) *Joker's Wild*   2. _____

3. A program that is NOT identified as a morning show is

   (a) *Joker's Wild*   (b) *Jeopardy*
   (c) *Headline Chasers* (d) *Tic Tac Dough*   3. _____

4. Which of the following sentences best expresses the main idea of the passage?

   (*a*) Situation comedies seem to have longer-lasting appeal than westerns or detective stories.
   (*b*) Other television programs come and go, but game shows seem to go on forever.
   (*c*) Talk shows and variety shows may be popular one year and unpopular the next.
   (*d*) Westerns were very popular for a long time.   4. _____

5. Which of the following titles best summarizes the content of the passage?

   (*a*) What to Watch on Television
   (*b*) Situation Comedies: The People's Choice
   (*c*) Changing Fads on Television
   (*d*) The Popularity of Game Shows on Television   5. _____

Answers

   When you choose an answer for a reading passage, be sure you base your answer on the passage as it appears in the test. Do not give your own opinion. Do not rely on a fact that *you* know but that does not appear in the reading. Stick to the passage as it is written—even if you think a fact is wrong. You might be sure from your own personal experience, for example, that one of the programs mentioned in #3 is an evening show, even though it is called a morning show in the passage. Don't base your answer on other information you might have. *Stick to the passage.* In this passage, *Jeopardy* is not identified as either a morning or an evening show. Now, let's look at the answers.

1. (*b*) With this kind of item, you must look back at the exact words in the passage. You find the sentence that contains the words *always available.* That sentence talks about situation comedies, and so (*b*) has to be the correct answer.
2. (*a*) Once again, the answer can be found in a single sentence. The key sentence begins, ''Some programs, like *Jeopardy* . . . .''
3. (*b*) Sometimes you will have to tell what something is NOT. Here all the programs except one are included in the sentence beginning. ''Weekday morning game shows . . . .'' The show *not* in this sentence is (*b*) *Jeopardy.*

   Notice that the letter of the answers to #3 and #4 is the same. That will sometimes happen. Never try to second-guess the tester. Don't think, for instance, that a certain answer is ''overdue'' or that ''three *c*'s in a row are impossible.''
4. (*b*) This question is a review of Section 4, ''Getting the Main Idea.'' Other types of programs are mentioned in the early sentences, but the passage deals mainly with game shows. Except for (*b*), the suggested answers are details.
5. (*d*) Choice (*a*) is too general. Situation comedies (*b*) are mentioned as having changes in popularity. Fads (*c*) fails to mention the heart of the paragraph: game shows. Only (*d*) accurately suggests the central point of the passage.

Use the following Practice to find details in a passage.

Practice: Finding Details

Read the following passage and answer the questions at the end.

"Do you want the job?" the interviewer asks. "You'll have to take care of 16 acres of lawn. You'll also have to care for 600 trees and hundreds of shrubs."

"That's all?" you ask.

"No. There's more. You'll have to tend two large gardens filled with flowering plants."

Just as you start to say, "No, thanks," the interviewer adds, "You won't have to do all the work yourself. You'll have a staff of 13, including gardeners, electricians, and janitors."

"That's better."

"And you'll have millions of people to check your skill. You'll be in charge of the White House lawn in Washington, D.C."

Actually, the job is already filled. The person in charge of the White House lawn is Mike Lawn. That's his real name, *Lawn*, which seems highly appropriate for his duties. Still, he has to spend about 40 percent of his time working at a desk. He can't wait to get outside and work along with his gardeners. The job isn't easy. He has to fight the same battles that homeowners face. Like home gardeners, he is bothered by fungi, insects, and drying out of the White House lawn. He provides fertilizer three times a year and soaks the ground in the growing season. Mike Lawn takes pride in his work and gets a lot of satisfaction from it.

If you visit the White House, be sure to notice the White House lawn and gardens.

KNOW THESE WORDS

appropriate: well-suited; right

fungi: kinds of plants without chlorophyll

Write the letter of your answer on the line at the right.

1. The number of people on Mike Lawn's staff is

(*a*) none   (*b*) 13

(*c*) 40   (*d*) not mentioned   1. _____

2. Mike Lawn most enjoys

   (*a*) working with the gardeners
   (*b*) sitting at his desk
   (*c*) soaking the ground in the growing season
   (*d*) winning the fight against insects   2. _____

3. According to the passage, the two gardens are

   (*a*) heavily planted with trees
   (*b*) filled with flowering plants
   (*c*) covered with grass
   (*d*) located far from the lawn area   3. _____

4. Mike Lawn applies fertilizer to the White House lawn

   (*a*) every other day
   (*b*) when the lawn is dried out
   (*c*) when he is not too busy
   (*d*) three times a year   4. _____

5. Which of the following sentences best expresses the main idea of
   the passage?

   (*a*) Mike Lawn is an employee of the U.S. government.
   (*b*) All lawns take a lot of work.
   (*c*) Mike Lawn has the perfect name because he works on lawns.
   (*d*) The White House lawn demands a lot of attention.   5. _____

Answers

Be sure to base your answers only on what the passage says. Find specific sentences to prove your answers.

1. (*b*) The imaginary interviewer says, ''You'll have a staff of 13.'' Since the interview is for Mike Lawn's job, all the facts in the interview apply to Lawn's job. Therefore, the correct answer is (*b*).
2. (*a*) Mike Lawn ''can't wait to get outside and work along with his gardeners.''
3. (*b*) The passage mentions ''two large gardens filled with flowering plants.'' That is the only specific mention of the gardens.
4. (*d*) Mike Lawn ''provides fertilizer three times a year.''
5. (*d*) In #1 through #4, the correct answer could be found and quoted. When you are looking for the main idea, however, you will seldom find a direct quote. You will have to keep the whole passage in mind. If you do, you will see that only (*d*) expresses the main idea. The other choices are faulty.
   (*a*) This is probably true, but it is not the main idea. In fact, Lawn's employer is not mentioned in the passage.
   (*b*) This statement is much too broad. The passage is not about ''all lawns,'' but about the White House lawn.
   (*c*) Although this is an interesting point, it is not the main idea of the passage.

Remember:

1. Details support the main idea, but details cannot be main ideas.
2. When answering a question calling for details, go back to the passage. Find the sentence that is directly related to the test item. Forget any ideas you may already have on the subject. *Stick to the passage.*
3. When answering a question calling for the main idea, be sure the idea suggested covers the passage as snugly as a roof covers a house. It should be neither too broad nor too narrow. It should not be wholly or partly off the topic.

On Your Own: Finding Details

Read the following passage and answer the questions at the end.

Our beaches are restless. They are on the move. During a strong wind or a storm, they may shift. Tons of sand may be moved in a short time. A house that stood a hundred feet from the ocean may find the water lapping at the door. In a few hours, a long, lovely beach may be gone. From Maine to Texas, our beaches are under attack.

A major cause of beach loss is a rise in the sea level. In the last century, the sea level has risen about a foot. In the next hundred years, it will rise at least two more feet, and perhaps as much as ten feet.

Nature is cruel to Eastern beaches, but people cause damage, too. Without thinking about what they are doing, they destroy beach grass. This is unfortunate, because beach grass is nature's ally in holding back the sea. Beach grass helps to anchor sand dunes in place, and the dunes provide protection. Yet people often trample beach grass. They run vehicles over the dunes, killing the vegetation. When the beach grass goes, there is no natural way of keeping the sand in place.

Many people build houses too close to the water. They are asking for trouble, because the movement of the sea is hard to stop. Sometimes they bring in new sand to help keep the sea away. But sand without beach grass soon washes out to sea. Sometimes they build concrete walls to protect their property. But the rolling, often violent sea cuts away the land beneath the wall. When the sea begins to approach buildings that are too close to the water, there is no protection that really works.

What should be done? Most experts agree that a first step is banning the construction of new buildings on threatened beaches. Federal and state governments are trying to stop new beach development, especially on barrier beaches. These are the narrow, sandy strips of land that lie off the East Coast mainland and help to protect it from the open ocean. Many expensive seaside homes have already been lost to the sea. Many more will follow.

KNOW THESE WORDS

ally: helper

dunes: small hills of sand

Write the letter of your answer on the line at the right.

1. In the past century, the level of the sea has risen

   (a) not at all   (b) one foot
   (c) two feet   (d) five feet   1. _____

2. A natural ally in the fight against beach destruction is

   (a) the wind   (b) tiny sea creatures
   (c) home builders   (d) beach grass   2. _____

3. When a concrete wall is built to protect a building, the usual result is that

   (a) the sea cuts away the land beneath the wall
   (b) neighbors object to the ugly appearance
   (c) beach grass grows at the base of the wall
   (d) the sea does no more damage   3. _____

4. A barrier beach is a

   (a) park for recreation
   (b) beach where swimming is not allowed
   (c) narrow, sandy strip of land
   (d) beach without houses   4. _____

5. Which of the following sentences best expresses the main idea of the passage?

   (a) Houses are often built too close to the water.
   (b) The barrier beaches are beautiful areas.
   (c) The sea is constantly threatening the shoreline from Maine to Texas.
   (d) Federal and state governments are trying to find ways of handling the problem of beach destruction.   5. _____

Bonus 1: Finding Details

Read the following passage and answer the questions at the end.

Ever since the coming of the Industrial Revolution, machines have taken over more and more of the jobs formerly performed by farmers and their animals. Third World countries have watched their industrialized neighbors and have tried to imitate them, transferring more jobs to machines. Yet the transfer has not been entirely successful. Many countries now realize that machines are too expensive and are beginning to appreciate once more the use of animals for transportation and other tasks.

Modern technology can, however, help improve the output of animals. Experts are finding ways to make the work of animals more effective. By changing the design of yokes and harnesses, they have increased the work ability of animals like oxen, donkeys, water buffaloes, and horses.

J. K. Garner visited Thailand in 1958 to help village farmers. He was shocked to see water buffaloes burdened with a wooden beam across the tops of their necks. The wood cut deeply into the flesh of the animals and the yoking was most inefficient. Garner strapped a horse collar onto a water buffalo and increased its pulling power amazingly. A breast strap improved efficiency even more.

In Latin America, improvements can be even greater. Latin American farmers yoke their cattle by the horns. Thus all the pulling is done by the animal's head, a weak part of the body. This procedure must be changed.

Improvements also need to be made in the vehicles pulled by the animals. Two-wheeled carts, for example, are especially difficult for animals. An unfortunate animal pulling a two-wheeled cart often has to carry 100 pounds of weight on its neck. The neck takes the shock of braking and turning. Potholes, bumps, stones—all make the life of the animal miserable.

There are opportunities for improvement all around the world. At first, tractors seemed a wise solution. Tractors can outpull draft animals. They don't need food. Unfortunately, they require a lot of maintenance. And they're expensive to begin with. They do not fit into the village life as efficiently as draft animals. It will be generations, if ever, before all draft animals are replaced by machines. Meanwhile, the world can make more humane, more efficient use of the animals that are available.

KNOW THESE WORDS

Industrial Revolution: the time in history when machines began to be widely used

technology: use of science

yokes: wooden frames placed on animals

draft animals: animals used to do heavy work

humane: merciful; civilized

Write the letter of your answer on the line at the right.

1. All the following animals were mentioned in the passage EXCEPT
   (*a*) horses   (*b*) camels
   (*c*) water buffalo   (*d*) oxen   1. _____

2. The wooden-beam yoke is

   (*a*) efficient but uncomfortable for the animal
   (*b*) inefficient but comfortable for the animal
   (*c*) better than a horse collar for pulling loads
   (*d*) inefficient and uncomfortable for the animal   2. _____

3. Farmers in Latin America use

   (*a*) a yoke by the horns   (*b*) a modified horse collar
   (*c*) the traditional wooden   (*d*) a crisscross breast strap
          beam   3. _____

4. Tractors are superior to draft animals in

   (*a*) appearance   (*b*) maintenance
   (*c*) pulling power   (*d*) fitting into village life   4. _____

5. Which of the following best expresses the main idea of the passage?

   (*a*) The Third World should industrialize immediately.
   (*b*) In general, draft animals are superior to machines.
   (*c*) J. K. Garner revolutionized farming techniques around the world.
   (*d*) Animals can play a major role in solving Third-World energy problems.   5. _____

6. Which of the following titles best summarizes the content of the passage?

   (*a*) Using Oxen for Farm Work
   (*b*) Helping Our Poorer Neighbors to the South
   (*c*) Solving Third-World Problems by Animal Power
   (*d*) Modern Technology vs. Village Ways   6. _____

Bonus 2

Read the following passage and answer the questions at the end.

At intervals, the world seems to experience energy crises. Reliance upon oil has made many nations vulnerable to a reduction of supplies or sometimes a cutoff. Wars in the Middle East have threatened the energy lifelines of industrialized nations throughout the world. Rising prices have brought dangerous inflation.

Scientists have long sought alternatives to oil. Fortunately, wood, coal, and natural gas have helped during periods of oil shortages. Tidal power and wind power have their advocates. Hydroelectric plants have provided inexpensive energy for many areas. Solar energy is the cheapest and most abundant of all energy, but it is not easy to capture and tame. In some parts of the world, solar energy is completely impractical. Energy from the earth's internal heat, geothermal energy, is suitable for only a few areas.

Now scientists are seeking a new energy source: ocean power. This is not the power of waves, tides, or waterfalls. This procedure extracts energy from ocean water. It depends upon the differences in temperature between water deep down and water at the surface. It is based on the principle that a turbine can be powered by the difference in temperature. It works best in the tropics where the difference is at least 40 degrees.

To run the turbine, engineers need a continuous flow of both warm and cold water. The warm water runs through an evaporator and returns to the sea. The cold water runs through a condenser and returns to the sea. Here, in a nutshell, is how the procedure works in an experimental station in Hawaii.

Warm surface water is pumped into an evaporator. This evaporator contains a fluid with a low boiling point, like ammonia or Freon. The warm surface water causes the fluid to boil and vaporize. This energy outburst spins a turbine and generates electricity. But this is only half the process. Otherwise, the energy production would halt after this first step. The cycle must be closed. The ammonia or Freon must be cooled again.

How can the evaporating fluid be cooled, so that it can go back to the evaporator and be vaporized again? Cold ocean water is needed. To get this cold water, engineers pipe it through a long tube. This tube runs 5,000 feet offshore to a depth of 2,000 feet, where the water is quite cold. The cold water runs through a condenser, where it meets the ammonia or Freon vapor. The cold water cools the ammonia or Freon and sends it back on its way to repeat the cycle all over again. The fluid moves from evaporator to condenser and back to evaporator again. The change in temperature has done the work.

Does this all sound too good to be true? Unfortunately, there are some problems. Land locations are costly and hard to find. The conversion plant is also expensive. There are other costs that threaten the practicality of the idea. Still, with oil in ultimately limited supplies, nations must keep looking for a source of energy that is renewable and nonpolluting. Other, similar ocean installations may find ways to reduce costs and make the project more manageable, like floating barges anchored at sea.

The world cannot afford to overlook any possible energy source. Current sources may just not meet our needs. Those who advocate wind power, for example, overlook one important fact. If we took all the available space and put windmills everywhere, we'd get less than 1% of our energy needs. Energy requirements in the coming decades will be staggering. Every possibility must be explored. The oceans are a new energy frontier.

KNOW THESE WORDS

intervals: time or space between
vulnerable: open to injury
inflation: sharp rise in prices
alternatives: choices between things

> **advocates:** those in favor of something
> **hydroelectric:** producing electricity from water power
> **solar:** of the sun
> **geothermal:** providing heat from the earth
> **turbine:** kind of engine
> **condenser:** machine for changing gas into liquid
> **conversion:** act of changing
> **practicality:** usefulness; workability

Write the letter of your answer on the line at the right.

1. All the following sources of energy were mentioned in the passage EXCEPT

   (*a*) wind   (*b*) tidal

   (*c*) chemical   (*d*) solar   1. _____

2. The experimental plant in Hawaii gets cold water from a depth of

   (*a*) 40 feet   (*b*) 200 feet

   (*c*) 2,000 feet   (*d*) 5,000 feet   2. _____

3. The energy source that could give us, at best, about 1% of our energy needs is

   (*a*) wind   (*b*) coal

   (*c*) natural gas   (*d*) tidal   3. _____

4. According to the passage, electric energy is gained from

   (*a*) cold water by itself   (*b*) the vaporization of ammonia or Freon

   (*c*) the condenser   (*d*) rainfall   4. _____

5. Which of the following best expresses the main idea of the passage?

   (*a*) The ocean will replace oil as a source of energy within the next decade.
   (*b*) Oil crises may trigger dangerous inflation.
   (*c*) Plants that convert differences in ocean temperatures to energy are expensive.
   (*d*) Ocean-water-power conversion plants are worth exploring as a good source of energy.   5. _____

7. Drawing Inferences

Up to now, you have been finding specific details in reading passages. The writer has presented these details directly. There is no mystery about them. If you look hard enough and carefully enough through the passage, you will find them.

But when you take a reading test, you will also be asked to draw inferences. That means you will be asked to infer certain answers from the information you are given.

"Inferences?" you ask. *"Infer?* I don't even know what the words mean."

The words may be unfamiliar, but don't worry. You have been drawing inferences all your life. You began to make a kind of inference when you were a baby. You have been getting better at the skill all the time. Yet many students panic when they are asked to draw inferences on a reading test. They don't know how to go about the task. The sections ahead will show you how to draw inferences from what you read.

What Are Inferences?

When did you first learn to draw inferences? Long ago—even before you can remember. Your first inferences were probably about food. When you saw an adult coming toward you with a jar of baby food, you knew it was time to eat. No words had to be spoken. You knew you were hungry. You recognized the jar and the label. Dinner! You had learned how to draw the right inference.

Today you use this skill on many occasions. If you see smoke, you infer that there is a fire. If you hear an ambulance siren wailing on the highway, you infer that there has been an accident. If you see a black cloud approaching from the west, you infer that there will be a storm. You don't think about the process each time. You don't say, "Wow! I'm drawing an inference!" But that's what you're doing.

An *inference* is a conclusion reached *without a direct statement or explanation.* If your friend says, "The Red Sox lost 11-2 last night," she has made a direct statement. But suppose that, rather than making a direct statement, she says, "Those poor Red Sox. Weak pitching. Three errors. Will they ever start winning again?" You may *infer* that the Red Sox lost last night, even though she hasn't said it.

Inferences need to be checked for accuracy. For example, the wailing ambulance siren on the highway may not mean an accident. The ambulance might be answering a false alarm. Or perhaps someone who is ill is being rushed to a hospital. All you can do is to try to draw correct, accurate inferences and then check them later if you can.

Strong and Weak Inferences

Inferences can be either strong or weak. Let's look at both kinds.

1. *Statement:* When the game was over, the home fans loudly cheered the players.

   Inference: The home team won.

2. *Statement:* Joe didn't arrive at our house on time.

   Inference: Joe dislikes our family.

One of these inferences is more likely to be accurate than the other. The first is a **strong inference.** Since the home fans are happy, their team probably won. You cannot be completely sure until you check further. However, the inference seems to be a sound one.

The second is a **weak inference.** There may be many reasons for Joe's lateness. He may have been caught in traffic. He may have gotten the time wrong. He may have stopped to buy a present for the family. He may be forgetful. All of these are possibilities. Joe may like the family very much, but he may still be late in arriving.

Question 1: How Do You Distinguish Between Strong and Weak Inferences?

Classify each of the following inferences by writing *strong* or *weak* on the line at the right.

1. *Statement:* The potatoes taste burnt.

   Inference: They were cooked too long or at too high a heat.   1. _____

2. *Statement:* Beth isn't going out for girls' basketball.

   Inference: She's afraid of not making the team.   2. _____

3. *Statement:* All the lights in our neighborhood went out at once.

   Inference: There's a general outage, or loss of electrical power.   3. _____

4. *Statement:* The newspaper wasn't delivered to our doorstep this morning.

   Inference: The workers at the newspaper have gone on strike.   4. _____

5. *Statement:* He failed the spelling test.

   Inference: He didn't study the words to be tested.   5. _____

6. *Statement:* He failed the spelling test.

   Inference: He had bad luck because of walking under
   a ladder.   6. _____

7. *Statement:* It's 3:00 A.M., and the factory seems closed.

   Inference: The factory doesn't operate 24 hours a day.   7. _____

8. *Statement:* This is the fifth time I've gotten poison ivy
   after picking blackberries in the woods.

   Inference: There must be poison ivy in the woods.   8. _____

9. *Statement:* I can't find my science textbook.

   Inference: It was stolen on the bus.   9. _____

10. *Statement:* Maria isn't coming to the dance.

    Inference: She has no friends at school.   10. _____

Answers

1. *Strong.* These are good reasons for potatoes tasting burnt.
2. *Weak.* Beth may have other reasons: lack of time, family responsibilities, desire for another activity.
3. *Strong.* Since *all* the lights have gone out, there is probably a general outage.
4. *Weak.* There are many possible reasons for not getting the paper: the delivery person didn't get up in time; the delivery person quit; the papers didn't reach the delivery person.
5. *Strong.* Failing to study is a common cause for failing a test.
6. *Weak.* There is no connection between failing a test and walking under a ladder.
7. *Strong.* If the factory is closed at 3:00 A.M., it seems clear that it does not operate around the clock.
8. *Strong.* Getting poison ivy five times in a row strongly suggests that there is poison ivy in the woods.
9. *Weak.* There are many other possible explanations: carelessness, leaving the book at home or at school, borrowing by someone else.
10. *Weak.* Maria may not be coming because she is ill, has something else planned, doesn't like dancing, or for some other reason.

Choosing the Strongest Inference

You have now worked with strong and weak inferences. Sometimes on tests you will be asked to pick out the *strongest* of a number of inferences. Use the Question-and-Answer method to explore this kind of test question.

Question 2: What Are the Clues to Drawing Inferences?

The following type of slot-completion passage is called a *cloze exercise.* In the blank space, write the letter of the phrase that makes the best sense in the context.

> There were no cars in the parking lot. The restaurant shades were drawn. An automobile with two couples drove into the parking area, paused a moment, and then _____ .
>
> (a) put out the lights
> (b) honked the horn
> (c) dropped off three passengers (d) drove off (e) blocked the restaurant door

Answer

The people in the car probably intended to eat at the restaurant. When they got to the parking lot, they found no cars there. Then they saw that the shades were drawn. They inferred that the restaurant was closed. You can probably infer that they left. The best answer is (d) *drove off.*

Inferring a Single Word

Some tests ask you to choose a single word to fill a blank. Study the example in Question 3.

Question 3: How Can You Infer the Meaning of a Single Word?

In the blank space, write the letter of the word that makes the best sense in the context.

> When Brenda returned from the long hike, her steps were slow, and her shoulders drooped. It was clear that she was _____ from her experience.
>
> (a) happy (b) weary
> (c) bright (d) bitter
> (e) bored

Answer

There are three main clues here: the long hike, Brenda's slow steps, and her drooping shoulders. What do these clues, taken together, tell you? Let's look at the five possibilities. It's true that under certain circumstances, any one of the answers could fit. But you are asked to infer the *best* answer.

The answers (a) *happy* and (c) *bright* seem completely out of place. The words are too cheerful to fit Brenda's appearance. On the other hand, (d) *bitter* and (e) *bored*, while less cheerful, don't fit either. Both suggest what Brenda's feelings were, but there is nothing in the two sentences about feelings or emotions. You don't know what Brenda's feelings were—and you can't read into the sentences more than is suggested. From what is written, you can only infer that Brenda was tired. Therefore, the best answer is (b) *weary.*

On Your Own 1: Drawing Inferences

In the blank space, write the letter of the correct answer for each numbered item.

1. A trademark is a name, a sign, or a picture that appears on a product to make it easy for a customer to _____ the product.

   (*a*) overlook   (*b*) sell   (*c*) remember
   (*d*) carry   (*e*) eat

2. Spring rains and melting snow had made the country roads difficult to drive on; there was _____ everywhere.

   (*a*) grass   (*b*) advertising   (*c*) ice
   (*d*) sleet   (*e*) mud

3. When Marilyn got on the scale, shook her head, and said "Oh, no!" I could tell that she was _____ .

   (*a*) delighted   (*b*) afraid   (*c*) unkind
   (*d*) thoughtful   (*e*) disappointed

4. Since Julie has been given a surprise party every year for the past three years, we think she _____ one this year.

   (*a*) expects   (*b*) forgets   (*c*) dislikes
   (*d*) enjoys   (*e*) prepares

5. Traffic is so heavy on Route 52 that the county has decided to _____ the road.

   (*a*) widen   (*b*) close   (*c*) pave
   (*d*) renumber   (*e*) narrow

Inferences in Longer Passages

You may be asked to draw inferences about the correct words to fill blanks in a longer passage. Study this kind of test question in the following Practice.

Practice: Drawing Inferences

Read the following passage. Then write the letter of the correct answer in each numbered blank.

> Winston Churchill was the great British leader in the Second World War. After the war, he 1. _____ to a quiet life of reading and painting. But he was still 2. _____. On his 80th birthday, a young photographer came to take his picture. After the young man had finished, he made a 3. _____ remark. He said he hoped he would photograph Churchill on his 100th birthday.
>
> Churchill replied, "I don't see why not, young man. You look reasonably fit to me."

1. (*a*) ran (*b*) walked
   (*c*) retired (*d*) fled
   (*e*) stumbled

2. (*a*) friendly
   (*b*) calm
   (*c*) unknown
   (*d*) likable
   (*e*) famous

3. (*a*) grim (*b*) polite
   (*c*) loud (*d*) stupid
   (*e*) wicked

Answers

First read the entire passage. Then you will have an idea of what it's all about. This passage tells a humorous story about Winston Churchill. Churchill playfully turns the tables on a young photographer. The young man says he hopes he'll photograph Churchill on Churchill's 100th birthday. Churchill jokes that he sees no reason why the young man shouldn't be around for that occasion.

When you have thought about the entire passage, you should be able to handle the parts.

1. (*c*) The best choice is (*c*) *retired*. The words *ran*, *walked*, and *stumbled* suggest physical action. Such action is out of place here. Nor is *fled* correct. There is no suggestion that Churchill was running away.
2. (*e*) Since Churchill was a famous wartime leader, you can infer that he was still *famous* at 80. There is no reason to make any choice except (*e*).
3. (*b*) You can infer that the young man was being kind when he spoke. Therefore, (*b*) *polite* is the only possible answer. The other choices do not make good sense.

On Your Own 2

Read the following passage and answer the questions at the end.

> Once upon a time, you could buy an entire house through a mail-order catalog. It would cost you less than $2,000. No, this isn't a fairy tale. In 1908, Sears, Roebuck & Co. began selling houses by mail. If you were interested in buying, you would glance through a special pamphlet at pictures of attractive houses. You would then send in an order and wait for the house.

The house arrived in sections, of course. Every board had been cut to size. All parts were numbered to fit. A 76-page instruction booklet gave you all the help you needed to complete the house yourself. Or you might hire a builder to put the numbered parts together.

These Sears houses have become precious museum pieces. Today's owners are proud of their treasures. One house that cost $2,000 in 1913 is now worth $148,000. There is a movement to keep these houses from being torn down.

Sears kept its Modern Homes Department until 1937. Then it stopped selling complete homes through the catalog. Sears could no longer make a profit from the sales.

1. Write the letter of the statement that best expresses the main idea.

   (a) Sears once sold attractive houses through the mail-order catalog.
   (b) Some owners hired a builder to put the house together.
   (c) Sears dropped mail-order house sales because of a loss of profit.
   (d) House owners should always see a picture of the house they plan to build.   1. _____

2. Which of the following titles best summarizes the content of the passage?

   (a) The True Story of Sears, Roebuck & Co.
   (b) An Interesting Story About Houses
   (c) The Importance of Following Instructions
   (d) Houses by Mail   2. _____

3. The $148,000 house cost $2,000 in (a) 1908 (b) 1913 (c) 1937 (d) 1976.   3. _____

4. The parts of the mail-order house can best be compared with (a) the pieces of a jigsaw puzzle (b) a 76-page instruction booklet (c) a carpenter's toolbox (d) an illustrated mail-order catalog.   4. _____

5. In the expression ''Today's owners are proud of their treasures,'' the word *treasures* applies to (a) jewelry (b) furniture (c) carpets (d) houses.   5. _____

6. There is a movement to keep the Sears houses from being torn down because the houses are (a) more comfortable than modern homes (b) owned by people who bought them many years ago (c) museum pieces (d) as bright as the day they were built.   6. _____

Bonus: Drawing Inferences

Read the following passage and answer the questions at the end.

Scientists have created new and improved varieties of fruits and vegetables. The changes in sweet corn, for example, have been almost miraculous. Most changes in plants provide larger fruits or vegetables.

Recent changes include a dark green seedless cucumber, a round eggplant, and a pencil-thin asparagus. A newly developed tomato is said to keep its flavor all winter at room temperature. There are differences in size and appearance, too. Experimenters have developed a pumpkin the size of one's fist and a 40-pound watermelon with beautiful yellow stars on its skin.

The strangest changes of all, though, involve new colors. Would you eat blue potatoes, purple beans, or pink cabbages? These exotic vegetables are not in most supermarkets, but they do appeal to gardeners who are looking for something different. A new kind of radish reverses the usual coloring. It is red inside and white outside. One grower is raising white beets. A new lima bean has an ivory pod streaked with red.

Some of the innovations will probably survive, while others will not. Blue potatoes, for example, are not very popular. They seem to repel many people, not attract them.

KNOW THIS WORD

innovations: new ideas

1. Write the letter of the statement that best expresses the main idea.

    (*a*) Changes in fruits and vegetables have not been popular with the public.
    (*b*) Plant experimenters have made many surprising changes in vegetables and fruits.
    (*c*) A well-balanced diet is a basic element in good nutrition.
    (*d*) Creation of a hardy tomato will probably change the way in which tomatoes are grown and harvested.   1. _____

2. An important reason for the changes made in fruits and vegetables is (*a*) greater public acceptance (*b*) better taste (*c*) curiosity (*d*) ease of cooking.   2. _____

3. A round eggplant and a pencil-thin asparagus differ from the traditional vegetables in (*a*) shape (*b*) color (*c*) size (*d*) taste.   3. _____

4. The passage suggests that some plant changes are made merely for the sake of (*a*) convenience of farmers (*b*) foreign markets (*c*) novelty (*d*) advertising.   4. _____

5. Blue potatoes probably repel people because the color is so (*a*) dark (*b*) bright (*c*) commonplace (*d*) unnatural.   5. _____

6. As used in paragraph 3, *exotic* means (*a*) tasty (*b*) unusual (*c*) nourishing (*d*) expensive.   6. _____

7. As used in paragraph 4, *repel* means (*a*) win over (*b*) bore (*c*) drive away (*d*) influence.   7. _____

8. Using Synonyms and Associated Ideas

In the previous section, you drew inferences from the wording of entire sentences or even paragraphs. Often, however, you will get more direct help. You will still be drawing inferences, but in doing so, you will use specific clues built into the passages.

Pairs of Words with Similar Meanings

What Are Synonyms?

A *synonym* is a word that has *nearly the same meaning* as another word. Here are ten examples of paired synonyms:

agree—consent	courage—bravery
boast—brag	near—close
break—smash	observe—watch
cheerful—happy	powerful—strong
complain—gripe	stumble—trip

Question 1: How Do You Distinguish Between Synonyms in Pairs?

In the following list of paired synonyms, the less common word is at the right. Complete each sentence after the list by inserting one of the underlined words. If you are unsure, use the synonym clue to help you.

acceptable—suitable	desire—crave
better—superior	high—lofty
blue—indigo	honest—upright
clear—evident	inventive—creative
cruel—ferocious	stop—cease

1. My old tennis shoes were good, but my new ones are _____ .

2. The eagle had built its nest in a(n) _____ tree.

3. Her workroom was decorated in striking shades of red and _____ .

4. Sally, who is very _____ , wrote a prize-winning poem about celery.

5. Do you _____ chocolate if you haven't had it for some time?

6. All writing must _____ when the bell rings.

7. The villain in the story is a(n) _____ pirate.

8. Your new party dress will be _____ to wear to the wedding reception.

9. The defendant smiled and tried to sound _____ on the witness stand, despite the strong case against him.

10. It was _____ to the jury that he had lied.

Answers

1. superior	6. cease
2. lofty	7. ferocious
3. indigo	8. suitable
4. creative	9. upright
5. crave	10. evident

Next, let's use the Question-and-Answer approach to see how the pairing of synonyms can help you in sentences and longer passages.

Question 2: How Do Synonyms Provide Clues to Meaning?

Try to use the pairing of synonyms to fill in the blank below. The words to be paired can appear in the same sentence or in different sentences.

A motorist asked Ted and me to help start his engine. We knew nothing about his problem and could not _____ him.

(*a*) tease (*b*) copy
(*c*) assist (*d*) anger
(*e*) control

Answer

The two words that must be paired are these:

- *help* in the first sentence
- the word to fill the blank in the second sentence

What is needed in the blank is a synonym for *help*. It isn't *tease, copy, anger,* or *control*. The correct answer is (*c*) *assist*.

Practice 1: Studying Paired Synonyms

Study the use of pairing in the following sentences.

The day was wet, and the farmer did not permit us to pick strawberries. He promised, however, that the next day he would _____ us to fill our buckets.	(a) prevent (b) chase (c) deny (d) enjoy (e) allow

Answer

The paired words are *permit* and the word needed to fill the blank. Since only *allow* is a synonym for *permit*, (e) is the correct answer.

Practice 2

Note how paired synonyms help reading comprehension.

Alfred Hitchcock was a master at making scary movies. *The Birds* is an example of a 1. _____ film. In it, familiar ideas are turned upside down. Birds that are usually peaceful are no longer 2. _____ , but dangerous. They attack human beings in great flocks.

Hitchcock was pleased with his achievements and 3. _____ of his fame. Once in a French airport he introduced himself as a producer.

"What do you produce?" asked the official.

Hitchcock replied, "Gooseflesh!"

1. (a) funny
   (b) forgotten
   (c) loud (d) sad
   (e) frightening

2. (a) wild (b) gentle
   (c) smart
   (d) colorful
   (e) noisy

3. (a) proud
   (b) doubtful
   (c) ashamed
   (d) fearful
   (e) unafraid

Answers

Always read the entire passage before starting to choose any answers. This passage is about Alfred Hitchcock, the movie director and producer. It begins by describing one of his films. It then mentions Hitchcock's opinion of his work and ends with a joke that Hitchcock made at a French airport.

After you have thought about the whole passage, turn to the individual items.

1. (e) The best choice is (e) *frightening*. It is paired with its synonym, *scary*. The other choices do not make sense.
2. (b) Although (b) *gentle* is not an exact synonym for *peaceful*, it is the best answer. Sometimes you will find that no answer seems perfect to you. When that happens, think carefully about the choices and pick the one that seems most nearly right.
3. (a) If Hitchcock was pleased with his achievements, he was (a) *proud*. The other choices are negative, except for *unafraid*, which doesn't make good sense.

On Your Own 1: Studying Synonyms

Read the following passage and answer the questions at the end. Note the use of helpful synonyms throughout the passage: *located—situated*; *wide range—variety*; *do well—thrive*; *hot—fiery*; *dangerous—destructive*.

> Big Bend National Park is located along the Rio Grande in southern Texas. It is situated in the curve of the river, far from any cities. The park contains a wide range of plant and animal life. This variety occurs because Big Bend includes both high mountains and low-lying deserts.
>
> Trees do well in the higher altitudes of the Chisos peaks. Many beautiful shrubs also thrive in the mountains. The desert floor is hot, especially in the summer. Temperatures often reach a fiery 100 degrees along the river itself.
>
> In summer, heavy, dangerous thunderstorms sometimes strike the Big Bend region. These destructive cloudbursts can quickly fill dry river beds and destroy bridges many miles away.

1. Write the letter of the statement that best expresses the main idea.

    (*a*) Big Bend National Park is a place of beauty, variety, and sometimes turbulent weather.
    (*b*) Trees grow well in the higher altitudes of Big Bend National Park.
    (*c*) Big Bend is an isolated park, far from any cities.
    (*d*) Both mountains and desert show a rich abundance of plant and animal life.   1. _____

2. Big Bend got its name because of its location

    (*a*) in the Chisos mountains
    (*b*) in a curve of the Rio Grande
    (*c*) near a bend in the borderline with New Mexico
    (*d*) near important highway bridges   2. _____

3. Temperatures of 100 degrees are common

    (*a*) in late spring
    (*b*) in the dry riverbeds
    (*c*) on the lower Chisos peaks
    (*d*) along the Rio Grande   3. _____

4. Summer weather in the Big Bend region can be characterized as
(*a*) quiet (*b*) surprisingly cool (*c*) consistently dry (*d*) sometimes
dangerous.   4. _____

5. As used in paragraph 2, *thrive* means (*a*) die (*b*) flourish (*c*) barely
survive (*d*) dry up.   5. _____

Using Associated Ideas

Another kind of clue to the word needed to fill a blank is less obvious than
paired synonyms. Sometimes you have to look for a word that is *associated*, or
connected, with a previous word or idea. The word is not a synonym, but it does
follow logically from what has already been said. Here's an example.

The new library has increased its circula-tion. All the _____ seem to like the new building.	(*a*) boys (*b*) girls (*c*) athletes (*d*) readers (*e*) merchants

You think of *readers* with libraries. All the other choices name groups that may
use the library, but nothing in the two sentences points specifically to them. Therefore, you need a word directly connected to the idea of a library. The answer must
be (*d*) *readers*.

Question 3: How Do Associated Ideas Provide Clues to Word Meanings?

In the blank space, write the letter of the correct answer.

1. Can you keep a _____? Promise that you won't tell anyone else.

   (*a*) joke   (*b*) coin   (*c*) credit card
   (*d*) secret   (*e*) news story

2. Many people from the area submitted paintings, drawings, sculpture, and craft
   projects. The _____ seemed more skilled than ever before.

   (*a*) officials   (*b*) sketches   (*c*) hostesses
   (*d*) electricians (*e*) artists

3. The lawn was beautifully cut. The plantings around the house looked well-
   tended and healthy. The _____ had done an excellent job.

   (*a*) farmers   (*b*) swimmers   (*c*) gardeners
   (*d*) butlers   (*e*) doctors

Answers

1. (*d*) A promise not to tell anyone is associated with a *secret*. Notice, too, that the word *keep* goes with the word *secret*. You don't "keep" a joke, for example. Any connections of this kind that you can make will help you get the right answer.
2. (*e*) Any answer might make sense under some circumstances, but you have to go by what is actually written. The *officials*, *hostesses*, and *electricians* may all have been skilled. However, there is nothing to relate them to the sending in of artwork. The only choice you can associate with the four kinds of art that are named—"paintings, drawings, sculpture, and craft projects"—is *artists*.
3. (*c*) Of the choices that are given, only *gardeners* cut lawns and tend plantings.

Now look for associations in the following brief passage.

Practice 3: Using Associated Ideas

Write the letter of the word that best completes the sentence.

> An unusual material had been used for the roof of the indoor tennis court. The builder had used canvas to fabricate the roof. Air pressure held the structure up.

As used in this passage, *fabricate* means (*a*) uncover (*b*) construct (*c*) decorate (*d*) paint.

Your answer 3: _____

Answer

First read the passage carefully and think about it. Then try each choice to see which one makes the best sense. You don't use canvas to *paint* a roof. You might use canvas to *decorate* it, but the passage as a whole suggests that the entire roof is being discussed. *Uncover* makes no sense at all. The passage deals with putting a roof on, not taking it off. The correct answer is (*b*) *construct*.

On Your Own 2: Studying Associated Ideas

Read the following passage and answer the questions at the end. Note how associated ideas help reading comprehension.

Many birds migrate twice a year. When these birds fly to their winter homes, they often cover great distances. Nearly half of our songbirds spend eight or ten weeks in the Northeast, building nests and raising their young. After a few months, they relinquish their nests, leave the familiar areas, and then head south. Some birds fly to Central or South America for the winter. There they look for familiar areas and spend six or seven months before returning north. They also spend months making the dangerous journeys between their summer and winter homes.

What happens if their wintering grounds are destroyed? If the birds cannot find suitable homes, they will not live through the winter. Many worldwide programs have been set up to protect migrating birds' northern and southern homes so that these birds will continue to survive.

KNOW THIS WORD

grounds: places favorable for birds

1. Write the letter of the statement that best expresses the main idea.

    (a) Birds risk their lives whenever they travel long distances.
    (b) Steps must be taken to preserve bird nesting areas in the Northeast.
    (c) Some birds migrate, while others do not.
    (d) Migrating birds need secure summer and winter homes to survive.   1. _____

2. As used in paragraph 1, *relinquish* means (a) leave behind (b) redecorate (c) destroy (d) mark.   2. _____

3. Raising their young is done by birds (a) in special nests prepared by homeowners (b) where there are no natural enemies (c) in their southern homes (d) in their northern homes.   3. _____

4. Migrating birds spend most of their lives (*a*) in flight (*b*) in the Northeast (*c*) in their wintering grounds (*d*) at their nesting sites.   4. _____

5. A good label for migrating birds is (*a*) carriers of the latest news (*b*) international travelers (*c*) citizens of the Northeast (*d*) friends of animals.   5. _____

Bonus: Reviewing Synonyms and Associated Ideas

Read the following passage and answer the questions at the end.

Have you ever heard of race walking? Not many people in the United States know about this unusual sport. Yet it is an Olympic sport and a favorite activity in many other countries around the world.

Race walking requires a peculiar gait. One foot must be on the ground at all times. The racer's leg must be straight at the knee when the leg is directly below the body. Race walking is not just a leisurely walk through the woods. It is hard work, with strong competition.

Race walkers often earn nothing but bursts of laughter. The requirements of the sport produce a very strange rolling walk, much like the odd saunter of the comedian Charlie Chaplin. But race walkers can go fast. They often embarrass joggers by passing them. One race walker recently covered a mile in five minutes and 41 seconds. That is good speed even for a runner.

Americans have not yet produced good Olympic competitors, but times are changing. More young people are being attracted to this demanding sport. If more race walking competitions are set up in the United States, Americans will have greater opportunities to perfect their skills.

---

1. Write the letter of the statement that best expresses the main idea.

   (*a*) The Olympic Games should include race walking.
   (*b*) Many young people are interested in race walking as a sport.
   (*c*) Race walking is a challenging sport fairly new to Americans.
   (*d*) Americans are excellent race walkers.   1. _____

2. Which of the following titles best summarizes the content of the passage?

    (*a*) A New Olympic Sport
    (*b*) How to Learn to Walk Faster
    (*c*) Expanding Olympic Competition
    (*d*) Race Walking: An Unusual Sport   2. _____

3. As used in paragraph 2, *gait* means (*a*) challenge (*b*) intensity (*c*) temperament (*d*) way of moving.   3. _____

4. As used in paragraph 3, *saunter* means (*a*) wit (*b*) comedy (*c*) a kind of stride (*d*) facial expressions.   4. _____

5. Race walking is (*a*) funny to watch (*b*) bad for the back (*c*) an ancient activity (*d*) faster than sprinting.   5. _____

6. Covering a mile in five minutes and 41 seconds is (*a*) a record for jogging (*b*) excellent time for a race walker (*c*) an average time at the Olympics (*d*) impossible for a race walker.   6. _____

9. Using Antonyms and Opposed Ideas

You have seen how helpful synonyms and associated ideas can be in answering test items. They help you to draw the right inferences. Other kinds of clues can also be useful. Sometimes, instead of words with similar meanings, you will work with words that have opposite meanings.

Pairs of Words with Opposite Meanings

What Are Antonyms?

An *antonym* is a word that means the *opposite* of another word. Here are some examples of antonyms:

calm—nervous	rough—smooth
give—take	sink—float
good—bad	up—down
hot—cold	wet—dry
love—hate	win—lose

Reading tests often include sentences that require antonyms. A sentence that needs an antonym in the blank usually has a key word that shows contrast:

Janet likes tennis, *but* Jennifer _____ it.

Even without a group of possible answers, the word *but* tells you that the answer is probably the antonym *dislikes*, or a word that means dislikes. Some other key words that show contrast are *not, though, although,* and *even if.*

A snake's skin is surprisingly dry, *not* wet and slimy.

Though the willow seems delicate, it is quite sturdy.

Although the morning of our picnic was stormy, by afternoon the weather turned sunny.

Even if he is angry inside, Ted keeps a calm exterior.

Question 1: How Can Antonyms Provide Clues to Meaning?

In the following list of paired antonyms, the less common word is at the right. Complete each sentence after the list by inserting one of the underlined words. If you are unsure, use the antonym clue to help you.

care—negligence   poor—prosperous

despair—optimism   prevent—enable

humble—haughty   scorn—idolize

important—petty   sensible—absurd

lacking—ample   thoughtful—tactless

1. Some clothing that looked _____ ten years ago seems sensible today.

2. Phil sometimes can't tell the difference between important and _____ _____ details.

3. The twins scorn rock-and-roll stars, but they _____ country singers.

4. Life can make even a(n) _____ person humble.

5. Janet is usually thoughtful, but her latest action was _____.

6. Though money is lacking, Mr. Wilson feels that his simple pleasures are _____ .

7. Many_____ men and women began life in poor sections of the city.

8. Proper care of equipment, not _____ , is necessary if we are going to keep our excellent safety record.

9. Some people might give in to a feeling of despair, but the disabled athlete still holds to her _____ .

10. If we can prevent vandalism, we will _____ the school to use less of its money for repairs.

Answers

In each item on the test, you had to find an antonym for a word in the sentence.

1. *absurd.* This is the opposite of *sensible.* The sentence contrasts the clothing of ten years ago with the clothing of today.
2. *petty.* This is an antonym for *important.* The words are paired to show contrast.
3. *idolize.* To *idolize* is the opposite of to *scorn.* In this sentence, the key word *but* tells you that an antonym is needed.
4. *haughty.* This is the opposite of *humble.* Notice how the key word *even* provides a clue that you need an antonym.
5. *tactless.* The antonym in the sentence is *thoughtful.* The key word *but* tells you that an antonym is needed.
6. *ample.* This is the opposite of *lacking. Though* tells you that a contrast is intended.
7. *prosperous.* This contrasts with *poor.*
8. *negligence.* This is the opposite of *care.* The key word *not* tells you that an antonym is needed.

9. *optimism.* This is the opposite of *despair.* The key word *but* tells you that an antonym is needed.

10. *enable.* To *enable* is the opposite of to *prevent. If* is used in the sentence to show contrast.

Next, use the following Practices to see how the pairing of antonyms can help you in sentences and longer passages.

Practice 1: Using Antonyms

Try to use the pairing of antonyms to fill in the blank below. The words to be paired can appear in the same sentence or in different sentences.

This report is not _____. Pages 2, 5, and 12 are missing.

    (*a*) accurate
    (*b*) attractive
    (*c*) enjoyable
    (*d*) readable
    (*e*) complete

Answer

The word to be paired is *missing.* What would be the effect of having missing pages? The report would not be (*e*) *complete.*

Practice 2

Read the following passage and answer the questions at the end.

The story of earmuffs is not just an ordinary one. In fact, it is quite unusual. The story goes back to 1873. It seems that Chester Greenwood of Farmington, Maine, had sensitive ears. When he was 15, he got a pair of ice skates as a present. Chester, however, liked warm weather and dreaded going out into the cold. To keep him warm when he did go outside, he covered his ears with cloth held by wire.

The idea took hold, and the town of Farmington went into the business of making earmuffs. Each year the townspeople celebrate Chester Greenwood's invention. They raise a flag with red earmuffs on a white background.

Through the years, the popularity of earmuffs has had its ups and downs. "It's like anything else," one manufacturer said. "We have excellent years and bad years."

In 1978, earmuffs were not very popular in the United States. A woman from Austria bought a pair of earmuffs to take home with her. People admired them, and she and her husband decided to sell earmuffs in Europe. Most American earmuffs had been dull in color. The Austrian couple made them in more flamboyant shades and sold them all over Europe. The fad drifted back to the United States.

Some details have varied, but Chester Greenwood's basic design for earmuffs has remained unaltered. Chester went on to invent other things, but on chilly winter days a lot of people are glad he invented this practical way to warm the ears—good, old-fashioned earmuffs.

KNOW THESE WORDS

sensitive: easily hurt

celebrate: recall with happiness

practical: useful

1. Write the letter of the statement that best expresses the main idea.

   (a) Earmuffs became more popular in Europe than in the United States.
   (b) The town of Farmington is famous as the home of the Greenwood earmuff.
   (c) Wearing earmuffs is a practical fad.
   (d) The earmuff has had a varied history from 1873 to the present.   1. _____

2. As used in paragraph 4, *flamboyant* means (a) dreary (b) red (c) showy (d) strange.   2. _____

3. As used in paragraph 5, *unaltered* means (a) constant (b) economical (c) attractive (d) typical.   3. _____

4. The earmuff flag is raised (a) on Chester Greenwood's birthday (b) by an Austrian couple (c) whenever earmuff sales have a good year (d) each year in Farmington.   4. _____

5. We may reasonably infer that earmuff sales go up and down as a result of (a) health reports (b) changes in fashion (c) labor troubles at the Maine factory (d) magazine articles.   5. _____

Answers

First read the entire passage. As you will see, it is all about earmuffs. It explains how and why Chester Greenwood invented earmuffs and then tells something about their later history.

After you have thought about the whole passage, you are ready to look at the individual questions.

1. (*d*) Only (*d*) suggests the idea of the total passage. Both (*a*) and (*b*) are details. Choice (*c*) is too general.
2. (*c*) *Flamboyant* is contrasted with *dull*. Therefore, we need a word that is opposed in meaning. *Showy* (*c*) is the best choice.
3. (*a*) *Unaltered* is contrasted with *varied*. The word *constant* is opposed in meaning. *Constant* (*a*) is the best choice.
4. (*d*) This is a detail from the passage: ''Each year the townspeople . . . raise a flag with red earmuffs on a white background.'' The selection says nothing about Chester Greenwood's birthday (*a*). The Austrian couple have nothing to do with the flag (*b*). Good and bad years are mentioned, but not in connection with the flag (*c*).
5. (*b*) The key sentence is ''The popularity of earmuffs has had its ups and downs.'' Popularity determines fashion. Therefore (*b*) is the best choice. The other choices are not mentioned in the passage.

On Your Own 1: Reviewing Antonyms

Read the following passage and answer the questions at the end.

The yearly Academy Awards ceremony was once a private affair. Now, because of television, it is very much a public affair. Hundreds of people gather in Hollywood to see the Oscars presented to outstanding actors, directors, and others involved in the motion picture industry. Millions more watch on television.

It all began on May 16, 1929, when 270 men and women sat down to dinner at the Hollywood Roosevelt Hotel. There was no secret about the winners. The names of the winners had been known for months. Janet Gaynor, for example, had won as Best Actress. Douglas Fairbanks presented her with the famous gold statuette.

The little statue was not then called an Oscar. Like a new actor, Oscar was unknown. About six years later, it somehow got that renowned name. A number of explanations have been offered for its origin, but nobody knows the true story for certain.

Nowadays the results of the Oscar voting are kept secret. Only two people know the winners before the names are announced at the ceremony. The counting of votes is not done by one group of people but by different groups. Nobody except two members of an accounting firm sees the final totals.

The information is not kept in open files. Winners' names are placed in sealed envelopes. The two accountants each carry a complete set of envelopes to the ceremony. One set is simply a spare to be used in case something happens to the other one.

KNOW THIS WORD

origin: beginning

1. Which of the following titles best summarizes the content of the passage?

   (a) How Oscar Got His Name
   (b) The First Academy Awards Winners
   (c) The Academy Awards Ceremony Through the Years
   (d) How the Oscar Winners Are Selected   1. _____

2. As used in paragraph 3, *renowned* means (a) strange (b) wonderful (c) much-disliked (d) famous.   2. _____

3. May 16, 1929, marks (a) Douglas Fairbanks' first winning of an Academy Award (b) the first time Oscar got his name (c) the first time the Awards were kept secret (d) Janet Gaynor's recognition as Best Actress.   3. _____

4. The number of people who know the Awards winners in advance is (a) 1 (b) 2 (c) 3 (d) a committee of six.   4. _____

5. Two envelopes are prepared for the ceremony (a) one for New York, one for Hollywood (b) as an extra precaution (c) one for the ceremony, one for the press (d) just because that is the custom.   5. _____

Bonus: Reviewing Antonyms

Read the following passage and answer the questions at the end.

To most of us, a snail in the garden is known only as a pest. But some clever people have turned a liability into an asset. They raise snails for food—or even for sport!

In Europe, snails are delicacies, enjoyed by hard-to-please diners in France, Italy, and elsewhere. Yet in the United States, snails have never been very popular. American snail farmers are trying to overcome this prejudice and are having some success. They are growing snails for an expanding market.

One resourceful Californian has a backyard full of snails. To prevent their escape, he has built a wooden fence ringed with a band of copper. The copper carries an electric current, which gives the snails a slight shock and keeps them in the yard. He sells his snails at an average price of 20 cents each to restaurants.

Some snail growers race their snails for sport. A snail in a hurry can travel about three inches a minute. You can see how the expression ''a snail's pace'' arose. Even though snails are sluggish, snail racing is a popular sport in some places, like Spain's Basque country.

The lowly snail is an object of aversion for most people in the United States, but for some people, here and abroad, it is beautiful!

KNOW THESE WORDS

asset: thing of value

delicacies: special foods

prejudice: unreasonable dislike

object: thing discussed

1. Which of the following titles best summarizes the content of the passage?

   (*a*) The Aversion to Snails
   (*b*) Snails: A Neglected Food Source
   (*c*) Snail Races: A Relaxing Sport
   (*d*) Snail Farming for Profit and Pleasure   1. _____

2. As used in paragraph 4, *sluggish* means (*a*) ugly (*b*) colorless (*c*) not active (*d*) weak.   2. _____

3. As used in paragraph 5, *aversion* means (*a*) mild curiosity (*b*) keen interest (*c*) preference (*d*) strong dislike.   3. _____

4. Snails are raced in (*a*) France (*b*) Spain (*c*) Italy (*d*) California.   4. _____

5. People are probably turned away from snails because of the snails' (*a*) taste (*b*) appearance (*c*) price (*d*) reputation.   5. _____

Using Opposed Ideas

Another clue to the word needed to fill a blank is less obvious than paired antonyms. Sometimes you have to look for a word or expression that is opposed in meaning to a previous word or idea. You are not looking for antonyms exactly, but only for opposite ideas. See the example on top of page 80.

> Harrison never seemed to tell a story directly and honestly. Even small details were _____ .
>
> (a) exciting
> (b) repeated
> (c) overlooked
> (d) false
> (e) remembered

There are no paired antonyms here, but the two sentences in the passage do contain opposite ideas. Harrison could never tell a story "directly and honestly." The word *never* tells you to seek a word that expresses the opposite of "directly and honestly." The answer is (d) *false*. (If you chose *overlooked*, think about it again. A person who overlooks something usually does it by accident. When an action is *in*direct and *dis*honest, there is *false*ness involved, not just a mistake.)

If you took the Bonus test on pages 78–79, you have already used this technique in answering question 2. The last paragraph of the passage on snails contrasts *aversion*, or strong dislike, with *beautiful*. These words are not antonyms, but they are opposed ideas. You have a *liking* for something that is beautiful and a *dislike* for something that is not. Words like *but, not, never, scarcely, neither, nobody, without, unless,* and *although* often point the way to an opposed idea.

Question 2: How Do Opposed Ideas Provide Clues to Meaning?

Write the letter of the correct answer for each numbered item.

1. Trainers of dolphins avoid speaking harshly to their animals. Their voices are always _____ .

   (a) loud   (b) gentle   (c) slow
   (d) discouraging   (e) boring

2. For a top tennis player, native ability is not enough. The will to win and the power to concentrate are also _____ .

   (a) needed   (b) discovered   (c) penalized
   (d) checked   (e) discussed

3. My keys have torn the pocket in my gray slacks. If I don't mend it, I may lose some change through the small _____ .

   (a) wallet   (b) cloth   (c) belt
   (d) opening   (e) purse

Answers

1. (b) The correct answer, *gentle*, is almost an antonym for *harshly*, but not quite. (The antonym would be *gently*.)
2. (a) If "native ability is *not enough*," then something else is *needed*. Certainly, (a) is the only choice that contains this opposed idea.

3. (*d*) Here the opposed ideas are not so obvious. A *pocket* is *closed* at the bottom. If a pocket is torn, the result is an *opening*. (If you answered *cloth*, think again. A pocket is usually made of cloth, but losing change "through the small cloth" makes little sense.)

Now look for opposed ideas in the following brief passage.

Practice 3: Using Opposed Ideas

Write the letter of the word that makes the best sense in the blank space.

I looked for the concert tickets everywhere, without success. The _____ disappointed my friend and me.	(*a*) concert (*b*) victory (*c*) loss (*d*) puzzle (*e*) time

Answer

The first sentence has to do with trying to find missing tickets (although neither the word *find* nor *missing* is used). The tickets seem to have been lost. The opposing ideas are finding—losing. Therefore, the answer is (*c*) *loss*.

Practice 4

Read the following passage and answer the questions at the end.

> Chocolate is one of the world's favorite foods. Very few people detest it. About 70 percent of today's candy bars are chocolate covered. Many candies and candy bars are all chocolate.
>
> Chocolate comes from cocoa beans, which come from the cacao tree. At the chocolate factory, the beans are cleaned and roasted. This roasting brings out the flavor and special smell of chocolate.
>
> After roasting, the outer shells are removed. The rest remains. The meat part of the bean, called the *nib*, is ground. The nibs melt and become chocolate liquor, which is more than half made up of cocoa butter.
>
> Cocoa butter is a natural fat. It is separated from the liquor. The remaining material is pressed, ground, and sifted. The end result is not a liquid. It is cocoa powder.
>
> To make semisweet chocolate, workers at the factory add sugar and flavoring to the chocolate liquor. To make milk chocolate, they replace some of the chocolate liquor with whole milk.

KNOW THESE WORDS

chocolate liquor: a sticky chocolate syrup

semisweet: slightly sweet

1. Which of the following titles best summarizes the content of the passage?

   (*a*) How Chocolate Is Grown and Processed
   (*b*) America's Sweet Tooth for Chocolate
   (*c*) Different Kinds of Chocolate Used in Candy
   (*d*) Life at the Chocolate Factory   1. _____

2. As used in paragraph 1, *detest* means (*a*) eat (*b*) dislike (*c*) study (*d*) serve.   2. _____

3. The *nib* is (*a*) another name for cocoa butter (*b*) the outer shell (*c*) the central part of the bean (*d*) the cacao tree.   3. _____

4. Semisweet chocolate contains all the following ingredients EXCEPT (*a*) chocolate liquor (*b*) milk (*c*) sugar (*d*) flavoring.   4. _____

5. The flavor and special smell of chocolate come from (*a*) grinding (*b*) sifting (*c*) pressing (*d*) roasting.   5. _____

Answers

First read the entire passage, which deals with the making of chocolate. Once you know the main idea, the individual answers become easier.

1. (*a*) This is the only choice that deals with the entire passage. All the others are details mentioned or hinted at.
2. (*b*) The opposed ideas are those of *favorite* and *detest*. If a food is a favorite, very few people would not like it. Therefore, the correct choice is *dislike* (*b*).
3. (*c*) The nib is called "the meat part of the bean," what remains after the outer shells are removed. The only possible answer is *the central part of the bean* (*c*).
4. (*b*) The passage specifically says that to make semisweet chocolate workers add sugar, flavoring, and chocolate liquor. Since the question calls for the omitted ingredient (by using the word *except*), the answer must be *milk* (*b*).
5. (*d*) The passage specifically says, "This roasting brings out the flavor and special smell of chocolate." Therefore (*d*) is correct.

On Your Own 2: Reviewing Antonyms and Opposed Ideas

Read the following passage and answer the questions at the end. In this review, you will have to use all the skills you have learned so far.

Most people take a dim view of mice. They are even repelled by the word *mouse*. Yet one of the most popular of all cartoon characters is a mouse—Mickey Mouse. Real mice have their fans, too, just as cats, dogs, and other pets do. These people do not avoid mice. In fact, some of them raise mice and show them at exhibitions.

England has a National Mouse Club. It was founded in 1895. Each year a championship contest is held to choose the best mouse in the show. The contestants are kept in little green cages. The judge reaches into each cage and pulls out a mouse by the tail. He doesn't put the mouse back immediately. He carefully scrutinizes its ears. He checks to see if it has a healthy coat. He measures the length of the tail. He doesn't keep the mouse from moving. He allows the mouse to run up and down his arm. This freedom tests the mouse's liveliness. The owner of the winning mouse wins a solid silver punch bowl.

These are no ordinary mice. Even their colors are interesting. One type of mouse has a single, solid color. This color may be black, blue, cream, red, silver, or white. Some mice have more than one color. There are many color varieties, with all kinds of combinations.

It costs ten cents to enter a mouse in a Mouse Club show. This is the same fee that was charged 50 years ago. Members enjoy getting together. They greet old friends. They talk about mice for hours on end. It may not be everyone's cup of tea, but the members of the National Mouse Club look forward eagerly to their annual show.

KNOW THIS WORD

dim: negative; poor

1. Write the letter of the statement that best expresses the main idea.

    (a) Mice come in many colors and combinations of colors.
    (b) In comparing mice, judges look for certain qualities.
    (c) Some people raise mice to show at yearly competitions.
    (d) Mickey Mouse is the most famous mouse of all.   1. _____

2. As used in paragraph 1, *repelled* means (a) disgusted (b) stimulated (c) amused (d) cheered.   2. _____

3. As used in paragraph 2, *scrutinizes* means (a) pets (b) photographs (c) covers (d) examines.   3. _____

4. One of the major appeals of the National Mouse Club competitions is the (a) sociability (b) publicity (c) storytelling (d) financial gains.   4. _____

5. "It may not be everyone's cup of tea" suggests that (*a*) tea, rather than coffee, is served at the contests (*b*) many people would not enjoy the mouse competition (*c*) many people at the contest go home disappointed (*d*) members of the National Mouse Club tend to be tea drinkers.

5. _____

Bonus 1: Reviewing Antonyms and Opposed Ideas

Read the following passage and answer the questions at the end.

We often read about Egyptian tombs. Scientists have found many treasures in these ancient sepulchers. Paintings and sculptures have told us about the way of life in Egypt thousands of years ago.

Not many people know about the exciting discoveries in our own backyard, right here in America. We have our own diggings, which have some fascinating stories to tell.

Scattered throughout many Midwestern states are huge mounds. Indians, called by scientists the *Mound Builders*, developed a thriving civilization in this region. They were not wild, barbaric savages. The mounds contain pottery, tools, stone carvings, and many things that tell of a comfortable life long ago.

Some of the mounds are 2,000 years old. When the mounds were being built, there were often Indian villages near them. These villages have been buried for centuries. A few of them are being dug up, or excavated. Scientists called *archaeologists* find kitchen materials, weapons for hunting, and jewelry. From these findings, they can even tell what kinds of food the ancient people ate.

Some of the mounds are in the way of interstate highways. The archaeologists are trying to uncover as much of the Mound Builders' story as they can before all clues are gone, lost in the construction of modern highways.

KNOW THIS WORD

thriving: growing

1. Which title best summarizes the content of the passage?

   (*a*) How the Mound Builders Resemble the Egyptians
   (*b*) Modern Highways: Enemies of Archaeology
   (*c*) A Midwestern Story
   (*d*) The Mound Builders and Their Achievements

1. _____

2. As used in paragraph 1, *sepulchers* means (*a*) graves (*b*) sandpiles (*c*) villages (*d*) riverbeds.   2. _____

3. As used in paragraph 3, *barbaric* means (*a*) painted (*b*) uncivilized (*c*) restless (*d*) good-tempered.   3. _____

4. We may infer that construction on interstate highways

   (*a*) completely conceals the Mound Builders' story
   (*b*) has also played a part in Egyptian archaeology
   (*c*) has revealed the sites of Indian villages
   (*d*) has done nothing but harm to archaeology   4. _____

5. The Mound Builders lived in what is now (*a*) Egypt (*b*) the Midwest (*c*) the South (*d*) the West.   5. _____

Bonus 2

Read the following passage and answer the questions at the end.

The appearance of Halley's Comet in 1986 stimulated interest in comets. People asked, "What are these recurring visitors from outer space? Why do they swing around the sun? Why do they return? Why do some comets take longer to come back than others?"

One astronomer called a comet "a dirty snowball." According to his theory, a comet consists of a huge ball of gases that have been frozen into icelike solids at very low temperatures. The snowball is "dirty" because bits of dust and gravel, made up of rock and metal, are frozen into the ball.

Far out in some parts of space, temperatures are close to absolute zero. There the ball stays frozen. But as the comet moves closer to the sun, it begins to warm up. The icy solids begin to evaporate into gas. Some of the solid particles of "dirt" are liberated and float within the hazy, gaseous, outer surface. The comet glitters, because all these substances reflect sunlight.

As the comet gets closer to the sun, its outer layer of haze increases in depth. A stream of particles from the sun, called the "solar wind," forces some of the comet's haze into a "tail," which always points away from the sun.

Comets are held in orbit by the sun's gravitation. Some have small orbits, bringing them back every few years. Others have elongated orbits, keeping them out in space for thousands of years. The most famous comet of all, Halley's Comet, returns about every 76 years.

Comets get smaller on each return sweep. They lose some of their volume each time. Halley's Comet, for example, is smaller than it was a thousand years ago. Someday it will not be visible without a telescope. Eventually, it may not return at all.

KNOW THESE WORDS

stimulated: aroused

absolute zero: complete absence of heat

elongated: lengthened

1. Write the letter of the sentence that best expresses the main idea.

   (*a*) What are comets made of and why do they keep coming back?

   (*b*) A comet is a kind of dirty snowball that contains gases frozen into solids.

   (*c*) The most famous comet of all, Halley's Comet, cannot be seen with a telescope.

   (*d*) Comets have different orbits, some quite short and others quite long.   1. _____

2. As used in paragraph 1, *recurring* means (*a*) unwelcome (*b*) dangerous (*c*) tiny (*d*) returning.   2. _____

3. As used in paragraph 5, *elongated* means (*a*) tiny (*b*) lengthened (*c*) yearly (*d*) unexplainable.   3. _____

4. The "solar wind" (*a*) creates the comet's tail (*b*) often reaches earth from a comet (*c*) doesn't reach the earth's orbit (*d*) is less than it was a thousand years ago.   4. _____

5. Halley's Comet (*a*) will always return to sweep around the sun (*b*) is growing larger and more impressive with each sweep (*c*) may someday disappear (*d*) returns once every 86 years.   5. _____

Bonus 3

Read the following passage and answer the questions at the end. In this review, you will have to use all the skills you have learned so far.

When the outstanding dancer Fred Astaire was interviewed for a job by a Hollywood producer, the movie "expert" turned him down, saying, "Can't sing. Can't act. Dances a little." Here's another blunder. When the scientific genius Albert Einstein was in school, his teachers considered him rather dull. And a final story. The famous Polish pianist Paderewski was told by a teacher that he'd never be a success as a performer because the middle finger on each hand was too short.

What lessons can be drawn from these three experiences? First, true genius cannot be suppressed. Somehow or other it will work its way out. Second, early estimates of a person's abilities may be unfair or just plain wrong. Third, when there is a real determination to succeed, obstacles fall by the wayside.

The famous motto *ad astra per aspera* can be translated as "to the stars through hardships." Astaire, Einstein, and Paderewski proved their critics mistaken.

1. Write the letter of the statement that best expresses the main idea.

   (*a*) Fred Astaire was a talented dancer.
   (*b*) True ability will always make itself known.
   (*c*) Some people never get discouraged.
   (*d*) Albert Einstein proved his teachers wrong.   1. _____

2. As used in paragraph 2, *suppressed* means (*a*) encouraged (*b*) publicized (*c*) smothered (*d*) released.   2. _____

3. When Paderewski's teacher told him he'd never be a success, the teacher was (*a*) being humorous (*b*) cheerful, though concerned (*c*) somewhat hesitant (*d*) gravely mistaken.   3. _____

4. *Ad astra per aspera* is used in the passage (*a*) as a motto for the three men's lives (*b*) to demonstrate the value of Latin (*c*) to send the reader to the dictionary (*d*) to point out that genius is always recognized early.   4. _____

5. The writer of the passage assumes that the reader (*a*) knows that the three men were successes (*b*) someday dreams to become like one of the men (*c*) sympathizes with the poor teachers of the three men (*d*) knows that Fred Astaire was a famous Shakespearean actor.   5. _____

10. Choosing Words That Summarize

> "The restaurant offered broccoli, carrots, lima beans, and green beans. These vegetables were all cooked and served with a cream sauce."

Notice that the first sentence mentions specific foods—broccoli, carrots, and so on. The second sentence labels all those foods as *vegetables* and adds some further information.

Writing One-Word Summaries

The word *vegetables* is a general word. In a way, it is a one-word **summary** that includes *broccoli*, *carrots*, *lima beans*, *green beans*, and more. Here are a few similar examples:

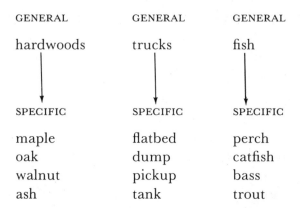

GENERAL	GENERAL	GENERAL
hardwoods	trucks	fish
↓	↓	↓
SPECIFIC	SPECIFIC	SPECIFIC
maple	flatbed	perch
oak	dump	catfish
walnut	pickup	bass
ash	tank	trout

Question 1: How Can You Distinguish Between General and Specific Words?

In each of the following groups of words, one word is general and can include, or *summarize*, the other, more specific words. Write the general word in the space provided.

EXAMPLE: apple, orange, banana, fruit, cherrry

_____fruit_____

ANSWER: The word *fruit* is a general word that can include *apple*, *orange*, *banana*, and *cherry*.

1. cake, pie, cookie, cupcake, dessert   1. _____

2. sedan, coupe, limousine, automobile, hatchback   2. _____

3. dog, poodle, setter, beagle, spaniel   3. _____

4. desk, furniture, table, chair, sofa   4. _____

5. hammer, chisel, tool, screwdriver, saw   5. _____

6. daffodil, tulip, lily, marigold, flower   6. _____

7. game, chess, tennis, volleyball, checkers   7. _____

Answers

1. dessert   2. automobile   3. dog   4. furniture   5. tool   6. flower   7. game

In the following passage, you are asked to find a general word that summarizes a list of specific words.

Practice 1: Studying General and Specific Words

In the blank space, write the letter of the correct answer.

On my mother's pantry shelf, you will find such items as basil, oregano, ginger, pepper, and dill. _____ like these help make her the best cook in our family.	(*a*) Spices (*b*) Beans (*c*) Grains (*d*) Fruits (*e*) Recipes

Answer

Words like *these*, *such*, *all*, and *other* are often good clues. So are phrases like *none of these*. In this passage, the key word is *these*. It helps tell you that a general word is needed in the blank—one that includes all the items mentioned in the first sentence. The correct answer is (*a*) *Spices*.

Practice 2

Read the following passage and answer the questions at the end.

> At the age of 54, Willie Shoemaker won the Kentucky Derby on a horse named Ferdinand. The competition was keen, with Badger Land and Snow Chief, in particular, threatening to win this important race. These two were favored to win over Ferdinand, but Willie Shoemaker had other plans.
>
> Ferdinand got off to a poor start and was running in last place, with other horses blocking the way to the lead. Shoemaker handled his horse brilliantly. He paced Ferdinand. He looked for openings and gradually overtook the leaders. He used the speed of other horses to motivate Ferdinand. On the homestretch, he found

daylight. He encouraged Ferdinand to go all out. Such tactics helped Ferdinand overtake the lead horse and cross the finish line a winner.

No one had given Shoemaker and Ferdinand much of a chance to win. But the veteran jockey and the spirited young horse thrilled the crowd.

KNOW THESE WORDS

overtook: passed

motivate: encourage

spirited: lively

1. Which of the following titles best summarizes the content of the passage?

   (*a*) A Good Combination
   (*b*) Left at the Post
   (*c*) An Unexpected Victory
   (*d*) Excitement at the Kentucky Derby   1. _____

2. A word that could be substituted for *two* in the first paragraph is
   (*a*) *jockeys* (*b*) *thoroughbreds* (*c*) *pacers* (*d*) *trotters*.   2. _____

3. *Tactics* refers to (*a*) Shoemaker's plan of action (*b*) Ferdinand's unusual speed (*c*) Badger Land's unexpected mistakes (*d*) Snow Chief's poor finish.   3. _____

Answers

First read the entire passage. You will notice that the words in 2 and 3 are summarizing words. They refer to things that have gone before.

1. (*c*) The heart of the passage is Shoemaker's upset of the favorites (*c*). Excitement at the Kentucky Derby (*d*) is too broad, while (*a*) and (*b*) are too narrow.
2. (*b*) *Two* refers to Badger Land and Snow Chief, the competing horses. The only possible answer is (*b*).
3. (*a*) *Tactics* refers to the ways in which Shoemaker moved up in the pack: pacing Ferdinand, looking for openings, using the speed of other horses. Ferdinand was indeed speedy (*b*), but his speed became part of Shoemaker's tactics.

On Your Own: Studying Words That Summarize

Read the following passage and answer the questions at the end.

Among tennis stars of the past quarter century, Arthur Ashe stands out, both as a player and as a person. In 1964, Ashe won the Eastern Grass Championship. In 1968, he won the National Singles Championship.

A month later, he won the U.S. Open Championship at Forest Hills. These tournaments were important milestones for him, but his greatest achievements may not appear in the record books.

A native of Richmond, Virginia, Arthur Ashe is a genuinely fine person. He is warm, friendly, relaxed, totally honest. These personality traits have won him friends around the world. He once said, ''Do I have the killer instinct? No, sorry. I just don't have the killer instinct. I play the game. That's me. I give it all I've got.''

Ashe has long been associated with the American Davis Cup team. In 1963, he played on the team that broke the Australians' streak of seven straight wins. Many years later, he came back as the nonplaying leader of the group, devoted as always to his country and to tennis.

In victory, he is modest. In defeat, he is mature. His opponents admire him for his sense of fair play. Throughout his career, his sportsmanship has made him a standout among modern athletes.

KNOW THESE WORDS

milestones: important events
instinct: feeling
modest: quiet; not bold
mature: gracious

1. Write the letter of the statement that best expresses the main idea.

   (*a*) Arthur Ashe won important championships in 1968.
   (*b*) The Davis Cup team that beat the Australians starred Arthur Ashe.
   (*c*) Arthur Ashe is a champion who has admirable human qualities.
   (*d*) It is better to be a good human being than a champion.   1. _____

2. A word that could be substituted for *personality traits* in the second paragraph is (*a*) *actions* (*b*) *thoughts* (*c*) *statements* (*d*) *qualities*.   2. _____

3. In the last paragraph, *sportsmanship* summarizes all the following qualities EXCEPT (*a*) modesty (*b*) publicity (*c*) maturity (*d*) sense of fair play.   3. _____

4. From this passage, we may infer that the killer instinct (*a*) is not necessary for success (*b*) was an important ingredient in Arthur Ashe's personality (*c*) makes more friends than enemies (*d*) won Arthur Ashe the Eastern Grass Championship in 1964.   4. _____

5. The Australians' streak of seven wins was broken by the American Davis Cup team in (*a*) 1963 (*b*) 1964 (*c*) 1968 (*d*) none of these.   5. _____

Bonus: Reviewing Words That Summarize

Read the following passage and answer the questions at the end.

How would you describe Quincy Jones? Is he an instrumentalist, a composer, an arranger, or a producer? None of these labels can sum up this remarkable man. He has been known for years to people who follow popular music. But his part in the *We Are the World* album and the "Hands Across America" project made him a national figure.

In addition to these accomplishments, Jones has written the music for many motion pictures, including *The Color Purple*, which won 11 Oscar nominations. He also wrote the score for Alex Haley's *Roots*, a hugely successful television miniseries. These achievements show his many-sided genius.

Quincy Jones was born March 14, 1933, on Chicago's South Side. Ten years later, his family moved to the Seattle area. It was there that he met Ray Charles, who was three years older than Jones and who in time would be a world-famous singer. The young musicians performed at small clubs and weddings. Through Ray Charles's influence, Quincy Jones began composing.

When Jones was only 15, his musical talent impressed Lionel Hampton, who invited him to join the Hampton band. Jones was ready to quit school to join, but Hampton's wife, Gladys, objected. Believing that he needed an education, she removed him from the band's bus. "Get that child out of here," she yelled. "Let him finish school."

These experiences made Quincy Jones more determined than ever to succeed. He finished high school, attended the Berklee College of Music in Boston on a scholarship, and finally did join Lionel Hampton's band. Soon, however, he struck off on his own. The future beckoned brightly.

KNOW THESE WORDS

project: work; task

scholarship: gift of money to use for education

1. Write the letter of the statement that best expresses the main idea.

   (*a*) Lionel Hampton played an important role in the success of Quincy Jones.
   (*b*) Ray Charles and Quincy Jones became close friends.
   (*c*) A college education is important for success in modern music.
   (*d*) Quincy Jones has had an exciting and successful musical career.   1. _____

2. The word *labels* at the beginning of the selection summarizes all the following EXCEPT (*a*) director (*b*) composer (*c*) arranger (*d*) instrumentalist.   2. _____

3. Among the achievements mentioned in the second paragraph was Quincy Jones's (*a*) work with Lionel Hampton (*b*) partnership with Ray Charles (*c*) work on Alex Haley's *Roots* (*d*) winning a scholarship to Berklee College of Music.   3. _____

4. In insisting that Quincy Jones get off the bus, Gladys Hampton was actually being (*a*) cruel (*b*) indifferent (*c*) kind (*d*) selfish.   4. _____

5. *We Are the World* is the name of a (*a*) biography of Quincy Jones (*b*) music album (*c*) song written by Quincy Jones (*d*) movie.   5. _____

11. Studying Cause and Effect

"I changed the oil and adjusted the carburetor. The car ran much more smoothly."

Notice that these two sentences are related. The second sentence follows from the first. The speaker *did* something. *As a result*, the car ran better. The first sentence gives the *cause.* The second sentence gives the *effect* (or result).

Cause: I changed the oil and adjusted the carburetor.

Effect: The car ran much more smoothly.

Cause-to-Effect Order

If you listen closely to conversation, you'll find many examples of statements in *cause-to-effect* order. Some of them are very simple, such as, "I'm tired (*cause*). I'm going to bed early (*effect*)."

Effect-to-Cause Order

Very often the effect is given before the cause. The statements are then in *effect-to-cause* order. In these cases, the first statement seems to raise the question, "Why?"

For example: "Maria demanded an apology. (Why?) She said that Carlos had left her name off the invitation list."

Here's another example:

Effect: Tom received the outstanding-player award. (Why?)

Cause: He had won every match in his senior year.

Question 1: How Do You Determine Cause-and-Effect Relationships?

After each pair of sentences, write **C-E** if the sentences are in cause-to-effect order. Write **E-C** if they are in effect-to-cause order.

1. The Joneses sold their piano. It needed more repairs than they were willing to make.   1. _____
2. Terry had left his bicycle outdoors for a week. The handlebars became rusty.   2. _____
3. Sheila was interviewed by a reporter from WSYR-TV. She had just returned from a convention of high school newspaper editors in Washington, D.C.   3. _____

4. A sudden snowstorm struck eastern Colorado. Hundreds of motorists were stranded on the highways.   4. _____

5. Marilyn's supporters ran an excellent campaign. She easily won election as class president.   5. _____

Answers

1. E-C   2. C-E   3. E-C   4. C-E   5. C-E

Words That Signal Cause-and-Effect Relationships

Sometimes a cause or an effect is shown by a key word or words. There were no such helpful words in the sentences in Question 1, but there often will be in longer passages. Here are two examples:

Cause-to-Effect: Sylvia went to bed early. *Consequently*, she missed the fireworks display.

Effect-to-Cause: Mr. Wong changed the lock on the door *because* he had lost his key to the old lock.

There are many other words that signal sentences dealing with cause and effect. Here are a few:

as a result	**for**	**therefore**
by this (that) method	**hence**	**this**
for this (that) reason	**since**	**this (that) is how**
in this (that) way	**so**	**thus**

In the following sentences, look for a key word that helps you see the cause-and-effect relationship.

Practice 1: Studying Cause-to-Effect Relationships

In the blank space, write the letter of the correct answer.

Shopping malls are usually located a distance from the center of cities, far from the heavy downtown traffic of the localities they serve. The malls can therefore be _____ fairly easily by automobile.	(*a*) overlooked (*b*) reported on (*c*) organized (*d*) sold (*e*) reached

Answer

The helpful word is *therefore* in the second sentence. It tells you that the second sentence is an effect of what is stated in the first sentence. The cause is the location of shopping malls. The effect (or result) is that malls can be easily (*e*) *reached* by car.

Practice 2

In each blank space, write the letter of the correct answer.

> The film career of Katharine Hepburn has been long and distinguished. She has never allowed herself to be filmed as a single, unchanging character. For that reason, she has been able to play a variety of 1. _____ that challenge the range of her abilities.
>
> In her early days, she often played a bright, witty, forceful leading lady. In more recent roles, she has appeared as a sprightly older woman. Throughout her career, she has maintained a solid reputation as a performer who understands her craft. As a result, she has 2. _____ the respect of the American public and critics alike.

1. (*a*) roles
   (*b*) interviews
   (*c*) theaters
   (*d*) fans
   (*e*) critics

2. (*a*) lessened
   (*b*) lost
   (*c*) retained
   (*d*) sought
   (*e*) rejected

KNOW THESE WORDS

distinguished: famous; outstanding
maintained: kept

Answers

First read the entire passage, which is about Katharine Hepburn and her long career as an acclaimed movie actress.

1. (*a*) If she didn't allow herself to be filmed as an unchanging character, then she took on a variety of *roles*. The other choices have nothing to do with her actual performances. *For that reason* is a clue to cause and effect. The correct answer is (*a*) *roles*.
2. (*c*) Since Hepburn "maintained a solid reputation," she must have *retained*, or kept, the respect of the public and critics. None of the negative choices—*lessened, lost, rejected*—makes sense. The cause-and-effect clue is *As a result*. The only appropriate answer is (*c*) *retained*.

Practice 3

Sometimes cause and effect are tested in other ways. Read the following passage and answer the questions at the end.

> In 1786, Thomas Jefferson urged the United States to adopt decimal currency, with its dollars and cents. Previously the British system of pounds, shillings, and pence had been used, a much more complicated system. Thirteen years later, during the French Revolution, the French designed and instituted the metric system. Like our decimal currency, the metric system is based on the

number 10, not 12 as in inches or 16 as in ounces. In our system, a yard is 36 inches and a mile is 5280 feet. In the metric system, a meter is 100 centimeters and a kilometer is 1000 meters. Adopting the metric system could have saved the United States untold billions of dollars in years to come.

KNOW THIS WORD

instituted: established; introduced

1. If the United States had adopted the metric system, (*a*) we would have regretted the decision (*b*) runners would not be trying to set new records for the mile (*c*) we would have gone back to the old system quickly (*d*) we'd still be getting our milk in quarts.   1. _____

2. Jefferson's attitude toward the metric system was probably one of (*a*) alarm (*b*) protest (*c*) approval (*d*) indifference.   2. _____

Answers

First read the entire passage, which is about the metric system.

1. (*b*) If the metric system had been adopted, the mile as a measurement would no longer be used. Note that some races in the United States do use the metric system: 100 meters, five kilometers, etc. If we had saved money, we would not have regretted the decision (*a*) nor gone back to the old system (*c*). We'd not be using the old measurement *quarts* (*d*).

2. (*c*) This question asks you to carry cause and effect one step further by deciding what Jefferson would have thought about the metric system. Since Jefferson obviously approved the metric idea when he suggested the use of dollars and cents, in all probability he would have approved the metric system of measurements in place of the illogical and confusing system we still use.

On Your Own: Studying Cause-to-Effect Relationships

Read the following passage and answer the questions at the end.

A half century ago, a book called *How to Win Friends and Influence People* won wide appeal among American readers. As a result, it kept its incredible popularity for many years. It still has its readers. The success of this book should not have surprised the critics, for Americans have always enjoyed self-help and how-to books.

Self-help books attempt to show readers how to overcome sadness, enjoy life more, find happiness, become popular, earn a better salary, or become wealthy. Indeed, some books seem to promise all six benefits. Self-help books of this kind are concerned with certain personal goals. The results often cannot really be measured. ''Am I happier now than I was two weeks ago?'' Can you truly tell?

There are, however, books that promise results that can be seen. These down-to-earth books explain how to garden successfully, how to catch fish, how to go camping, how to improve your tennis game, how to use power tools, how to build a greenhouse, how to do home repairs, and so on. The list is almost endless, for new how-to books continue to pour into the bookstores.

KNOW THIS WORD

concerned (with): about

1. Which of the following titles best summarizes the content of the passage?

   (a) *How to Win Friends and Influence People:* A Continuing Best-Seller
   (b) The Continuing Success of How-to and Self-Help Books
   (c) How Books Can Play a Role in Self-Improvement
   (d) Books: A Key to Success in Life   1. _____

2. We may infer that *How to Win Friends and Influence People* (a) made the best-seller lists (b) though widely used, was a financial disappointment to the author (c) was a flash in the pan, a brief success (d) was rewritten later as a book on how to manage money.   2. _____

3. We may infer that people who read self-help books (a) find their lives dramatically changed (b) do not bother with how-to books (c) find the long-term results negative (d) may or may not benefit from them.   3. _____

4. How-to books differ from self-help books because (a) self-help books are easier to read (b) self-help books are harder to read (c) self-help books are usually lighter and more amusing (d) the results of reading how-to books can be measured.   4. _____

5. All the following how-to skills were mentioned EXCEPT (a) gardening (b) fishing (c) swimming (d) camping.   5. _____

Bonus: Reviewing Cause-to-Effect Relationships

Read the following passage and answer the questions at the end.

Most great singers have had singing lessons since childhood. Occasionally, though, a great voice comes through untrained—a voice that is unbelievably, naturally beautiful. Mahalia Jackson had such a voice. Without having had a lesson, she was able to captivate listeners with her magnificent voice that never seemed strained or forced.

Mahalia Jackson was a gospel singer. She preferred to sing hymns rather than operatic arias or popular songs. Since financial rewards did not concern her, she rejected many opportunities to become wealthy. She sang for simple country people and for royalty. But she never changed her style or her point of view.

At one point, after much urging, her husband persuaded her to try out for a regular stage role. She reluctantly paid 25 cents for a song sheet and went to the audition. The judges offered her the part, for they were highly impressed. At this point, however, her husband got a job, and she turned down the offer. She wanted to go on singing at concerts.

Mahalia Jackson was a down-to-earth person without a trace of conceit. She considered her singing talent a gift from God and accepted it humbly. She would assist box-office clerks and would even help sell tickets out front, if necessary. Consequently, she was loved by all her associates.

Perhaps Mahalia Jackson's greatest moment was singing ''The Star-Spangled Banner'' at President John F. Kennedy's inauguration. The national anthem may never have been sung better.

KNOW THESE WORDS

arias: songs sung by solo voices

audition: hearing to test a singer's voice

inauguration: ceremony for installing a person in office

1. Write the letter of the statement that best expresses the main idea.

   (*a*) Mahalia Jackson had a highly successful career on her own terms.
   (*b*) Mahalia Jackson's greatest thrill was singing at President John F. Kennedy's inauguration.
   (*c*) Mahalia Jackson could have become a very wealthy woman.
   (*d*) A natural voice is better than a trained one.   1. _____

2. After all her success, Mahalia Jackson always remained
(*a*) critical (*b*) natural (*c*) shy (*d*) uncertain.   2. _____

3. As used in paragraph 1, *captivate* means (*a*) bore (*b*) arouse
(*c*) enchant (*d*) calm.   3. _____

4. As used in paragraph 3, *reluctantly* means (*a*) gratefully (*b*) joyfully
(*c*) carefully (*d*) unwillingly.   4. _____

5. If Mahalia saw that a young singer was very nervous before a
concert, she would probably (*a*) amuse her (*b*) cheer her
(*c*) ignore her (*d*) rehearse her.   5. _____

12. Studying Sequence

The Importance of Logical Sequence

In telling a story or explaining a process, *the sentences must be in order*. They must be in *sequence.* Look at the following sentences:

> We removed all the old paint from the table. Then we covered the wood with a clear varnish to show the beautiful oak grain.

The first sentence tells about an action. The second sentence describes what follows the first action. You couldn't reverse the two steps or the two sentences. If you did, you would apply the varnish before removing the old finish!

There are a number of clues to look for when you're working with sequence.

Question: What Are the Clues to Sequence?

In each blank space, write the letter of the correct answer.

The polls closed at 9:00 P.M. Soon after that, television reporters began to 1. _____ the results. Townsend and Pruitt at first seemed to be running very close in the race for mayor. Then, as the results from more and more voting places came in, Townsend began to pull away from his rival. By midnight it was all over. Pruitt, realizing he had lost, 2. _____ his opponent.

1. (*a*) reject (*b*) lie about (*c*) forget (*d*) announce (*e*) try out

2. (*a*) ignored (*b*) challenged (*c*) defeated (*d*) laughed at (*e*) congratulated

---

Answers

1. (*d*) When the polls closed and the results came pouring in, television reporters would give totals and *announce* the results. That is the usual sequence of events.
2. (*e*) A candidate who wins by a large margin will usually be *congratulated* by the loser.

Notice the clues to sequence in the Question test. Words and phrases like *after*, *then*, and *by midnight* help you keep track of the sequence of events on election night. There are many such words that show the order in which things happen. Here are a few:

after	finally	next
as soon as	first	second
at last	later	then
before	meanwhile	while

Practice 1: Studying the Clues to Sequence

Read the following passage and answer the question at the end.

> Thompson was a success from the first. As a law clerk, he attracted the attention of the senior partner and was promoted within a month. He kept rising higher and higher in the firm until he reached the zenith of his career, full partner.

The sequence of events tells us that *zenith* means (*a*) midpoint (*b*) modest success (*c*) highest point (*d*) end.

Your answer 1: _____

Answer

The use of *success*, *promoted*, and then *higher and higher* suggests that Thompson's career was on a steadily upward curve. The answer is *highest point* (*c*).

Practice 2

Read the following passage and answer the questions at the end.

> Peggy Fleming was one of the world's great figure skaters. The story of her achievements is a long list of triumphs in major international competitions. In 1960, at the age of 12, she won her first title, the Pacific Coast juvenile figure skating championship. Her success continued when, a year later, she won an influential women's competition on the West Coast. The importance of her victories continued to escalate.
>
> Fleming looked forward to the 1964 Olympics. There, at the age of 15, she placed sixth among the greatest amateur figure skaters in the world. After the Olympics, she added title after title to her string of victories. She won the U.S. title at Lake Placid, New York, in February 1965. But national recognition was not enough. She kept moving up the ladder from national to international fame.
>
> Peggy Fleming captured five straight national championships, but her greatest goal was to win at the Olympics in 1968. That year, in Grenoble, France, she skated out on the ice for the beginning of her most prestigious competition. She skated with perfect grace and form, taking the gold medal that had been her dream and her ambition.

KNOW THIS WORD

recognition: praise

1. Which of the following titles best summarizes the content of the passage?

   (*a*) Peggy Fleming: World-Class Figure Skater
   (*b*) The Joys and Sorrows of Figure Skating
   (*c*) The Importance of Victory in the Olympic Games
   (*d*) Peggy Fleming's Recipe for a Successful Career in Skating   1. _____

2. The sequence of preceding events suggests that *escalate* means (*a*) make nervous (*b*) lessen (*c*) grow rapidly (*d*) remain.   2. _____

3. As used in paragraph 3, *prestigious* means (*a*) undesired (*b*) graceful (*c*) nerve-wracking (*d*) honored.   3. _____

4. It can be said of Peggy Fleming that (*a*) her dream came true (*b*) her competition was weak (*c*) she reached the top too soon (*d*) her success was due more to hard work than natural ability.   4. _____

5. National recognition was not enough for Peggy Fleming because it was too (*a*) late in coming (*b*) local (*c*) little advertised (*d*) easy.   5. _____

Answers

First read the entire passage, which tells about Peggy Fleming's success as an amateur figure skater. If you understand the whole passage, you will do better on the individual items.

1. (*a*) The passage is all about the achievements of Peggy Fleming. The correct title should include her name. We can eliminate (*b*) and (*c*). Choice (*d*) is not implied. The passage doesn't give us her recipe.
2. (*c*) Since Peggy has been winning, we have a sequence of victories. Thus, *escalate* must mean grow rapidly (*c*).
3. (*d*) All events have been leading to the Olympics. *Prestigious* must mean influential (*d*).
4. (*a*) Peggy started young and obviously had the dream of winning the figure-skating event in the Olympics. When she did, we can be sure her dream had come true.
5. (*b*) National recognition is contrasted with international fame in the next sentence. We may assume, then, that Peggy thought winning national titles was good but limited. *Local* (*b*) is the correct answer.

On Your Own: Studying Sequence

Read the following passage and answer the questions at the end.

On July 4, 1986, Americans celebrated the Statue of Liberty's 100th birthday. Parades, speeches, fireworks, and other activities contributed to the gaiety of the occasion. The celebration caused reporters and columnists to look back a century to the similar jubilation that marked the dedication of the statue.

The Statue of Liberty was dedicated in 1886, but the story begins earlier. The idea for a statue was first suggested at a dinner party by Edouard de Laboulaye, a French historian. A guest at the party was Frederic Auguste Bartholdi, a young sculptor.

Most people who attended the dinner party soon forgot the idea, but Laboulaye and Bartholdi remembered. In 1871, Bartholdi came to the United States to interest Americans in a statue that would link France and the United States in friendship. Many people in France had already been convinced and had contributed money to the project. Americans were also persuaded to donate to a fund for the statue. Much of the money came from schoolchildren.

After the idea had been accepted, Bartholdi set to work. He toiled for many years. His friend Laboulaye died before the statue was completed. At last, in 1885, the statue was sent to the United States. It had to be shipped in sections and then assembled.

From that time on, 1886, the Statue of Liberty has stood as a symbol of freedom to millions of immigrants entering New York Harbor.

KNOW THESE WORDS

gaiety: joy

dedication: official opening

1. Which of the following titles best summarizes the content of the passage?

   (a) Frederic Auguste Bartholdi, Sculptor
   (b) The 100th Birthday of the Statue of Liberty
   (c) The Story of the Statue of Liberty
   (d) How Schoolchildren Made the Statue of Liberty Possible   1. _____

2. The sequence of preceding events suggests that *jubilation* means
   (*a*) announcements (*b*) disputes (*c*) pride (*d*) rejoicing.   2. _____

3. Bartholdi made his first trip to the United States to talk about the
   Statue of Liberty in (*a*) 1865 (*b*) 1871 (*c*) 1885 (*d*) 1886.   3. _____

4. Which of the following statements is NOT true?

   (*a*) The 100th birthday of the Statue of Liberty was celebrated
        in 1986.
   (*b*) Edouard de Laboulaye was on hand when the Statue of Liberty
        was dedicated.
   (*c*) Schoolchildren contributed a great deal of money to the Statue
        of Liberty.
   (*d*) The Statue of Liberty stands in New York Harbor.   4. _____

5. The Statue of Liberty was shipped in sections because (*a*) it was
   too large (*b*) the United States had better means of assembling it
   than France (*c*) the completed statue was to be a surprise for Americans (*d*) assembling it cost less in the United States.   5. _____

Bonus: Reviewing Sequence

Read the following passage and answer the questions at the end.

"The Martians are coming." Science fiction stories often show the United States threatened by aliens from outer space. Such aliens are fanciful dangers, but there are very real invaders that menace our well-being. These are insect pests that cross our borders on vegetable matter from foreign countries.

A traveler arrives at John F. Kennedy International Airport from the Dominican Republic. She has brought in a beautiful, ripe mango, pleasing to look at and delicious to eat. The federal inspector at the airport immediately confiscates the fruit. When the lady protests, he points to two tiny punctures in the smooth surface of the fruit. He digs his knife into each puncture and exposes a worm. He explains that the worm is actually the larva of a Caribbean fruit fly. The larvae from this mango could become full-fledged flies, extremely dangerous to crops.

In just five hours of an average day, the inspector takes from arriving passengers hundreds of fruits and seeds, from tiny peppercorns to large coconuts. These are loaded with harmful insects, snails, and other undesirable intruders.

The arriving pests are often more dangerous in the United States than they are in their native countries. They have left behind their natural enemies and are ready to go wild in the lush farmland and orchards of the United States. A bug may be completely harmless abroad but a deadly threat here.

Some of the deadly pests that arrived in the past are the San Jose scale, the cotton boll weevil, the gypsy moth, the Japanese beetle, and the Dutch elm fungus.

In 1980, the Medfly arrived in the Santa Clara Valley of California and set off a nightmare chain of events. The flies probably arrived as larvae in a piece of fruit. Farmers panicked as they imagined their precious crops destroyed. Helicopters began spraying insecticide over 1300 square miles weekly. Residents worried about their health. Governor Edmund G. Brown, Jr., was criticized for spraying too much and spraying too little. It took two years and $100 million to eradicate the fly. It could have been worse. If the Medfly had been allowed to go unchecked, it would have infested 80% of the U.S. citrus crop at a loss of more than half a billion dollars in sales.

With the increase in air travel, the job of preventing unwanted pests from infesting our country gets more difficult. Inspectors cannot allow airline passengers and cargoes from other countries to bring dangerous invaders to our country.

KNOW THESE WORDS

aliens: outsiders

fanciful: imaginary

menace: threaten

larva: immature form of an insect (*plural:* larvae)

lush: fertile; rich

panicked: became terrified

1. Write the letter of the statement that best expresses the main idea.

   (*a*) Science fiction can alert us to dangers from outside.
   (*b*) The Medfly is an extremely dangerous insect pest.
   (*c*) Inspectors at John F. Kennedy International Airport do a good job.
   (*d*) Insect invaders from other countries are a constant threat.   1. _____

2. As used in paragraph 2, *confiscates* means (*a*) takes away (*b*) inspects (*c*) tastes (*d*) discusses.

2. _____

3. As used in paragraph 6, *eradicate* means (*a*) understand (*b*) analyze (*c*) destroy (*d*) locate.

3. _____

4. As used in paragraph 7, *infesting* means (*a*) surrounding (*b*) overrunning (*c*) arousing (*d*) discovering.

4. _____

5. The Martians are mentioned at the beginning of the passage to (*a*) begin the thought about invaders (*b*) arouse greater interest in science fiction (*c*) show that Martians don't really exist (*d*) suggest that Martians are a greater threat than insect invaders.

5. _____

6. The mango mentioned in the article came from (*a*) California (*b*) the Dominican Republic (*c*) the Santa Clara Valley (*d*) the Netherlands.

6. _____

7. When an insect pest arrives here from abroad, (*a*) the natural balance of nature is destroyed (*b*) native birds immediately keep the new insect in check (*c*) it is usually sprayed by helicopter (*d*) it is seldom discovered by plant inspectors.

7. _____

8. It could reasonably be said that Governor Brown of California (*a*) started the spraying too early (*b*) started the spraying too late (*c*) used far too much insecticide (*d*) couldn't avoid criticism.

8. _____

9. The people in California worried about their health because of (*a*) unripe fruit (*b*) the danger from stinging flies (*c*) the spraying (*d*) the anger of the farmers.

9. _____

10. All the following are mentioned as serious foreign pests EXCEPT (*a*) the gypsy moth (*b*) the cotton boll weevil (*c*) the chestnut blight (*d*) the Dutch elm fungus.

10. _____

13. Understanding Figurative Language

Dan, our basketball center, is seven feet tall.
Dan is as tall as a giant.   (*Simile*)
Dan is a giant.   (*Metaphor*)
When Dan plays, Pride is playing on our team.   (*Personification*)
Some teammates call Dan "the Shoulders."   (*Synecdoche*)
Others call him "Mr. Leather himself."   (*Metonymy*)
When Dan stands up, clouds gather around his head.   (*Hyperbole*)
Dan was a trifle tall for the opposing six-foot center.   (*Understatement*)
Chuck calls seven-foot-tall Dan "Shorty."   (*Irony*)

There is a great difference between the first statement above and all the rest. The first is a straightforward, *literal statement*. It means just what it says. The others are examples of ***figurative language***, or ***figures of speech***. Dan isn't actually a giant, nor is he as tall as a giant. When he stands up, clouds don't really gather around his head. Calling a tall man "Shorty" is a tongue-in-cheek statement.

Why do you often use figurative language, which describes things as they really aren't? Is it a kind of lying? Is it careless, inaccurate speech? Not at all! Figurative language helps make what you say more vivid. It adds power, humor, and feeling to your speech. While literal language just tells the facts, figurative language lights up these facts and makes them more colorful.

Comparison is the basis of most figurative language, as in the first three examples following.

Simile: The salesperson was as persistent as a mosquito.

(A simile compares things by using the words *like* or *as*. The salesperson is compared with a mosquito. In the opening example, Dan is compared with a giant.)

Metaphor: Cheryl tossed Peter a warning glance.

(A metaphor compares things without using *like* or *as*. Cheryl's act of glancing is compared with tossing a ball. In the opening example, Dan is compared with a giant, but *like* or *as* is not used.)

Personification: Duty shouldn't whisper but shout.

(In personification, something is compared with a person by giving it human qualities. Here, duty is compared with a person who can whisper and shout. In the opening example, Pride is given the human quality of being able to play.)

Association is another basis for figurative language, as the next two examples demonstrate.

Synecdoche: The hired hands herded the 30 head of cattle.

(Synecdoche substitutes a part for the whole or the whole for a part. *Hands* really represents people and *head* really represents cattle. In the opening example, *shoulders* represents Dan.)

Metonymy: The defendant made a plea to the bench for clemency.

(Metonymy substitutes one word for another closely associated with it. *Bench* is substituted for *judge.* In the opening example, *leather* is associated with *basketball*.)

Figurative language includes other examples of playing with reality.

Hyperbole: When Carla saw Jim's Halloween costume, she nearly died laughing.

(Hyperbole is a form of exaggeration, often humorous. *Nearly died* is an exaggeration. Carla was not really near death. In the opening example, clouds didn't really gather around Dan's head.)

Understatement: Vince had a pretty good day, scoring four touchdowns in the second half.

(Understatement is the opposite of hyperbole. By saying less, it often says more. Vince's achievements are excellent, not just *pretty good.* In the opening example, Dan is not a *trifle tall*; he's overpoweringly taller than the opposing center.)

Irony: I can't wait to begin the dreary job of cleaning up the basement.

(Irony says one thing and suggests another. The speaker obviously isn't eager to begin the job: *can't wait* is ironic. In the opening example, *Shorty* ironically pays a tribute to Dan's height.)

The preceding list is given for completeness, so that you will have a feeling for figurative language. In the examples that follow, you will not be expected to know the specific names of the various figures of speech, but you will be expected to identify figurative language when it occurs.

Metaphor is the most common of all. It exists in all your conversations and friendly letters. It is everywhere, though you rarely recognize it. Note the following examples of metaphor.

> The *light in her eyes went out* when she heard the news.
> Juan doesn't want to *shoulder* any more burdens.
> I *slipped* a little in math last month but *shot up* in English.
> After the test, Donna wanted to *unwind* in the swimming pool.
> I *caught* a cold overnight and took two weeks to *lose* it.
> Shy Emma *dropped* a *blockbuster* into the conversation.
> Bud is a *lion* on the football field but a *mouse* in class.

Question: How Do You Identify Figurative Language?

Which of the following sentences contain a figurative expression? Write each figurative expression.

1. Sheila has been chosen president of our class.   1. _____

2. Drop me a note when you get home.   2. _____

3. When his arguments are challenged, Ben is a rock.   3. _____

4. The school bus was late this morning.   4. _____

5. From the air, the farmland of the Midwest looked like a
giant checkerboard.   5. _____

Answers

Let's examine the possible answers.

1. This is a literal statement of fact.
2. *Drop* is a physical action. Here it is used figuratively, as though a note can physically be dropped.
3. Ben isn't really a *rock*. He is figuratively said to resemble a rock in an argument.
4. This is a literal statement of fact.
5. The farmland is being compared figuratively with a *checkerboard*. It is not a checkerboard.

Practice 1: Completing Figurative Statements

Write the letter of the answer that most appropriately completes each statement.

1. Juan was as carefree as a (*a*) child in a meadow of flowers
(*b*) high school senior before an examination (*c*) tiger stalking its
prey (*d*) customer at a supermarket.   1. _____

2. The new houses sprang up like (*a*) water over the dam
(*b*) plants in a drought (*c*) dandelions after a spring shower
(*d*) a circus parade.   2. _____

3. The balloon fell as slowly as (*a*) a rain of hail (*b*) a feather fluttering
down on a still afternoon (*c*) a train slowly puffing out of a station
(*d*) the flow of lava during a volcanic eruption.   3. _____

4. Pam was as unpredictable as (*a*) a soap opera (*b*) moonrise over
a lake (*c*) her sister (*d*) lightning.   4. _____

5. Tony looked as forlorn as (*a*) the last leaf on the tree (*b*) a surfer
at the beach (*c*) a tree in the forest (*d*) a singer at a concert.   5. _____

Answers

Let's examine the possible answers.

Although alternative choices may be made, the following answers are probably most appropriate. If you have a good reason for choosing another, state it. This is partly a matter of taste. The value lies in the discussion.

1. (*a*) A child is likely to be carefree in a meadow of flowers. A high school senior is more likely to be nervous than carefree before an examination (*b*). A tiger stalking its prey is tense and concentrated (*c*). A customer at a supermarket is likely to be concentrating on prices and products (*d*).
2. (*c*) Dandelions spring up quickly after a spring shower. The other alternatives are inappropriate.

3. (*b*) The slow descent of the balloon is closest to the slow descent of a feather. Hail doesn't fall slowly (*a*). The comparison of a lumbering train with a balloon is farfetched (*c*). Lava doesn't fall; it flows (*d*).
4. (*d*) Of all the possibilities, lightning is the most unpredictable.
5. (*a*) The last leaf on the tree, lonely and battered by weather, looks forlorn. The other examples do not fit.

Practice 2

Read the following passage and answer the questions at the end.

There is one kind of story that is a perennial favorite of readers as well as television and movie viewers. Westerns rise and fall in popularity. Science fiction has its day in the sun and then fades for a time. But spy stories seem to be always with us. Secret operatives of the CIA, the KGB, and other alphabetical agencies cross swords with each other in their never-ending quest for secrets of the other side.

There is an incredible real-life story connected with World War I. The heroes of this story were not trained agents and double agents. They were simple people who never carried a weapon or went in disguise in enemy territory. They were Belgian railway workers.

In 1914, Germans overran Belgium and occupied the country. They replaced Belgian stamps with German stamps, but to identify the country of use they printed *Belgien* over the original stamps. Along with the country overprint was the denomination—for example, *8 Cent*. These overprints gave Belgian patriots the opportunity to act as spies in the middle of the enemy.

Railway workers were in the perfect position to observe troop movements. They knew how many troop trains were on the way to the front, but they had to find a way to notify others. They devised a code that was a marvel of ingenuity and one almost impossible to spot. They inked in portions of the overprint to indicate what was happening. Filling in the top of the *B* in *Belgien*, for example, indicated a train was on the way to the front. Filling in the *e* of *Cent* indicated it was a heavy artillery unit.

Thirteen overprint modifications were used to convey a great deal of useful information. The stamps were eventually forwarded to the ringleaders in Brussels, who organized the information and passed it to France and Britain through a neutral nation.

> After a time, the German authorities began to suspect something was afoot, but they were powerless to stop the scheme. They hadn't the time to screen tens of thousands of postcards each day in search of tiny dots and smudges. By the end of the war, more than 16,000 pieces of information had been successfully transmitted to the Allies. The brilliant spies were just ordinary people.

KNOW THESE WORDS

operatives: secret agents
devised: invented; made up
ingenuity: cleverness
convey: pass along
afoot: happening

1. Write the letter of the statement that best expresses the main idea of the passage.

   (*a*) Simple railway workers outwitted German authorities in World War I.
   (*b*) Spies usually use postage stamps for transmitting information.
   (*c*) German authorities overprinted their own stamps for use in Belgium.
   (*d*) Spies must be clever to survive.   1. _____

2. Which of the following sentences contains a figurative expression?

   (*a*) They were Belgian railway workers.
   (*b*) Westerns rise and fall in popularity.
   (*c*) They inked in portions of the overprint to indicate what was happening.
   (*d*) They replaced Belgian stamps with German stamps.   2. _____

3. Which of the following sentences contains a figurative expression?

   (*a*) Secret operatives cross swords with each other.
   (*b*) The heroes of this story were not trained agents and double agents.
   (*c*) They were simple people who never carried a weapon or went in disguise in enemy territory.
   (*d*) Filling in the *e* of *Cent* indicated it was a heavy artillery unit.   3. _____

4. The expression "Science fiction has its day in the sun" means that science fiction (*a*) usually deals with the solar system (*b*) is more popular on television than in the movies (*c*) is unusually popular for a time (*d*) celebrates the anniversary of the first successful science fiction series on television.   4. _____

5. Filling in the *e* of *Cent* meant that (*a*) a train with prisoners was passing through (*b*) the train was a heavy artillery unit (*c*) a hospital train was passing through (*d*) a train was headed back to Germany.   5. _____

6. The strength of the code was its (*a*) use of several different code books (*b*) use by the Germans (*c*) simplicity (*d*) limited use.   6. _____

7. The use of *screen* in "the time to screen tens of thousands of postcards" is an example of (*a*) simile (*b*) personification (*c*) exaggeration (*d*) metaphor.   7. _____

8. As used in paragraph 1, *perennial* means (*a*) unusual (*b*) fanciful (*c*) timely (*d*) long-lasting.   8. _____

9. As used in paragraph 1, *quest* means (*a*) trip (*b*) search (*c*) excitement (*d*) advertisement.   9. _____

10. As used in paragraph 5, *modifications* means (*a*) numbers (*b*) changes (*c*) communications (*d*) stamps.   10. _____

Answers

Let's examine the possible answers.

1. (*a*) The main idea should make the point that the railway workers outwitted the authorities. Choices (*b*) and (*c*) are important details, but not the main idea. Choice (*d*) is too general.
2. (*b*) The figurative expression is *rise and fall*. Westerns do not physically rise and fall.
3. (*a*) The figurative expression is *cross swords*. The operatives don't actually use swords when they oppose each other.
4. (*c*) *To have a day in the sun* is a figurative expression meaning to be popular (in the sun) for a short time (a day).
5. (*b*) This is a detail specifically mentioned in this sentence: "Filling in the *e* of *Cent* indicated it was a heavy artillery unit."
6. (*c*) The code was so simple but so difficult to control that it succeeded where a more complicated code might have failed.
7. (*d*) A comparison without *like* or *as* is a metaphor. In the expression, checking each of the many postcards is compared with passing them through a screen, or grid, that could separate out those bearing a code.
8. (*d*) If the other stories rise and fall in popularity, *perennial* must mean long-lasting.
9. (*b*) If the operatives were after secrets, *quest* must mean search.
10. (*b*) Since different ways of sending messages are mentioned, *modifications* must mean changes.

On Your Own: Studying Figurative Language

Read the following passage and answer the questions at the end.

"I can't play any musical instrument!" This sad comment, often heard in otherwise musical families, is an untruth. The reality is that there is one musical instrument that everyone can play: the kazoo. If there were an advertisement for openings in a kazoo band, it would have to say, "No talent needed." As Barbara Stewart, kazoo authority, says, "It takes about four seconds to learn. For slow learners, it may take six seconds."

Nearly everyone is familiar with the kazoo, "an open-ended tube with a membrane-covered side hole." Many people have, at one time or other, actually played a kazoo. As writer Ben Fanton has said, "It has often been used as a stocking-stuffer at Christmastime by parents who've deeply regretted their action about an hour after sunrise on Christmas morning." The father may hit the roof, but the kids play blissfully on.

Some people take the kazoo seriously. Barbara Stewart is not one of them, though she collects kazoos in all shapes, sizes, and in many different materials. She is a professional kazooist, who has formed "the world's largest kazoo quartet." It's the largest because it actually has *five* members! Members of the group have, at times, been serious music students, but when they join the group, fun conquers all. Her group is dressed formally in tuxedos—but is barefooted! The group has appeared on the *Tonight* show; *Good Morning, America*; *PM Magazine*; and other television programs. The performers poke fun at serious music. At their performances, audience members enter into the spirit of fun and throw socks at them. "I got a nice pair of argyles once," Barbara proudly declares.

Despite her fun with the kazoo, Barbara Stewart has a serious reply when asked why people should bother with the kazoo. "It's fun! People are ready for a good time, and it's a good-times instrument. Everybody can do it, and a lot of people have wanted to do something musical and have gone through the dreadful experience of grade-school music where they are asked please not to sing. Playing the kazoo brings out creativity."

Indeed, throughout the country, senior citizens form kazoo bands that entertain the ill in nursing homes and perform in shopping malls and other places of assembly. To see the look of intense concentration and satisfaction on the faces of these performers is to realize that the kazoo has a place in music.

If you'd like to become a kazoo performer yourself, you may benefit from the advice offered by Barbara Stewart. ''Practice, practice, practice . . . but not near the neighbors.''

KNOW THESE WORDS

blissfully: happily
argyles: variety of socks
creativity: originality

1. Which of the following titles best summarizes the content of the passage?

    (a) Barbara Stewart and Her Kazoo Band
    (b) The Kazoo: An Instrument for Everyone
    (c) The Kazoo: A Favorite Gift at Christmas
    (d) How to Collect Kazoos   1. _____

2. The figurative expression *hit the roof* means (a) dent the ceiling (b) play the kazoo loudly (c) become very angry (d) speak softly.   2. _____

3. An example of figurative language is the expression (a) *audience members throw socks* (b) *''I can't play any musical instrument''* (c) *Barbara Stewart has a serious reply* (d) *fun conquers all.*   3. _____

4. An example of figurative language is the expression (a) *poke fun* (b) *members throw socks* (c) *Barbara proudly declares* (d) *senior citizens form kazoo bands.*   4. _____

5. All the following television programs were mentioned in the passage EXCEPT (a) *PM Magazine* (b) *Good Morning, America* (c) the *Today* show (d) the *Tonight* show.   5. _____

6. Parents at Christmas may regret their choice of stocking-stuffer because of (a) expense (b) fights (c) disappointments (d) noise.   6. _____

7. Calling the group of five ''the world's largest kazoo quartet'' is intended to (a) annoy (b) amuse (c) provoke (d) calm.   7. _____

Bonus: Reviewing Figurative Language

Read the following passage and answer the questions at the end.

When your grandfather was a boy, he probably took your grandmother to an ice-cream parlor. Here, for little more than a dime, he could treat the young lady to an ice-cream soda, a sundae, a malted milk, or some other delightful dessert. Probably, the ice-cream parlor was situated in a corner of a drugstore. It had marble counters and metal gooseneck arms that dispensed carbonated bubbly water. There were containers of many kinds of syrups. The person behind the counter was called a *soda jerk*. He was the master of such delightful concoctions as the *brown cow*, a root-beer soda with ice cream floating in it.

The name *soda water* tells something of its origins. Naturally carbonated water flows out of the ground in mineral springs around the world. These mineral springs have long lured people in search of a cure for indigestion or other ills. Then in 1767, the scientist Joseph Priestley created the first soda water not taken from natural mineral springs. Soon other experimenters were finding new ways to create the bubbly water that is the basis of so many soft drinks. In 1825, Elias Durand decided to tap the public interest in sparkling waters. He opened a drugstore in Philadelphia that served carbonated water, at that time still considered a helpful medicine.

A few years later, another Philadelphian, Eugene Roussel, decided to bottle soda water of different flavors. His first offering was a popular lemon soda, sold at the fountain of his perfume shop. Other manufacturers entered the race, and new flavors were introduced. Meanwhile, at soda fountains, enterprising owners added sweet cream to make the drink more appetizing.

Then came one of the most important events in the history of soda water. In October 1874 at the semicentennial celebration of Philadelphia's Franklin Institute, a concessionaire named Robert Green sold so many soda-water drinks with cream that he ran out of cream. He rushed to a nearby shop to buy some vanilla ice cream. He planned to melt the ice cream and use it as cream. His customers were too thirsty to wait, and so he put the ice cream right into the soda water. The ice-cream soda was born. It has never lost its popularity.

Not far away, Charles E. Hires was experimenting with selling dried roots, bark, herbs, and flowers for making a drink he called *root beer*. He also made his own. By 1892, more than two million bottles of his soft drink were being sold annually. Then came a host of other drinks: Moxie, Dr. Pepper, and Coca-Cola. When the Eighteenth Amendment forbade the sale of alcoholic beverages, the soft-drink market exploded.

The soft-drink market today is a gigantic business, with many competitors pushing their wares on television and in newspapers and magazines. There are still many fast-food places where ice-cream sodas may be ordered. There are soft-drink dispensing machines in every corner of the land. But the old-time ice-cream parlor in a corner of a drugstore is largely a thing of the past.

KNOW THESE WORDS

dispensed: poured out

concoctions: combinations of materials

lured: tempted

semicentennial: occurring after fifty years

concessionaire: owner of a refreshment stand

wares: things for sale

1. Which of the following titles best summarizes the content of the passage?

   (*a*) Why the Soft-Drink Industry Is Popular in Hot Climates
   (*b*) The Invention of Carbonated Water
   (*c*) A Historic Moment in the History of Soda Water
   (*d*) The Story of Soda Water and the Ice-Cream Parlor   1. _____

2. An example of figurative language is the expression (*a*) *ice-cream soda* (*b*) *carbonated water* (*c*) *gooseneck arms* (*d*) *popular lemon soda.*   2. _____

3. An example of figurative language is the expression (*a*) *tap the public interest* (*b*) *soda-water drinks with cream* (*c*) *many kinds of syrups* (*d*) *helpful medicine.*   3. _____

4. *The soft-drink market exploded* means (*a*) the sale of soft drinks fell off (*b*) soft drinks were suddenly more popular than ever (*c*) only certain kinds of soda were popular (*d*) Americans preferred fast-food shops to ice-cream parlors.   4. _____

5. As used in paragraph 3, *enterprising* means (*a*) adventurous (*b*) wealthy (*c*) worried (*d*) nervous.   5. _____

6. The first drugstore with a soda fountain was opened by (*a*) Joseph Priestley (*b*) Elias Durand (*c*) Robert Green (*d*) Charles E. Hires.   6. _____

7. The author of this passage would probably (*a*) disapprove of Robert Green's actions (*b*) prefer root beer to lemon soda (*c*) like to see ice-cream parlors return (*d*) hope for a job advertising soft drinks.   7. _____

8. The ice-cream soda was born (*a*) in 1825 (*b*) through the genius of Charles E. Hires (*c*) by accident (*d*) in a drugstore.   8. _____

14. Distinguishing Fact from Opinion

Hank Aaron is the record holder for most home runs in a career.

Hank Aaron is the greatest baseball player who ever lived.

How similar these two statements are, yet how different! Both sentences make statements. Both use the verb *is* to make the statements. Both are talking about Hank Aaron, a major-league baseball player. But the similarity stops there. The first sentence is a statement of *fact.* It can be checked by a glance at the record books. The second is a statement of *opinion.* It cannot be checked or verified. You may well agree with the second statement and say, ''Yes, that's true.'' But there is a world of difference between the *greatest baseball player* and *a baseball record holder.*

''Well, that's pretty obvious,'' you're probably saying. When you look at two sentences side by side, you can see the differences. But surprisingly enough, in everyday living, opinions are often accepted as fact. There is nothing wrong with having or listening to opinions. The danger is that you may confuse an opinion with a fact.

People will argue for hours about who is the best quarterback in professional football or who is the greater president, George Washington or Abraham Lincoln. Now these arguments may bring out a lot of factual information, but they can never be resolved. The answers are all opinions.

Statements of opinion can be interesting and informative, but they can also cause confusion and even harm. ''Georgette is a snob.'' ''Juan is conceited.'' ''Maureen is thoughtless.'' ''Dave is stingy.'' Labeling people can be an especially dangerous habit, since people are far too complicated for easy tags. Nobody can avoid using occasional labels, but speakers and listeners should recognize these labels for what they are—opinions, NOT statements of fact.

Some opinions are better than others. If Dave often avoids paying his fair share, the label *stingy* may seem appropriate. But there may be financial reasons for Dave's actions, situations you know nothing about. If you wanted to be a bit more careful, you might say, ''At times, Dave holds back on paying his fair share and seems to me to be stingy.'' This is, at least, a more accurate way of analyzing the situation. It talks about Dave's actions, identifies your opinion, and doesn't make a flat statement about his character.

Certain kinds of words characterize opinions as opposed to factual statements. There are emotional, ''loaded'' words like *pleasant, disagreeable, likable, fussy, silly, careless, uninformed.* There are easy labels like *genius, fool, tattletale,* and *chatterbox.* There are judgment words like *greatest, best, worst, stupid,* and *boring.* There are sweeping, all-or-nothing words like *always, never, nobody, everybody, all,* and *none.*

If you want to experience judgment words in action, listen to television or movie critics on television. Their criticisms are loaded with personal judgments, opinions rather than statements of fact. If you generally share your favorite reviewer's taste, you will probably find his or her opinions helpful. But they are still opinions.

Question: How Can You Distinguish Fact from Opinion?

Tell whether each of the following is a factual statement or an opinion. Write *F* for a fact and *O* for an opinion.

1. The potato, the pumpkin, and the pineapple originally came from South America.   1. _____

2. The Incas of South America were the greatest farmers the world has ever known.   2. _____

3. In 1795, Napoleon offered a prize for a practical way of preserving food.   3. _____

4. A French inventor, Nicholas Appert, devised the process of canning.   4. _____

5. Modern freezing methods of preserving food are better than canning or bottling.   5. _____

Answers

Let's examine the possible answers.

1. This is a factual statement. Note that a statement may be in factual form and yet be in error. "The potato, the pumpkin, and the pineapple originally came from Europe" is a statement in factual form. It can be checked and shown to be erroneous.
2. This is a statement of opinion. Note that an opinion may be one that nearly everyone agrees with, but it is still an opinion. Most Americans would agree with the following statement: "The United States is the best country in the world to live in." Though an excellent statement for most of us, it is still an opinion.
3. This is a factual statement that can be checked for accuracy.
4. This, too, is a factual statement capable of verification.
5. The word *better* is strictly a judgment word. This is an opinion.

Practice 1: Studying Facts and Opinions

Read the following passage and answer the questions at the end.

> What is pitch? Technically speaking, pitch is the position of a tone in the musical scale. It is determined by the frequency of vibration of the source of the tone. In everyday terms, pitch is characterized by such terms as *low* and *high*. If you fill a jar with water, you can hear the change in pitch. At first the sound is low, but it gradually becomes higher as the jar is filled. Similarly, if you hear a train approach, its whistle gets higher and higher until the train passes you. Then the pitch gets lower as the train pulls away.
>
> Pitch is measured by the number of vibrations, or cycles, per second. If the pitch of a sound is too high or

too low, the human ear cannot hear the sound. Older people tend to "lose" higher-pitched sounds. Dog whistles, which cannot be heard by the human ear, prove that dogs can hear higher-pitched sounds than we can.

In the musical scale, the pitch of the note A is very important. All the musical instruments are tuned, or adjusted, in relation to an A. It is therefore very important to standardize the pitch of that note.

In 1810 at the Paris Opera, the note A had stood at 423 cycles per second but had climbed to 431.7 by 1822. Singers insisted that the latter number raised the pitch beyond their ability to sing. The pitch was temporarily lowered to 425.8. Then the number began to creep up again, reaching 449 in 1855. According to one writer, "This was, until recently, the horrifying standard of the Berlin Philharmonic."

In 1858, the French government set up a commission of musicians and scientists to establish some kind of agreement. The commission settled upon an A of 435 cycles per second. An international conference at Vienna accepted this decision in 1889. This was indeed a major achievement of far-reaching importance.

Did the decision settle the problem for all time? No. Deviations began to creep in, and A moved upward again. As it approached 450 cycles per second, Adelina Patti, at the end of the 19th century, led a singers' protest. In response to the protest, London pitch was reduced to 435.5, a drop of more than a quarter tone. The A of most symphony and opera orchestras today ranges between 440 and 444.

In general, the pitch of A has been rising since the time of Mozart and Beethoven, when A stood between 415 and 429. When opera fans now hear Mozart's *The Magic Flute*, they are hearing the entire piece as much as a half tone higher than in Mozart's time. A modern-day soprano has to soar to F over high C, but an 18th-century soprano had to go no higher than the note we hear as E. As Donald Henahan comments, "For some voices that could be enough of a difference to shorten careers."

"Modern-day sound is more beautiful than the sound of 200 years ago," say some critics. True, raising the pitch of A often brings brilliant, memorable sounds, but it can place a terrible burden on singers.

KNOW THESE WORDS

deviations: differences
memorable: worth remembering

1. Which of the following titles best summarizes the content of the passage?

   (*a*) Musical Pitch: A Movable Standard
   (*b*) How Musical Pitch Was Finally Standardized
   (*c*) The Leadership of France in Determining Pitch
   (*d*) Why Singers Have Problems with High Notes   1. _____

2. Which of the following is an opinion?

   (*a*) Pitch is the position of a tone in the musical scale.
   (*b*) Older people tend to ''lose'' higher-pitched sounds.
   (*c*) This was indeed a major achievement of far-reaching importance.
   (*d*) If the pitch of a sound is too high or too low, the human ear cannot hear the sound.   2. _____

3. Which of the following is an opinion?

   (*a*) In 1810 at the Paris Opera, A had stood at 423.
   (*b*) Pitch is measured by the number of vibrations per second.
   (*c*) The A of most symphony and opera orchestras today ranges between 440 and 444.
   (*d*) ''Modern-day sound is more beautiful than the sound of 200 years ago.''   3. _____

4. As used in paragraph 3, *standardize* means (*a*) make uniform (*b*) study intensively (*c*) raise (*d*) lower.   4. _____

5. If pitch is not set at an agreed-upon number, there is a tendency for it to (*a*) arouse the curiosity of audiences (*b*) creep upward (*c*) work to the advantages of singers (*d*) please the conductors of orchestras.   5. _____

6. The pitch of A stood at 423 in (*a*) 1810 (*b*) 1822 (*c*) 1858 (*d*) 1889.   6. _____

7. Mozart's *The Magic Flute* (*a*) was harder to sing in Mozart's time (*b*) is the favorite of most good sopranos (*c*) has always been a favorite opera (*d*) was easier to sing in Mozart's time.   7. _____

8. The illustration of the jar is used to demonstrate (*a*) the purity of musical sounds (*b*) the similarity between a train whistle and a dog whistle (*c*) variations in pitch (*d*) a sound that cannot be heard by the human ear.   8. _____

9. Donald Henahan is probably a (*a*) physical scientist (*b*) music critic (*c*) companion of Mozart (*d*) 19th-century singer.   9. _____

10. Setting A at 450 (*a*) is popular with the Paris Opera (*b*) was common in Mozart's time (*c*) is unfair to singers (*d*) is more common in France than in Germany.   10. _____

11. Each of the following statements contains an example of figurative language EXCEPT

   (*a*) Deviations began to creep in, and A moved upward.
   (*b*) A modern-day soprano has to soar to F over high C.
   (*c*) Older people tend to ''lose'' higher-pitched sounds.
   (*d*) Pitch is measured by the number of vibrations per second.   11. _____

12. Which of the following statements contains the best example of figurative language?

   (*a*) If you fill a jar with water, you can hear the change in pitch.
   (*b*) Dog whistles, which cannot be heard by the human ear, prove that dogs can hear higher-pitched sounds than we can.
   (*c*) In 1810 at the Paris Opera, A had stood at 423 cycles per second but had climbed to 431.7 by 1822.
   (*d*) In 1858, the French government set up a commission of musicians and scientists to establish some kind of agreement.   12. _____

Answers

   First read the entire passage. As you will see, it is all about musical pitch. Understanding the entire passage makes the individual questions easier.

   1. (*a*) The passage deals with the variations in pitch through the ages, as demonstrated by the numbers assigned to the musical note A. ''A movable standard'' accurately sums up the variations. Choice (*b*) is not true. Pitch is still not fully standardized. Choices (*c*) and (*d*) are details, not main ideas.
   2. (*c*) ''A major achievement,'' though probably a sound observation, is still an opinion. Some might debate how ''far-reaching'' the decision was. The other choices are factual and can be verified.
   3. (*d*) The word *beautiful* tends to identify an opinion. There are as many definitions of beauty as there are people. This is not verifiable as are the other choices.
   4. (*a*) Since pitch has moved up and down, there have been attempts to make pitch uniform, to *standardize* it. The other choices do not fit the context.
   5. (*b*) This is a detail: ''In general, the pitch of A has been rising since the time of Mozart and Beethoven.''
   6. (*a*) This is a detail: ''In 1810 at the Paris Opera, A had stood at 423.''
   7. (*d*) This requires an inference based upon the lower pitch of Mozart's day and the comment that ''raising the pitch . . . can place a terrible burden on the singers.''
   8. (*c*) If the pitch changes as the jar is filled, we can infer that the demonstration is mentioned to show how pitch changes.
   9. (*b*) A comment about singers' careers is best made by a music critic, who knows more about music and singers than does an average physical scientist (*a*). The physical scientist would, of course, know a great deal about pitch but not necessarily about performers. The context indicates that Donald Henahan is living today, making choices (*c*) and (*d*) absurd.

10. (c) Setting the pitch of A too high can "shorten careers." Therefore, we can conclude it would be unfair to singers. There is no indication that the Paris Opera uses a setting of 450 (a). Choice (b) is incorrect. Pitch was lower in Mozart's time. Since the German standard was higher than the French, (d) is wrong.

11. (d) Choice (d) is a straightforward, literal statement. The figurative expressions in (a) are *creep in* and *moved upward*. *Soar* is figurative in (b). "*Lose*" is figurative in (c).

12. (c) This is the opposite of 11. Here you must pick out the sentence with the figurative expression. *Stood* and *climbed* in (c) are figurative.

On Your Own: Studying Facts and Opinions

Read the following passage and answer the questions at the end.

A symphony orchestra seems to be a perfect example of agreeable people always working harmoniously together. The conductor raises his baton. All eyes are on him. He begins to conduct and the music flows magically. Yet to reach this point is not always easy. The pitch to which the instruments are tuned is sometimes a source of anguished argument. Should A be fixed at 440 cycles per second, which is considered standard, or at 442.5 cycles per second, which is used by the Chicago Symphony Orchestra? The difference may seem to be insignificant, but to the trained ear, it may be troublesome.

Who sets the pitch of an orchestra? In many orchestras, the oboe sets the pitch of A, and all other instruments follow suit. Musical experts believe that the oboe's tone is "purer," less complex than that of other instruments like the violin. At the New York Philharmonic, however, the A is sounded by the principal clarinetist. The person who sets the pitch inevitably enjoys a higher status than others and some envious criticism.

A device is now often used to avoid quarrels about the ability of any musician to sound the right pitch as the guide for the orchestra. The Metropolitan Opera Orchestra, for example, uses an electronic "black box," a lap-held instrument that sounds a perfect tone of 440 cycles per second. Though the principal oboeist is the keeper of the box, her role is purely mechanical. She activates the box, and the box sounds the standard A.

"This is terrible," say some musicians who have been called the *Anti-A Team*. "A machine is running our lives." Whether criticized or not, the black box does provide a standard pitch that reduces arguments and disagreements. It is a superior solution.

KNOW THESE WORDS

anguished: painful
inevitably: unavoidably

1. Write the letter of the statement that best expresses the main idea.

   (*a*) Symphony orchestras are examples of harmony in action.
   (*b*) A problem with orchestras is deciding who sets the pitch.
   (*c*) The oboeist, rather than the clarinetist, determines pitch in most orchestras.
   (*d*) The pitch of A should be set at 440 cycles per second.   1. _____

2. Which of the following is a factual statement?

   (*a*) The music flows magically.
   (*b*) At the New York Philharmonic, however, the A is sounded by the principal clarinetist.
   (*c*) "This is terrible."
   (*d*) It is a superior solution.   2. _____

3. Which of the following is an opinion?

   (*a*) In many orchestras, the oboe sets the pitch of A, and all other instruments follow suit.
   (*b*) She activates the box, and the box sounds the standard A.
   (*c*) "A machine is running our lives."
   (*d*) The Metropolitan Opera Orchestra, for example, uses an electronic "black box."   3. _____

4. The violin is not generally used to set the pitch of A because its tone is too (*a*) loud (*b*) soft (*c*) complex (*d*) simple.   4. _____

5. The electronic "black box" (*a*) sounds a perfect tone (*b*) is universally approved (*c*) is used by all major orchestras (*d*) is activated by the clarinetist.   5. _____

6. The *Anti-A Team* refers to musicians who (*a*) are not real music lovers (*b*) prefer a pitch of 442.5 cycles per second (*c*) are members of the New York Philharmonic (*d*) are opposed to electronic setting of pitch.   6. _____

7. Which of the following statements is the best example of figurative language?

   (*a*) The conductor raises his baton.
   (*b*) The difference may seem to be insignificant.
   (*c*) At the New York Philharmonic, however, the A is sounded by the principal clarinetist.
   (*d*) All eyes are on him.   7. _____

Bonus: Reviewing Facts and Opinions

Read the following passage and answer the questions at the end.

The 1920s were a time of outlandish fads. There were dance marathons, with couples dancing on and on past the state of exhaustion. There were flagpole sitters, who competed to see how long they could live at the top of a flagpole. Then at the end of the decade came a fad that topped all others in popularity: miniature golf. In many areas, an entire 18-hole course was set up in a vacant lot. All over the country, miniature golf courses sprang up like mushrooms.

These were not simple putting greens. There were tunnels to go through, bridges to go over, tricky angles to master, and hazards of every description. There were hollow logs, castles with moats, windmills with tricky vanes, and sphinxes with passages between their paws. The designer's ingenuity was unlimited.

Garnet Carter of Georgia saw the possibilities and began to set up miniature courses called *Tom Thumb* courses. By 1930, there were 3,000 Tom Thumb links and more than 20,000 other courses. The courses sprang up overnight and became so popular that movie attendance fell nearly 25 percent. The studios ordered their stars not to go near their competitors' territory.

The bubble burst almost as quickly as it had developed. Garnet Carter sold his business in October 1930 at a considerable profit. He must have been a prophet. The popularity of the fad quickly died away. One after another, the miniature courses closed until they were nearly all gone. The fad had a brief revival in the 1950s, but it never achieved the popularity of the past. Though there are still some miniature courses throughout the country, most of the potential customers are at home, watching television.

KNOW THESE WORDS

outlandish: strange

marathons: endurance contests

decade: period of ten years

hazards: golf-course obstacles

revival: renewal of interest

1. Which of the following titles best summarizes the content of the passage?

    (a) Fads and Fancies of the 1920s
    (b) The Incredible Success of Miniature Golf
    (c) Miniature Golf: Its Ups and Downs
    (d) Garnet Carter's Brainstorm   1. _____

2. Which of the following is an opinion?

    (a) By 1930, there were 3,000 Tom Thumb links and more than 20,000 other courses.
    (b) In many areas, an entire 18-hole course was set up in a vacant lot.
    (c) The 1920s were a time of outlandish fads.
    (d) One after another, the miniature courses closed until they were nearly all gone.   2. _____

3. As used in paragraph 2, *ingenuity* means (a) cleverness (b) luck (c) wealth (d) time.   3. _____

4. The author of the passage probably put *profit* and *prophet* close together (a) to keep the readers attentive (b) for a lighthearted play on words (c) as a way of emphasizing the short-lived popularity of miniature golf (d) to indicate that fads come and go.   4. _____

5. The castles, windmills, and sphinxes were added to golf courses to make the courses (a) easier (b) less expensive (c) faster (d) more challenging.   5. _____

6. It can fairly be said that Garnet Carter was in the miniature-golf business (a) for the fun of it (b) by accident (c) through a friend (d) for a short time.   6. _____

7. All the following were mentioned as fads EXCEPT (a) dance marathons (b) miniature golf (c) hula hoops (d) flagpole sitting.   7. _____

8. Which of the following statements contains an example of figurative language?

    (a) There were tunnels to go through.
    (b) All over the country, miniature golf courses sprang up like mushrooms.
    (c) Garnet Carter sold his business in October 1930 at a considerable profit.
    (d) One after another, the miniature courses closed until they were nearly all gone.   8. _____

9. Each of the following statements contains an example of figurative language EXCEPT

   (*a*) The bubble burst almost as quickly as it developed.
   (*b*) The popularity of the fad quickly died away.
   (*c*) In many areas, an entire 18-hole course was set up in a vacant lot.
   (*d*) The courses sprang up overnight and became so popular that movie attendance fell nearly 25 percent.

   9. _____

10. The expression *sprang up like mushrooms* means that the golf courses (*a*) were suddenly numerous (*b*) used plastic mushrooms as part of the decoration (*c*) did especially well in warm, humid climates (*d*) became an important part of the environment.

    10. _____

15. Recognizing Propaganda

Senator Albertson is a stubborn, inflexible, thoughtless voter on any legislation dealing with the environment.

Senator Albertson is a consistent, high-minded supporter of positive legislation dealing with the environment.

On three occasions, Senator Albertson has introduced bills to clean up harbors and rivers throughout the country.

Can you see how different each statement is? The first is a highly unfavorable comment. The second is favorable. The third states the facts. The first two are slanted statements of opinion. The last is a factual statement.

Propaganda has been defined as "ideas, facts, or allegations spread deliberately to further one's cause or to damage an opposing cause." The first two statements above may qualify as propaganda. Propagandists are everywhere. They urge you to buy certain products, attend particular movies, vote for their candidates. They use a variety of devices, but they all have one purpose: to get you to act in a certain way.

Not all propaganda is evil. Propagandists often have a worthy goal. You yourself have undoubtedly been a propagandist at times. Though propaganda may urge you on to good actions, you should still be aware of the techniques used. Then you can choose your course of action on the basis of clear thinking. The following list gives examples of propaganda techniques.

Testimonial: Movie star Robert Newman urges you to vote for Senator Albertson.
    (Robert Newman may be an expert in acting techniques, but he is not necessarily an expert in politics.)

Bandwagon: Everybody is going to the Judy Carpenter concert. Don't be left out!
    (Don't jump on the bandwagon and do what "everybody else is doing." Think for yourself. The majority may be wrong. Be on guard against words like *everybody* and *nobody*, *always* and *never*, *all* and *none*. These words often try to sweep the easily influenced along.)

Name-Calling: (The first statement at the beginning of this section is an example of name-calling. Name-calling sheds more heat than light.)

Glittering Generalities: ("Virtue" words or phrases like *Americanism, public spirit, friend of the people*, and *economical* are often used to sway voters and consumers. The second statement at the beginning of this section uses glittering generalities.)

Plain Folks: Hiya, my neighbors and good friends. It's great to be back in the heart-land of America, where all you good people live.

(Here the propagandist is pretending to be just like the rest of us: down-to-earth, no pretense, a regular fellow.)

Snob Appeal: This exclusive handbag, as shown in the expensive shops of London and Paris, is for the discriminating woman.

(This device reverses the appeal of *plain folks*. Instead, this one tries to flatter the consumer by making her think she is special.)

Scientific Slant: Seven out of ten doctors interviewed preferred Nopane to ordinary aspirin.

(Appealing to science and scientists is a popular advertising device. In the example above, who knows how the interviewed doctors were chosen? Sometimes scientific names like *hexachlorophene* are introduced to make the claims sound more impressive.)

Stereotypes: My opponent was once a professional football player. We all know that football players are brutal, insensitive wild men.

(*Stereotype* is a term taken from printing. It is an oversimplified mental picture of an entire group. Off the field, a football player may be a thoughtful, sensitive, highly intelligent individual. Giving an individual a label in advance is prejudice. Not all nurses, for example, are kind and compassionate. Not all teenagers are flighty, mixed-up, and unpredictable. Not all poets are dreamers. Not all young brides are poor cooks. Not all gruff old men have hearts of gold. Television often perpetuates stereotypes of family members, police personnel, soldiers, criminals, small-town citizens, "street people," and other groups.)

Question: How Can You Recognize Propaganda?

In each of the following pairs, one statement is straightforward and factual. The other is propaganda. Write the letter of each example of propaganda.

1. A. Candidate Sandra Michael is a highly responsible legislator, ethical and perceptive, ideally equipped to handle the urban challenges we shall all face in the years ahead.

   B. On three occasions, Sandra Michael has voted to provide low-income housing in the abandoned sections of our city.   1. _____

2. A. The front office of the Bears has announced that there will be a rally of Bears fans at the stadium on Monday night.

   B. Everybody is rooting for the Bears to win the Super Bowl. Join your fellow fans and come to the rally at Bears Stadium on Monday night.   2. _____

3. A.   Well, you nice people, I'm going to let you in on a secret and show you why this kitchen knife is the best little ole product you can get.

   B.   Today I am introducing and demonstrating a new kitchen knife.   3. _____

4. A.   The Prowler is a new eight-cylinder luxury car with a great many extra features as outlined below.

   B.   The owner of a Prowler enters a new world of elegance undreamed of by the average car owner.   4. _____

5. A.   Penny Walker, winner of two Academy Awards, uses Glitter, the new shampoo.

   B.   Penny Walker, winner of two Academy Awards, uses Glitter, the new shampoo. The same awareness and discrimination that brought her movie fame has led her to try Glitter and say, "I'll never use another product."   5. _____

Answers

Let's examine the possible answers and identify the examples of propaganda.

1. A.   "Virtue" words or phrases like *highly responsible*, *ethical*, *perceptive*, and *ideally equipped* identify this as propaganda rather than a literal statement of fact.
2. B.   This is an appeal to get on the bandwagon and join all the other fans. *A* merely gives the information.
3. A.   *You nice people* and *little ole product* reveal a use of the plain-folks device. The folksy, friendly manner is common with certain high-pressure salespeople.
4. B.   This is an example of snob appeal, stimulating the desire to be unique, special.
5. B.   Penny Walker is not necessarily an expert on shampoos. Of course, winning two Academy Awards does suggest that she is a competent actress. The two talents do not necessarily go together.

Practice: Recognizing Propaganda

Read each of the following passages and answer the question at the end of each.

1. "Please let me take the car to the dance," pleaded Roberto. "Joey says I'm a good driver. Ellen likes to have me drive. I promise to be more careful than last time."

   In his effort to get permission to use the family car, Roberto (*a*) uses previous experience as a reason (*b*) quotes his friends as testimonials (*c*) appeals to his parents' easygoing nature (*d*) tells why he wants to go to the dance.   1. _____

2. The sign on the restaurant said, ''Welcome, all you good people. Come in where your friends are. Enjoy a good, tasty, nourishing meal without fancy sauces or frills—just good honest value at a price you can afford.''

The sign appeals to each of the following EXCEPT (a) economy (b) plain folks (c) bandwagon (d) snobbishness.

2. _____

3. The television ad declared, ''Allsport, the after-shave lotion for men, is not just a smooth, soothing, cooling aid for tired skin. It also has a masculine scent that women find attractive and other men secretly admire.''

To persuade consumers to buy the product, the advertisers use (a) an appeal to masculine hopes and dreams (b) recommendations by others (c) outright lies (d) the prestige of science.

3. _____

Answers

Let's examine the possible answers.

1. (b) By mentioning Joey and Ellen, Roberto is using the testimonial device, as though his two friends are experts on driving.
2. (d) It appeals to economy by saying *at a price you can afford*. Therefore, (a) is wrong. By using such phrases as *all you good people* and *your friends*, it is using the plain-folks device. Therefore, (b) is wrong. *Come in where your friends are* tells prospective customers to get on the bandwagon. Therefore, (c) is wrong. The sign nowhere appeals to snobbishness (d). Quite the opposite!
3. (a) Mention of women's and men's reactions to the product appeals to a man's wish to be attractive to women and popular with men.

On Your Own: Recognizing Propaganda

Read the following passage and answer the questions at the end.

Support Andy Lewis, your classmates' choice for President of the Student Council. All right-thinking students have been impressed by his integrity, his hard-working seriousness combined with a keen sense of humor that delights his friends. As you all know, his opponent is Martha Callahan. She is a sweet, pleasant girl, but she lacks the leadership ability so often demonstrated by Andy. The next year will be a crucial one for all the students of Central High. Many changes in the curriculum and student organization have been promised. They will sap the energy of everyone. It will be comforting to realize that we have as our premier student representative a person who can lead all of us, his dear friends, at a difficult time. The election is this coming Tuesday. Don't fail to vote—for the person who is so highly qualified: Andy Lewis.

1. Which of the following titles best summarizes the content of the passage?

   (a) An Election at Central High
   (b) Andy Lewis: An Outstanding Candidate
   (c) The Problems of President of the Student Council
   (d) The Friends of Andy Lewis   1. _____

2. Which of the following statements may be classified as propaganda? Which are more direct statements of fact? Write *P* for each example of propaganda and *F* for each fact.

   (a) All right-thinking students have been impressed by his integrity, his hard-working seriousness combined with a keen sense   2.
       of humor that delights his friends.   *a.* _____
   (b) As you all know, his opponent is Martha Callahan.   *b.* _____
   (c) Many changes in the curriculum and student organization
       have been promised.   *c.* _____
   (d) It will be comforting to realize that we have as our premier
       student representative a person who can lead all of us, his dear
       friends, at a difficult time.   *d.* _____
   (e) The election is this coming Tuesday.   *e.* _____
   (f) Don't fail to vote—for the person who is so highly qualified:
       Andy Lewis.   *f.* _____

3. As used in the fourth sentence of the passage, *she is a sweet, pleasant girl* is (a) actually insulting (b) a tribute to a nice girl (c) a secret slap at Andy Lewis (d) NOT an example of propaganda.   3. _____

4. Which of the following is an example of figurative language?

   (a) His opponent is Martha Callahan.
   (b) She lacks the leadership ability so often demonstrated by Andy.
   (c) They will sap the energy of everyone.
   (d) The election is this coming Tuesday.   4. _____

5. As used in the fifth sentence of the passage, *crucial* means (a) happy (b) amusing (c) interesting (d) important.   5. _____

Bonus: Reviewing Propaganda

Read the following passage and answer the questions at the end.

> For an up-to-date, reliable, accurate reference source, buy the *New National Dictionary*. All over the country, college professors are recommending this outstanding book to their students. In thirty-three colleges sampled, the *New National Dictionary* is by far the

most popular dictionary sold to serious students of language. For those with a discriminating taste and a sincere love for scholarship, this new edition will meet all needs.

This new edition contains more than 12,000 words not listed in the previous editions. New words from science, like *Jarvik heart*, make their first appearance, as do other new words like *computer hacker*, *anchorperson*, and *workaholic*. Definitions are crisply clear, models of sharp observation, brilliantly phrased. Sample sentences show how the words are used in the senses defined. The dictionary clearly distinguishes subtle differences between one synonym and another.

There are many other attractions in this superlative example of modern scholarship. An improved pronunciation guide takes some of the hesitation out of deciding how a word should be pronounced. Instead of hunting in special supplements, readers now find biographical and geographical names in the all-inclusive body of the text. Major literary characters also appear in the main listing, along with important foreign phrases. Because maps are best treated in a section of their own, a supplement provides detailed maps of every corner of the globe. This is truly a magnificent new book.

Follow a librarian's advice. Put this high-powered, intelligently organized brilliant new dictionary on your shelves. Don't let your children be outpaced by their friends who already own this new reference tool.

KNOW THESE WORDS

computer hacker: computer enthusiast
outpaced: outdone; left behind

1. Write the letter of the statement that best expresses the main idea.

   (*a*) Dictionaries are the most useful of all reference books.
   (*b*) The *New National Dictionary* is a dictionary worth buying.
   (*c*) A new dictionary should contain the new words that have entered the language.
   (*d*) The *New National Dictionary* has been especially designed for children, not adults.

   1. _____

2. Which of the following statements may be classified as propaganda? Which are more direct statements of fact? Write *P* for each example of propaganda and *F* for each fact.

   (*a*) All over the country, college professors are recommending this outstanding book to their students.

   (*b*) In thirty-three colleges sampled, the *New National Dictionary* is by far the most popular dictionary sold to serious students of language.

   (*c*) For those with a discriminating taste and a sincere love for scholarship, this new edition will meet all needs.

   (*d*) This new edition contains more than 12,000 words not listed in the previous edition.

   (*e*) New words from science, like *Jarvik heart*, make their first appearance.

   (*f*) Definitions are crisply clear, models of sharp observation, brilliantly phrased.

   (*g*) Sample sentences show how the words are used in the senses defined.

   (*h*) There are many other attractions in this superlative example of modern scholarship.

   (*i*) Follow a librarian's advice.

   (*j*) Put this high-powered, intelligently organized brilliant new dictionary on your shelves.

   2.
   a. _____
   b. _____
   c. _____
   d. _____
   e. _____
   f. _____
   g. _____
   h. _____
   i. _____
   j. _____

3. An example of figurative language is the expression (*a*) *how a word should be pronounced* (*b*) *this new edition* (*c*) *every corner of the globe* (*d*) *accurate reference source.*

   3. _____

4. The figurative expression *anchorperson* suggests (*a*) the person who is responsible for getting advertisers to support a television program (*b*) an expert in boating and marine affairs (*c*) the main broadcaster in a news program (*d*) an officer in the United States Navy.

   4. _____

5. *This is truly a magnificent new book* is an example of (*a*) a factual statement (*b*) an opinion (*c*) an obvious lie (*d*) a figurative expression.

   5. _____

6. All the following are listed as new words in the dictionary EXCEPT (*a*) *Jarvik heart* (*b*) *anchorperson* (*c*) *computer hacker* (*d*) *chocoholic.*

   6. _____

7. According to the passage, the dictionary publishers (*a*) sampled thirty-three colleges (*b*) designed entirely new maps (*c*) sold more books to libraries than to schools (*d*) used high-quality paper for the new dictionary.

   7. _____

8. The number of new words included is (*a*) about a thousand
   (*b*) more than 12,000 (*c*) 33,000 (*d*) not mentioned.   8. _____

9. The word *workaholic* has been formed on *alcoholic* and probably
   means a person who (*a*) hates any kind of strenuous effort
   (*b*) finds it difficult to keep a job (*c*) neglects other activities for
   work (*d*) works best at certain times of day.   9. _____

10. From the descriptions given, the new dictionary (*a*) seems like
    an improvement over the previous edition (*b*) should be
    especially useful for those interested in the language of television
    (*c*) has more biographical and geographical names than other
    dictionaries (*d*) is used more often by college professors than
    college students.   10. _____

11. As used in paragraph 1, *discriminating* means (*a*) especially keen
    (*b*) fairly undeveloped (*c*) hasty but reliable (*d*) ordinary.   11. _____

12. As used in paragraph 3, *superlative* means (*a*) new (*b*) planned
    (*c*) interesting (*d*) excellent.   12. _____

16. Studying the Author's Role

All the members of the unruly mob pushed and shoved their way through the jammed shopping streets, their blank faces reflecting the emptiness of their lives.

All the members of the good-natured crowd moved cheerfully along the popular shopping streets, their happy faces reflecting the joys of the holiday season.

Writing is done by people, not machines. People have points of view. They have human strengths and failings and sometimes human prejudices. They have personal likes and dislikes and individual ways of seeing things. The writers of the two sentences above are describing the same scene. One writer sees only the negative side of the picture. He or she uses negative words like *unruly*, *pushed*, *shoved*, *blank*, and *emptiness*. The other writer sees the positive side of the picture. He or she uses positive words like *good-natured*, *cheerfully*, *happy*, and *joys*. Two different writers have given two entirely different interpretations of the same event. When you read something, remember that there is a human being behind the printed page.

The Author's Tone

"Watch out!"

If you shout a warning to a friend who doesn't see an oncoming car, the tone of your voice will suggest sharp concern. In writing, *tone* is suggested by the words used. In the first sentence at the beginning of this section, the negative words give the sentence a tone of angry disapproval. In the second sentence, the positive words give the sentence a tone of heartwarming approval.

To achieve an emotional tone, authors use happy words, sad words, angry words. To achieve a tone of impartiality, fairness, and evenness, authors use factual words, objective words, literal words. Unskilled authors are usually not aware of the tone they are giving their writing. Skilled authors, however, are usually aware of the tone in their writing and try to control it.

Question 1: How Can You Determine an Author's Tone?

Read the following sentence and answer the question at the end.

My heart leaps up when I behold
    A rainbow in the sky.   (William Wordsworth)

The tone of this sentence can best be described as (*a*) loud and demanding (*b*) quietly joyous (*c*) bitterly sarcastic (*d*) strangely mistrustful.

Your answer: _____

Answer

The poet's reaction to the rainbow is one of pleasure. He suggests that pleasure through a beautiful figure of speech (page 108). The tone of his description is quiet, thoughtful, joyous (*b*).

Practice 1: Studying an Author's Tone

Read the following sentence and answer the questions at the end.

> Clumsy Denny came last to the picnic, forgot the lemonade, spilled ketchup on my T-shirt, poked me in the eye during volleyball, and thoroughly enriched what had promised to be a good day.

1. A word that seems to conflict with the author's tone is (*a*) *clumsy* (*b*) *spilled* (*c*) *poked* (*d*) *enriched*.   1. _____

2. The author probably introduced that word for (*a*) humor (*b*) excitement (*c*) the sake of Denny (*d*) approval.   2. _____

Answers

1. (*d*) Since Denny has done everything wrong to the author, the word that seems out of place is *enriched*.

2. (*a*) An author will sometimes do the opposite of the expected to bring a smile to the reader's face. The use of *enriched* instead of the more likely *spoiled* is meant to jolt the reader and make a humorous point. (The author's purpose is dealt with later in this section.)

The Author's Attitude

Closely related to tone is the author's ***attitude*** toward what he or she is writing. If the author is angry about the subject, the tone will be sharp, bitter. On the other hand, if he or she is happy, the words will reveal that feeling. William Wordsworth's attitude toward the rainbow is one of admiration and joyful appreciation.

Practice 2: Studying an Author's Attitude

Read the following sentence and answer the question at the end.

> The perfect weather, warm surf, excellent accommodations, and outstanding food made our weekend at Fripp Island a vacation to remember.

The author's attitude can best be described as one of (*a*) mild disapproval (*b*) sophisticated indifference (*c*) qualified anger (*d*) enthusiastic approval.

Your answer: _____

Answer

Words like *perfect, warm, excellent, outstanding,* and *a vacation to remember* clearly signal that the author's attitude is one of enthusiastic approval (*d*).

The Author's Purpose

> The new attractions at Epcot make this brother of Walt Disney World a satisfying place to visit again and again, especially during less crowded months like May and November.

When authors write, they have a **purpose**: to entertain, amuse, confirm, inform, describe, contradict, persuade, protest, poke fun at, or explain. In the sentence above, the author is trying to persuade readers to visit Epcot. His or her attitude toward Epcot is favorable. The tone of the sentence is quietly factual.

Practice 3: Studying an Author's Purpose

Read the following ad and answer the questions at the end.

> Hurry! For three more days, you may still buy a wide selection of videocassette recorders at simply unbelievable prices. Don't miss the opportunity of a lifetime. We cannot keep the offer open much longer.

1. The author's purpose in writing this ad is to (*a*) explain (*b*) persuade (*c*) describe (*d*) entertain.   1. _____

2. The tone of this ad can best be described as (*a*) instructional (*b*) scholarly (*c*) urgent (*d*) thoughtful.   2. _____

3. The author's attitude is one of (*a*) uncritical approval (*b*) partial acceptance (*c*) delighted amazement (*d*) mild distaste.   3. _____

Answers

1. (*b*) The author wants to sell videocassette recorders and is trying to persuade his or her readers to act.
2. (*c*) Use of words like *hurry, opportunity of a lifetime,* and *open much longer* suggests an urgent tone.
3. (*a*) The author's breathless plea to buy the product suggests an attitude of uncritical approval.

The Author's Assumptions

> Since women should avoid any job requiring physical strength, Linda's parents urged her to become a secretary.

An *assumption* is something taken for granted. It may or may not be true. In the sentence above, the author is assuming that women cannot handle jobs requiring physical strength. The assumption is false and out-of-date. Yet the author apparently accepts the erroneous idea as true. Authors make all kinds of assumptions, either consciously or unconsciously. Identifying these assumptions is a step to better reading.

Here are some examples of assumptions that make their way into writing from time to time.

An only child lives a life of loneliness and unhappiness.

If a movie critic likes a movie, it will be a success.

All boys naturally like to watch football on TV.

Girls generally like school more than boys do.

All politicians are unreliable and always forget their promises after they are elected.

Practice 4: Studying an Author's Assumptions

Read the following and answer the question at the end.

> Floriana, that new perfume sponsored by the movie star Marsha Major, goes on sale tomorrow. It is an unusual new product, especially designed by Miss Major herself. It combines several floral scents in a fascinating way. It is, as you would expect, quite expensive. I'm sure it is excellent.

The author assumes that (*a*) perfumes have floral scents (*b*) the advertising for Floriana is better than average (*c*) Floriana must be good since it is expensive (*d*) movie stars should not sponsor commercial products.

Your answer: _____

Answer

The author is not talking about other perfumes; therefore (*a*) is wrong. There is no comparison of the advertising for various products; therefore (*b*) is wrong. There is no suggestion that movie stars should avoid sponsoring commercial products; therefore (*d*) is wrong. There is a strong implication that the author considers something to be good if it is expensive (*c*). Though expense is often linked with quality, the linkage does not always hold true. This is a weak assumption.

Practice 5: Studying an Author's Role

Read the following passage and answer the questions at the end.

A gardener was bothered by the dandelions in his lawn. He wrote to the county agricultural agent and got some suggestions for removing them. The suggestions didn't work. He wrote again. No luck. Then he wrote a third time. This time the harried county agent wrote back wearily, ''Learn to love them.'' This is good advice for everyone.

The writer Samuel Pickering, Jr., once wrote, ''The real American Beauty is not the rose but the dandelion.'' Why did he come out so strongly for the lowly dandelion? There are many good and sound reasons.

The dandelion came from somewhere in Europe, but nobody knows where or when. Like the immigrants, the ''huddled masses,'' it found a new and better life in the New World. It rolled up its sleeves and went to work. It made the wastelands bloom. Where there was formerly a barren patch of exhausted soil, there came a field of dandelions, tossing their golden heads in every breeze. Where other flowers feared to tread, the dandelion grew well. When other flowers fell to the onslaught of storms and rough weather, the dandelion lay still, waiting for the sun. Even a hailstorm couldn't break the spirit of the dandelion. Appropriately, the dandelion's name is pure poetry. It comes from two French words meaning *lion's tooth*.

The dandelion is a friendly plant. It can furnish nourishing greens when it is young. Children can weave a garland of flowers with the showy heads and stems of mature plants. It is a respectable member of the community, opening and blooming at sunrise, then going to bed when the sun goes down. It has 100–200 tiny florets in every bloom. Then as the flower matures, the florets turn to silver, forming a beautiful globe. A passing breeze or a child's breath sends off the seeds, with their little parachutes. Someone has observed that the change from flowers to seeds can be fancifully described in this way: "The suns of the dandelions turned into moons."

Why not make the dandelion our national flower? It is not limited to any state or region. It is everywhere—in the deserts of Arizona, the orange groves of Florida, the mountains of Colorado. It is a bright sign of hope—on any day in the year. If the winter snows beat against your windowpane, take heart. Somewhere the dandelion is blooming.

KNOW THESE WORDS

barren: lifeless; empty

tread: walk; set foot

garland: wreath of flowers

florets: small flowers, part of a larger flower

1. Which of the following titles best summarizes the content of the passage?

   (*a*) The Dandelion: An Insufficiently Appreciated Flower
   (*b*) How to Raise Dandelions
   (*c*) Plants, Weeds, and Flowers
   (*d*) The Pleasures of Growing Dandelions   1. _____

2. The author's purpose in writing this passage was to (*a*) suggest ways of growing dandelions (*b*) change people's views about dandelions (*c*) emphasize the practical value of dandelions (*d*) show how dandelions resemble immigrants.   2. _____

3. The tone of this passage is (*a*) serious but well-intentioned (*b*) bland and colorless (*c*) lighthearted and entertaining (*d*) hilariously funny.   3. _____

4. The author's attitude toward dandelions may best be described as (*a*) indifferent (*b*) antagonistic (*c*) rather silly (*d*) favorable.   4. _____

5. The author assumes that (*a*) the reader has an interest in flowers (*b*) the reader is a gardener (*c*) the dandelion is a bit too common (*d*) roses are not as colorful as dandelions.   5. _____

6. In the figurative expression "The suns of the dandelions turned into moons," the word *suns* refers to the (*a*) seeds (*b*) tiny individual florets (*c*) full-blooming flower heads (*d*) flowers at night.   6. _____

7. Which of the following statements contain figurative language? Write *F* for each example of figurative language.

7.

   (*a*) He wrote to the county agricultural agent.

   a. _____

   (*b*) This is good advice for everyone.

   b. _____

   (*c*) It rolled up its sleeves and went to work.

   c. _____

   (*d*) There came a field of dandelions, tossing their golden heads in every breeze.

   d. _____

   (*e*) Where other flowers feared to tread, the dandelion grew well.

   e. _____

   (*f*) Even a hailstorm couldn't break the spirit of the dandelion.

   f. _____

   (*g*) It has 100–200 tiny florets in every bloom.

   g. _____

   (*h*) As the flower matures, the florets turn to silver.

   h. _____

   (*i*) A passing breeze or a child's breath sends off the seeds, with their little parachutes.

   i. _____

   (*j*) Somewhere the dandelion is blooming.

   j. _____

8. Which of the following is an opinion?

   (*a*) A gardener was bothered by the dandelions in his lawn.

   (*b*) He wrote again.

   (*c*) ''The real American Beauty is not the rose but the dandelion.''

   (*d*) It is not limited to any state or region.

   8. _____

9. One reason that the dandelion may not be fully appreciated is that it (*a*) is not particularly pretty (*b*) grows everywhere without care (*c*) is too difficult to establish in a traditional garden (*d*) is sometimes fragile.

   9. _____

10. If the gardener wrote to the county agent about dandelions a fourth time, the agent would probably (*a*) send a copy of the second letter he or she had written (*b*) visit the gardener (*c*) send some other flower seeds (*d*) fail to answer.

   10. _____

11. As used in paragraph 1, *harried* means (*a*) overworked and upset (*b*) friendly and helpful (*c*) energetic and lively (*d*) intelligent and reliable.

   11. _____

12. As used in paragraph 3, *onslaught* means (*a*) gentle arrival (*b*) empty threat (*c*) heavy snows (*d*) vigorous attack.

   12. _____

Answers

First read the entire passage. As you will see, it is all about dandelions, written by a highly sympathetic author. Understanding the entire passage makes the individual questions easier.

1. (*a*) This captures the point of the passage. There is nothing about raising dandelions (*b*) or (*d*). Choice (*c*) is too general and indefinite.

2. (b) The author nowhere talks about cultivating or growing dandelions (a). The passage mentions qualities of dandelions other than the *practical* (c). The resemblance of dandelions to immigrants is a minor detail (d). The author is trying to make people look at dandelions in a new and positive way (b).

3. (c) The opening paragraph, with its lighthearted anecdote, sets the tone. The passage is entertaining without being hilariously funny, serious, or colorless.

4. (d) The author loves dandelions as is shown by the admiring descriptions of the dandelion's appearance and durability.

5. (a) The author's vivid picture of dandelions and their place in nature would appeal especially to those with an interest in flowers. One doesn't have to be a gardener (b) to have an interest in flowers.

6. (c) The passage says that the change is from flowers to seeds. The seeds would resemble moons, not suns. Therefore (a) is wrong. The individual florets would not look like suns (b). Since the flowers close at night (d) is wrong.

7.   The figurative expressions are these:
   (c) The dandelion is personified, compared with a person who rolls up his or her sleeves.
   (d) The heads are compared with the metal gold.
   (e) The dandelion is again personified, compared with a person walking.
   (f) The dandelion doesn't actually have a spirit.
   (h) The florets do not actually turn to silver.
   (i) The floating seeds are compared with parachutes.

8. (c) Since beauty is in the eye of the beholder, the statement is an opinion.

9. (b) If something is commonplace, it is often unappreciated.

10. (d) Since the agent gave a harried "final answer" by saying, "Learn to love them," the agent would probably fail to answer if a fourth query arrived.

11. (a) Since the agent has already replied twice before to the same question and since he or she writes wearily, we can assume that the agent is *overworked and upset*.

12. (d) *Gentle arrival* (a) doesn't suit storms and rough weather. A dangerous storm with rough weather is no empty threat (b). The storms are not necessarily snowstorms (c). We can be sure the onslaught is a dangerous, vigorous attack (d).

On Your Own: Studying an Author's Role

Read the following passage and answer the questions at the end.

"Mosquito!"

The cry inside a house sends everyone on a chase, trying first to find and then to swat this unpopular pest. A buzzing in the ears in a darkened bedroom is a most unwelcome sound. Snapping on the lights often fails to reveal the wily intruder.

A mosquito may weigh 35 millionths of an ounce, but its power for damage is awesome. Mosquitoes cause 300 million cases of malaria yearly around the world, killing a million African children alone. Yellow fever and encephalitis are other diseases associated with mosquitoes.

Nearly everyone has been attacked by a mosquito. People talk about mosquito *bites* or mosquito *stings*, but neither word is quite accurate. The mosquito actually saws her way through the skin into the flesh, then pumps up the blood into her stomach. She can double her body weight in a little more than two minutes. The "bite" itself is probably painless, but the victim experiences pain in about three minutes. By that time, the mosquito has gone. The pronoun *she* indicates that the blood-suckers are female. Male mosquitoes live on nectar and plant juices. They seem to be gentle, law-abiding citizens.

The peculiar zigzag flight of the mosquito is not aimless. She is looking for a warm-blooded meal ticket. Moist air plumes arise from a warm-blooded animal. The mosquito follows this plume, going back and forth to keep on the right track. Movement, lactic acid, and other chemical cues guide the mosquito to her deadly meeting. The best natural defense against attack is to lie still: calm, cool, and dry. But when we hear a mosquito, we rush about, sweating, raising our body temperatures and blood pressures, making ourselves more discoverable by the mosquito. Insect repellents don't actually repel mosquitoes. They block the sensory apparatus that helps mosquitoes find us.

Most people think that tropical diseases are carried only by mosquitoes in the tropics. When Napoleon sent an army to the area we now call the Louisiana Purchase, it was almost wiped out by mosquito-borne yellow fever. In 1803, we were able to buy the Louisiana Territory from France largely because of this episode. There have been epidemics of yellow fever in places like New Orleans, Philadelphia, and New York City. Malaria was a killer during the American Civil War, persisting as late as World War II. In most of the United States, we haven't succeeded in eradicating the mosquitoes that carry these plagues. We have succeeded in getting rid of the diseases for the most part, but the mosquitoes that could do the damage are still with us. The disease encephalitis, however, is still a serious problem in parts of North America.

The name *mosquito* comes from Latin through Spanish. It literally means little fly. There is another word derived from the Latin word *musca*, or fly. That word is *musket*. Some people think the pain a mosquito can cause is a lesser version of the pain caused by a musket shot. If there were a vote for the most unwanted of all the world's creatures, the mosquito would have a spot near the top of the list.

KNOW THESE WORDS

> **awesome:** causing fear
> **sensory:** of the senses
> **apparatus:** equipment

1. Write the letter of the statement that best expresses the main idea.

   (*a*) Only the female mosquitoes attack warm-blooded animals.
   (*b*) Mosquitoes do most damage in Africa.
   (*c*) The mosquito is a worldwide pest, fragile but durable.
   (*d*) To protect yourself from mosquitoes, keep calm.   1. _____

2. The author's purpose in writing this passage is to (*a*) warn Americans against yellow fever and malaria (*b*) provide general information about the mosquito (*c*) explain the difference between bites and stings (*d*) recommend more research into the disease-carrying mosquito.   2. _____

3. The tone of this passage is (*a*) urgently persuasive (*b*) bitterly sarcastic (*c*) quietly indifferent (*d*) direct and straightforward.   3. _____

4. The author's attitude toward mosquitoes may best be described as (*a*) disapproving (*b*) admiring (*c*) despairing (*d*) confused.   4. _____

5. The author assumes that (*a*) most people have experienced mosquito bites (*b*) mosquitoes are less dangerous than large game animals (*c*) yellow fever is more serious than malaria (*d*) once seen, mosquitoes are easily killed.   5. _____

6. Which of the following is an example of figurative language?

   (*a*) A mosquito may weigh 35 millionths of an ounce.
   (*b*) She can double her body weight in a little more than two minutes.
   (*c*) Most people think that tropical diseases are caused only by mosquitoes in the tropics.
   (*d*) Some people think the pain a mosquito can cause is a lesser version of the pain caused by a musket shot.   6. _____

7. Which of the following is an opinion?

   (*a*) Mosquitoes cause 300 million cases of malaria yearly around the world.
   (*b*) The pronoun *she* indicates that the bloodsuckers are female.
   (*c*) They seem to be gentle, law-abiding citizens.
   (*d*) They block the sensory apparatus that helps mosquitoes find us.   7. _____

8. The best word to describe the attack of the mosquito is (a) *bites* (b) *saws* (c) *stings* (d) *squeezes*.   8. _____

9. The disease mentioned as still being a serious problem in North America is (a) malaria (b) yellow fever (c) encephalitis (d) influenza.   9. _____

10. There have been epidemics of yellow fever in each of the following cities EXCEPT (a) Boston (b) New York (c) Philadelphia (d) New Orleans.   10. _____

11. As used in paragraph 2, *wily* means (a) friendly (b) unexpected (c) crafty (d) harmless.   11. _____

12. As used in paragraph 6, *eradicating* means (a) increasing (b) studying (c) finding (d) eliminating.   12. _____

Bonus: Reviewing an Author's Role

Read the following passage and answer the questions at the end.

> Little Boy Blue,
> Come blow your horn,
> The sheep's in the meadow,
> The cow's in the corn.
>
> You surely have heard this favorite nursery rhyme, and you have probably visualized what a meadow looks like. You have seen many fields alive with wildflowers, but the chances are that you have not seen a *natural* meadow. What you have probably seen is an old field that was once cultivated and has since been neglected. A natural meadow is a permanent grassland. In most parts of the country, what you might call a *meadow* will become a woodland in twenty years or less if left untended.
>
> Natural meadows occur only in areas where shrubs and trees cannot thrive. Otherwise, these woody plants take over and crowd out the wildflowers. Natural grasslands thus occur in areas where environmental factors prevent the growth of woody plants. *Alpine* meadows occur on mountains where the climate is unfavorable for trees or shrubs. *Coastal* meadows border the sea because the salt spray inhibits the growth of woody plants. *Desert* meadows depend upon low precipitation to keep away trees. Fires and recurring droughts prevent the growth of woody plants on the *prairies*.

Farmers, loggers, and other workers on the land have created temporary meadows. If a farmer's field is left idle for a few years, it becomes a meadow, alive with wildflowers. Cattle grazing on a field may provide ideal conditions for a meadow. Farmers may help by eliminating any trees that seem to gain a foothold. The nation's roads have created thousands of small meadows. The areas beside the roads may be cut once or twice a year, killing woody plants before they get a chance to survive. Some areas on the Blue Ridge Parkway of North Carolina have been designated wildflower areas and qualify as meadows. Young trees and shrubs are eliminated from these fields. These small sections are beautiful through the summer.

Variations of the meadow may be found in odd and unexpected places. The embankments along railroad tracks harbor many lovely wildflowers. Some hardy plants survive even in the roadbed itself, between the railroad ties. If a lawn is left untended for a while, wildflowers will begin to appear amidst the grasses. Even city wastelands will grow wildflowers from seeds spread by the wind or dropped by birds.

Every area has what is called *climax vegetation*, the plants that eventually take over if the area is undisturbed. In the Northeast, for example, the climax vegetation might be a beech-maple forest or a hemlock-pine forest. The meadow is a climax in only parts of the country. But people have altered the natural processes and have given us meadows everywhere—even if some of these are doomed to be taken over eventually by oaks, poplars, or hickories.

KNOW THESE WORDS

droughts: long dry spells

embankments: raised earthen structures supporting railroad tracks

untended: uncared for

1. Which of the following titles best summarizes the content of the passage?

   (a) The Prairie: A Magnificent Natural Meadow
   (b) All About Meadows—Natural and Temporary
   (c) The Part Played by Farmers and Loggers
   (d) Beauty Along the Railroad Tracks

   1. _____

2. The author's purpose in writing this passage is to (a) explain what a true meadow is (b) congratulate farmers and loggers for creating meadows (c) suggest that gardeners try creating meadows instead of lawns (d) emphasize the part played by climate in creating a meadow.

2. _____

3. The author inserts the Little Boy Blue verse at the beginning to (a) add some humor (b) provide a moment of relaxation (c) show that Mother Goose rhymes can deal with nature (d) suggest that *meadow* is a word we know from childhood.

3. _____

4. The tone of this passage is (a) stiff (b) hurried (c) relaxed (d) angry.

4. _____

5. The author's attitude toward meadows may best be described as (a) uncertain (b) approving (c) disapproving (d) indifferent.

5. _____

6. The author assumes that (a) readers have seen fields of wildflowers (b) farmers create meadows for the beauty of the wildflowers (c) children especially enjoy wildflowers (d) native wildflowers are better than flowers in a garden.

6. _____

7. The figurative expression *to gain a foothold* means (a) trip careless hikers (b) be trampled underfoot (c) grow a foot or two apart (d) begin to grow successfully.

7. _____

8. Which of the following is an opinion?

    (a) A natural meadow is a permanent grassland.
    (b) Otherwise these woody plants take over and crowd out the wildflowers.
    (c) These small sections are beautiful throughout the summer.
    (d) Some hardy plants survive even in the roadbed itself, between the railroad ties.

8. _____

9. If a house is deserted in the Northeast and the lawn is completely uncared for, it will eventually be taken over by (a) tall grasses (b) small shrubs (c) trees (d) none of these.

9. _____

10. All the following are mentioned as natural meadows EXCEPT (a) alpine (b) coastal (c) high plains (d) desert.

10. _____

11. As used in paragraph 3, *inhibits* means (a) discourages (b) supports (c) allows (d) spreads.

11. _____

12. As used in paragraph 3, *recurring* means (a) seriously damaging (b) happening again (c) completely unexpected (d) generally mild.

12. _____

17. Predicting Outcomes

"What happens next?"

Often, after you have finished a story, you wonder about the outcome. After finishing *Gone with the Wind*, for example, you may wonder whether Scarlett O'Hara ever did win back Rhett Butler. A promised sequel may provide the answer. The popularity of movie sequels like *Back to the Future II* and *III* suggests that readers and moviegoers want to know what happened next.

Predicting outcomes in reading passages is an important skill. When you predict the outcome of a reading passage, a story, or a movie, you are drawing a special kind of inference (page 55). You are noticing trends and guessing their direction. This technique is called *extrapolation* and is often used in statistics to suggest future developments. The United States census, for example, uses extrapolations to help predict the future. Proceeding from the known to the unknown is a commonplace activity of columnists, news commentators, and social planners. Most laws, budgets, and other financial decisions are based on conjectures about the future, or the outcome of current trends.

Here's an example of predicting outcomes in literature. "The Secret Life of Walter Mitty," by James Thurber, is a short story about a dreamer. Walter Mitty daydreams constantly, even in the midst of other activities. During the story, he imagines himself a Navy airplane commander, a famous surgeon, a sharpshooter, and a pilot of war. The slightest external stimulus can send him off into his own private world. The story ends with Walter Mitty imagining himself facing a firing squad. "Then, with that faint, fleeting smile playing about his lips, he faced the firing squad; erect and motionless, proud and disdainful, Walter Mitty the Undefeated, inscrutable to the last."

"What happens next?" We have little doubt that Walter Mitty the Undefeated will return briefly to the real world and then escape again to one of the many worlds of his imagination. The clues are all in the text.

Question: How Can You Predict Outcomes?

Read the selection and choose the answer that suggests the most likely outcome.

1. At noon, the climber looked up at the summit of Mt. Jefferson barely a thousand feet above. The day was clear. The weather was fine. The climber put his pack on and smiled to himself.

What probably happened next?
(*a*) The climber decided to set up camp and head for the summit the next day.
(*b*) The weather suddenly turned bad, and the climber reluctantly started back down. (*c*) The climber made the summit in good time. (*d*) Another climber came along, and the two walked onward.

Your answer 1: _____

2. The car was rolling along on Interstate 26. Beth enjoyed the excellence of the road and the beauty of the mountain scenery. Suddenly the engine made a strange sound, then chugged, and died away altogether. Beth rolled to a stop on a wide shoulder.

What probably happened next?
(*a*) Unexpectedly, the car started up again. (*b*) Beth opened the hood, took out a wrench, and removed the air filter. (*c*) A flame under the hood caused Beth to leave the car. (*d*) Beth checked the gas gauge.

Your answer 2: _____

Answers

1. (*c*) Since the distance was short and all conditions excellent, the climber probably made the summit. There is no reason to suggest that another climber came along. Predicting outcomes is based on probabilities. Life is, of course, unpredictable and unexpected things do happen, but probability is still the best guide.
2. (*d*) The first and most likely possibility was an empty gas tank. After that had been checked, Beth might explore other reasons that her car stalled. Though the car might have started up again or caught fire, these are less probable outcomes.

On Your Own 1: Predicting Outcomes

Read the selection and choose the answer that suggests the most likely outcome.

1. Mark Hanna, an American politician, overheard one of his office boys say, ''I wish I had Hanna's money and Hanna was in the poorhouse.'' Hanna called the boy to his office and said, ''If you had your wish and my money and I was in the poorhouse, what would you do?'' Quickly the boy replied, ''The first thing I'd do would be to get you out of that poorhouse.''

What probably happened next?
(*a*) Mark Hanna chuckled and gave the boy a raise. (*b*) The boy added, ''But first I'd get a new suit.'' (*c*) Mark Hanna in cold fury told the boy never to appear in his office again. (*d*) Mark Hanna adopted the boy as his own son.

1. _____

2. Chauncey Depew and Mark Twain were both to speak at a banquet. Twain was a marvelous speaker and kept the audience entertained for 20 minutes. Depew got more and more nervous. Twain was a difficult act to follow. When Depew finally got up, he said, ''Before the banquet, Mark and I agreed to trade speeches. He has just delivered mine and I'm grateful for the reception you have accorded it. I regret that I have lost his speech and cannot remember a thing he had to say.''

What probably happened next?
(*a*) Mark Twain called Depew a lying scoundrel. (*b*) Depew then pulled out a long speech and bored the audience for 20 minutes. (*c*) The audience loudly booed. (*d*) Depew sat down with much applause.

2. _____

3. The American composer Aaron Copland was browsing in a book-store when he noticed a woman buying his book *What to Listen for in Music*. She also picked up a Shakespearean play and paid for both. As she was leaving, he asked warmly, ''Would you like me to autograph your book?'' Taken aback for a moment, the woman asked, ''Which one?''

What probably happened next?
(*a*) Copland called the woman a fool. (*b*) The woman said, ''Autograph both.'' (*c*) Copland himself was momentarily speech-less. (*d*) The storekeeper sold Copland a Shakespearean play.   3. _____

On Your Own 2: Predicting Outcomes in a Reading Passage

Read the following passage and answer the questions at the end.

The increasingly popular cat is the source of many mysteries and legends. Anyone who has observed a cat's inscrutable stare wonders what lies beyond those unblinking eyes. It is not surprising that throughout history, cats have often held a place of honor. In ancient Egypt, the cat was revered. Cat mummies have been discovered.

The special abilities of cats are commonplace. Incredible stories about a cat's ability to find its way home from hundreds of miles away hint at the cat's special abilities. That homing instinct is only part of the story. Cats are survivors, able to endure cruel abandon-ment much more successfully than dogs. Cats are quick, alert, and resourceful. They tolerate their human owners and sometimes even show some affection, but they are their own masters. Perhaps the most uncanny ability of all, though, is a cat's ability to land right-side up after a fall.

Why does a cat land upright? It has a built-in gyroscope located in the inner ear. If a cat starts to fall while upside down, it quickly determines its position, twists in midair, and rights itself, all within two or three feet.

When it does fall, why is a cat less likely to be hurt than a human being? First of all, it lands on four feet, thus distributing the impact more effectively than if it landed on two. There is another related ability. The cat lands with limbs flexed, further distributing the impact through muscles and joints. It is a protective spring, preventing the jarring impact of a rigid body. Parachutists practice a similar skill. They try to land on their toes with knees and hips flexed. Then they roll over, keeping the impact away from their rigid, breakable bones.

There is another surprising side to this story. Though cats have an excellent chance of surviving a fall from any height, they do better from a nine-story building than from a four-story building. How can this be so? It runs counter to common sense.

During the first part of a fall, the cat has its four limbs straight down to spread the impact over a large surface. But there is a still larger surface: the cat's body. Instinctively, the cat makes the most of the advantage. After a certain time of falling, the speed levels out and becomes steady. The cat's inner devices recognize this change. The cat spreads its legs like a good skydiver and increases the area of resistance to the air, reducing the speed. It is like a flying squirrel. There is another advantage: the cat lands with its full body and larger surface to absorb the impact. Though cats will suffer a fracture from four stories, they are less likely to break a limb from nine stories or above.

In a study made of 13 cats that had the misfortune to fall nine or more stories, only one suffered a fracture. Cats falling from lower heights survived with an occasional broken limb.

Why are cats so much better able than dogs to survive falls? One scientist suggests that through their long history, cats were used to climbing trees. Dogs weren't. Gradually cats ''learned'' to fall better than dogs because the unsuccessful cats didn't survive to pass on their genes.

Cats are worthy of admiration.

KNOW THESE WORDS

inscrutable: not easily understood, mysterious
revered: loved and respected
tolerate: put up with
uncanny: strange
gyroscope: a device for keeping moving things level
flexed: bent

1. The main idea of the passage is that (*a*) people have never learned how to fall (*b*) cats have many unusual abilities, including the ability to fall successfully (*c*) cats and dogs are both excellent pets, but cats have certain advantages (*d*) when a person falls, he or she should stretch out arms and legs for maximum surface.   1. _____

2. If left behind after a stop for gasoline a hundred miles away from its home, the cat (*a*) would never find its way back to its home (*b*) would return home within a week (*c*) would probably starve to death rather quickly (*d*) might find its way back home.   2. _____

3. If a cat fell from a ten-story building, it (*a*) would probably fracture all four limbs (*b*) could not survive (*c*) would keep its limbs straight down to distribute the impact (*d*) would probably survive unharmed.   3. _____

4. If a cat lost its footing on a slippery rock and fell ten feet to the ground, it would (*a*) prefer water to grass (*b*) land with only the rear feet down (*c*) land on all four feet (*d*) probably suffer a fracture.   4. _____

5. If a cat had trouble with its inner ear, it (*a*) could not right itself (*b*) would have difficulty hearing high sounds (*c*) would lose all appetite (*d*) would not come when called.   5. _____

6. The cat would land with all four limbs stretched out after a fall of (*a*) six feet (*b*) twenty feet (*c*) six stories (*d*) eleven stories.   6. _____

7. An example of figurative language is (*a*) *flexible spring* (*b*) *rigid body* (*c*) *breakable bones* (*d*) *lower heights*.   7. _____

8. A falling cat was NOT compared with a (*a*) helicopter (*b*) flying squirrel (*c*) skydiver (*d*) parachutist.   8. _____

9. The sentence beginning "They tolerate their human owners" suggests that cats tend to be (*a*) warm and outgoing (*b*) cruel and untamable (*c*) cool and proud (*d*) stupid and noisy.   9. _____

10. The word *learned* is in quotation marks because (*a*) a scientist used the word (*b*) the cats haven't learned as human beings learn (*c*) their skill is taught by their mothers (*d*) learning always requires books.   10. _____

Bonus: Reviewing Reading Skills

Read the following passage and answer the questions at the end.

All living things exist in a subtle balance with one another. Here's an example. If too few deer are born, the number of predators drops off. If deer are plentiful, the predators increase to keep things in balance. Too many deer destroy the food source and bring starvation unless the balance can be restored.

When a new plant or animal is introduced into a stable community, the balance may be upset, and the results may be disastrous. When rabbits were introduced into Australia, the lack of natural enemies caused rabbit populations to explode, to the detriment of the entire countryside. When the water hyacinth was introduced into Florida waters as a ''pretty plant,'' it turned up everywhere, choking rivers and lakes. Some newcomers are harmless, but the risks are great.

There are many other examples of misplaced plants and animals that have threatened agriculture and the economy. Dutch elm disease has almost killed off the American elm tree. A tiny pest, the Mediterranean fruit fly, has caused untold damage to California citrus trees. About a hundred years ago, a fungus from Europe stowed away on nursery plants from Asia. It attacked the native chestnut tree. By 1950, native chestnut trees had virtually disappeared from the country.

The story of the sea lamprey is a tale of the unintentional introduction of a new species. In November 1921, a fisherman pulled from Lake Erie a large lake trout with a ferocious two-foot parasite attached to the fish's body. This ugly creature, the lamprey, increased to become a major menace to fishing in the Great Lakes. How did it get there?

A native of the North Atlantic, the sea lamprey had reached Lake Ontario through the St. Lawrence River. It could never reach the other Great Lakes, however, because of Niagara Falls. When the Wellington Canal was built between Lakes Erie and Ontario, the sea lamprey found its way into Lake Erie, with the other lakes now within reach. Within 25 years, the lamprey reduced the lake-trout catch by 90%.

How can we summarize the problems brought on by the introduction of aliens into stable communities? One: We bring these ecological disasters on ourselves. Two: Most invasions are irrevocable. Once a new species arrives and thrives, it stays. Three: The invaders expand in the new unthreatening environment. Four: There are no natural controls. The most dangerous invaders have arrived from native ecosystems that are complex. In such an environment, natural checks and balances keep populations under control. In a new environment, the checks are gone. Five: when an ecosystem is changed from one of great diversity to one of simplicity, the invader has an easy time. A wheat field is less diversified than the native plants it has displaced. Simplification provides empty niches for the newcomers to fill.

Strict quarantine regulations at airports and other ports of entry help keep out many potential invaders, but still they come, attached to bales of fabric, smuggled in by shortsighted travelers, airborne across borders. Fire ants do not respect borders. Full public cooperation and vigilance are essential to prevent new and dangerous invaders from upsetting ecological niches.

KNOW THESE WORDS

subtle: delicate

predators: creatures that prey on other animals

detriment: damage

virtually: practically

aliens: not native elements

ecological: relating to the interrelationship of organisms and environment

irrevocable: unchangeable

ecosystems: communities of plants and animals

diversified: varied

niches: places of individuals in their environments

1. The main idea of the passage is that (*a*) new species of plants or animals introduced into a settled environment may be disastrous (*b*) two major American trees, the elm and the chestnut, have been devastated by blights (*c*) deer must be protected from predators at all costs (*d*) every newcomer becomes a deadly pest.   1. _____

2. If a tourist arrived at Kennedy airport from Asia with a new kind of melon, (*a*) he or she would be welcomed as a resourceful traveler (*b*) the melon would be taken away (*c*) he or she would be arrested immediately (*d*) nothing would happen.   2. _____

3. When the Australian rabbit population increased so drastically, (*a*) rabbit fur became the major export (*b*) rabbits began using kangaroo dens (*c*) Australians tried to reduce the number of rabbits (*d*) rabbits became the national animal.   3. _____

4. After many years of attack on the sea lamprey, it probably (*a*) was finally eliminated (*b*) became a valuable food source for hungry Americans (*c*) left the Great Lakes of its own accord (*d*) was still present.

4. _____

5. If the Wellington Canal had never been built, in all probability the sea lamprey (*a*) would still exist in the Great Lakes in its present numbers (*b*) would not have reached the Great Lakes (*c*) would have become a major pest in the Atlantic (*d*) would have attached itself to ocean liners.

5. _____

6. When an invader enters a stable community, (*a*) it has little chance of surviving (*b*) all the native plants and animals attack it (*c*) it stays (*d*) scientists rarely recognize the problem.

6. _____

7. The one that has the greatest danger of being harmed by an alien invader is (*a*) a cornfield (*b*) an old woodland (*c*) a stable meadow (*d*) a tropical rain forest.

7. _____

8. The most efficient agent in keeping all plant and animal forces in balance is (*a*) the Department of Agriculture (*b*) the scientists at major colleges (*c*) the Food and Drug Administration (*d*) nature.

8. _____

9. The native chestnut tree was attacked by (*a*) bacteria (*b*) viruses (*c*) a fungus (*d*) none of these.

9. _____

10. Which of the following is an opinion?

    (*a*) The water hyacinth has choked Florida rivers.
    (*b*) The Mediterranean fruit fly has damaged the citrus industry.
    (*c*) Inspectors at U.S. airports are lax in their inspections.
    (*d*) The Wellington Canal paved the way for the sea lamprey in Lake Erie.

10. _____

18. Reading for Information

Reading for enjoyment is one of the major pleasures of life, but there is another kind of reading. It is reading for information. You might call it "bread-and-butter reading" or "survival reading." This kind of useful reading influences how well you do in school, at home, or on the job. It has an impact on every part of your life. In this section, you will meet some of these everyday reading challenges and gain some insights into how to handle them more effectively.

Table of Contents

The first group of challenges includes many skills used in working with books. At the top of the list is the *table of contents*.

Question 1: How Do You Use a Table of Contents?

Turn to pages vii–ix at the front of this book and answer the following questions.

1. Of the following topics, the one that comes first in the table of contents is (*a*) *Studying Cause and Effect* (*b*) *Drawing Inferences* (*c*) *Studying Sequence* (*d*) *Finding Details*.   1. _____

2. For additional practice in reading skills, you would turn to Part (*a*) I (*b*) II (*c*) III (*d*) IV.   2. _____

3. All the following are included in the *Review of Reading Skills* EXCEPT (*a*) main idea (*b*) sequence (*c*) propaganda (*d*) humor.   3. _____

4. A review of the role of Anglo-Saxon, Latin, and Greek in our vocabulary is probably included to help students (*a*) understand the functions of prefixes, roots, and suffixes (*b*) analyze unfamiliar words (*c*) form new words (*d*) do all of the preceding.   4. _____

5. *Reading Practice Test 1* begins on page (*a*) 158 (*b*) 193 (*c*) 201 (*d*) 257.   5. _____

Answers

1. (*d*) *Finding Details*, which is #6, precedes the others.
2. (*c*) Part III, which contains the reading practice tests, provides extra practice in reading.
3. (*d*) Humor is nowhere mentioned in the table of contents.
4. (*d*) Section 2, *Building Vocabulary*, helps students with all of the first three choices.
5. (*c*) Part III, which begins on page 201, contains this material.

Index

The table of contents is an excellent guide to broad topics and the organization of a book. If you are seeking a specific bit of information, however, you must turn to the alphabetical *index* at the back of the book. If you are looking up information on a chow in a book about dogs, for example, you will find the page or pages covering that particular breed in the index.

Question 2: How Do You Use an Index?

Read the following excerpt, or portion, of an index and answer the questions at the end.

Metaphor, 25
Middle English, 8, 22
Midland speech, 38
Milton, John, 8
Miracle Worker, The, 60
Morphology, 4–5
Movable type, 16

New words, 19–20
News Gothic, 17
Nonverbal communication, 63–69, 78
Northern speech, 38
Noun, 6, 43
Numbers, 12

Obsolete English, 36
Odysseus, 18
Old English, 8
Origins of language, 1
Overworked words, 50

Pantomime, 65
Paradise Lost, language of, 8
Paradox, 80–81
Parts of speech, 5–6, 43
Phonetic alphabet, 10
Phonetics, 9–10
Pictographic writing, 12–13, 14
Pioneers, English of, 19, 24–25
Play, language, 26–27, 32
Poetic words, 37
Poetry, 26, 37
"Pooh-pooh" theory, 1
Prefix, 22–24
Presymbolic language, 67
Primitive languages, 1
Printing, 13, 16–18
Problem solving, 84–86
Pronunciation, 8, 9, 12, 13, 14, 37, 43, 61
Pun, 27

Rationalizing, 82–83, 86
Reasoning, faulty, 81–84
    cause and effect, 81–82
    half-truth, 83–84
    rationalizing, 82–83
Regional variation, 37–39
Reports
    and clear thinking, 80
    contrasted with judgments, 76–77, 78
    verifiable, 76
Rhyme, 8
Right word, 29–30

Semantics, 57–79

Shakespeare, William, 8, 33, 36
Shaw, George Bernard, 10, 38
Shortening words, 33
Sign language, 2
Signals in grammar, 4–5
Signs, 62, 78
Simile, 25
Slang, 32–35, 36
Socrates, 63
Sounds, 9–10, 12, 14, 26–27
Southern speech, 38
Specialized language, 35–36, 61–62
Speech, 2–4, 9–10
    areas, 38–39
    and colloquial English, 31–32
    patterns, 4–5
Spelling, 8, 13, 42, 52
Spoken language, 2–3, 9–10, 12, 31–32
Standard English, 30–31
Structural grammar, 5–6
Structure of English, 4–7, 58
Substandard English, 30
Suffix, 23–24
Symbols, 9, 11–16
    signs and, 62
    words as, 59–63, 78, 80
Synonyms, 49–50, 73, 75
Syntax, 4–5

Thinking and language, 80–86
Times Roman, 17
Tone, 67–69, 78
Traditional grammar, 5–6
Transformational grammar, 5–6
Type faces, 17

Varieties of English, 3, 29–39
Verb, 6
Vocabulary, 19
    growth, 35, 40–56
    use, 35
    variations, 37
Vowel sound, 9, 16

Word
    form, 4–5, 43
    order, 4–5
    origins, 19–24, 33
Word study exercises, 10, 18, 28, 39,
        56, 69, 79, 86
Words often misused or confused, 52–55
Written language, 3, 8–18, 32

"Yo-he-ho" theory, 1

1. You would find information about sign language on page (*a*) 2
   (*b*) 4 (*c*) 62 (*d*) 78.   1. _____

2. All the following names are mentioned EXCEPT (*a*) Socrates
   (*b*) William Shakespeare (*c*) George Bernard Shaw (*d*) Adam
   Smith.   2. _____

3. From the excerpt, you may infer that rationalizing is a form of
   (*a*) pronouncing words (*b*) colloquial English (*c*) faulty reasoning
   (*d*) speaking rhythmically.   3. _____

4. Patterns of speech are discussed on pages (*a*) 9–10 (*b*) 4–5 (*c*) 38–
   39 (*d*) 31–32.   4. _____

5. From the index excerpt, you may infer that it was taken from a
   book dealing principally with (*a*) social studies (*b*) pronunciation
   (*c*) language (*d*) poetry.   5. _____

Answers

1. (*a*) *Sign language* appears in alphabetical order and is easy to find.
2. (*d*) A check of the alphabetical listing shows that *Adam Smith* is not included.
3. (*c*) *Rationalizing* appears in two places: in its own place in the alphabet and under *Reasoning, faulty.*
4. (*b*) Although *patterns* does not appear by itself in the alphabetical listing, it does appear under *Speech.*
5. (*c*) Practically every item deals with language in some form or other. *Pronunciation (b)* and *Poetry (d)* are details. *Social studies (a)* is neither mentioned nor implied.

Card Catalog

What the index does for a single book, the library **card catalog** does for all books. It provides a handy alphabetical index for finding a book on the library shelves. Your public library or school library may have its card catalog in microfilm or microfiche machines. There are three types of cards: author cards, title cards, and subject cards. The following excerpts from catalog cards illustrate all three types.

Author Card

> Keillor, Garrison
>   Lake Wobegon days/Garrison Keillor
> New York, Viking c 1985
>   337 p.

Title Card

> Lake Wobegon days
> Keillor, Garrison
>   Lake Wobegon days/Garrison Keillor
> New York, Viking c 1985
>   337 p.

Subject Card

> 796.426   MARATHON RUNNING—TRAINING
> Schreiber, Michael
> Training to run the perfect marathon/by
> Michael Schreiber
> ill. by J.T. Sevier—Santa Fe, NM
> J. Muir Publications c 1980

Three important abbreviations used on these cards are the following:

> p.—pages
> c—copyright
> ill.—illustrated

The number at the upper left of the subject card is a Dewey Decimal number, which will help you to locate the book on the shelves.

Question 3: How Do You Use Catalog Cards?

All questions refer to the excerpts from catalog cards.

1. J.T. Sevier is (*a*) an author (*b*) a publisher (*c*) an editor (*d*) an artist.   1. _____

2. The Schreiber book would probably be classified as a (*a*) history of the marathon (*b*) criticism of how marathons are promoted (*c*) how-to book about running (*d*) fictional account of a great runner.   2. _____

3. Viking and J. Muir are (*a*) authors (*b*) librarians (*c*) publishers (*d*) runners.   3. _____

4. If you were looking for a book on quilting, you would look for (*a*) author cards (*b*) title cards (*c*) subject cards (*d*) both author and title cards.   4. _____

5. Knowing the copyright date would be most important if you were looking for a book on (*a*) repairing furniture (*b*) science (*c*) writing fiction (*d*) chess.   5. _____

Answers

1. (*d*) The clue is the abbreviation *ill.* J.T. Sevier is the artist who illustrated the book.
2. (*c*) *Training to Run the Perfect Marathon* obviously emphasizes how to train. The other choices don't fit.
3. (*c*) J. Muir Publications clearly indicates that J. Muir is a publisher. You may infer that Viking is also a publisher.
4. (*c*) Author and title cards do not help in finding a particular *subject*.
5. (*b*) Advances in science make this subject the one requiring the most up-to-date book. Books of a few years ago may be out-of-date.

Readers' Guide to Periodical Literature

The ***Readers' Guide to Periodical Literature*** is another kind of alphabetized index, this time for material found in magazines. At the beginning of each volume of the *Readers' Guide*, you will find a list of abbreviations used. Abbreviations used in the selection below include the following:

Ap—April

My—May

Je—June

il—illustrations

pors—portraits

18:158-9—Volume 18, pages 158-9

Question 4: How Do You Use the *Readers' Guide?*

Examine the following excerpt from the *Readers' Guide** and answer the questions at the end.

Music, African
    See also
    Phonograph records—African music
Music, American
    See also
    Compact discs—American music
    Jazz music
          Dictionaries and encyclopedias
    The New Grove dictionary of American music. J. Idema.
      Smithsonian 18:158-9 Ap '87
Music, Caribbean
    Sounds of the Caribbean. D. Palmer. il *Black Enterp*
    17:42-4 My '87
Music, Church *See* Religious music
Music, Electronic
    See also
    Computers—Musical use
    Musical instruments, Electronic
    Videotapes—Electronic music
Music, Experimental
    See also
    Compact discs—Experimental music

---

* From *Readers' Guide to Periodical Literature*, 1987. Copyright © 1987 by the H.W. Wilson Company. Materials reproduced by permission of the publisher.

Music, Latin American
Music. See issues of *Américas* beginning May/June 1984
The spicy bite of Latin music. F. Hernandez. il *Essence* 17:30
  Ap '87
Music, Spanish
  See also
  Phonograph records—Spanish music
Music and animals *See* Animals and music
Music and children
  See also
  Phonograph records—Children's music
Music and fashion *See* Fashion and music
Music and literature
A movie star goes to Watts to make sure the Bard gets a good
  rap [work of J. Agutter] K. Hubbard. il pors *People Wkly*
  27:83–4 Je 29 '87
Music and the blind
Blind boy, 3, learns to play 50 songs on piano [J. Gardner]
  D. M. Cheers. il pors *Jet* 72:22–3 My 25 '87
Blind piano player, 3, visits Stevie Wonder [J. Gardner] il
  pors *Jet* 72:18 Je 22 '87
Blind since birth and barely 4, Jermaine Gardner happily
  hits all the right keys—and heartstrings. K. Hubbard. il
  pors *People Wkly* 27:53+ Je 22 '87
Music and the handicapped
  See also
  Pianists, Handicapped
Music critics and criticism
  See also
  Opera reviews
  Operetta reviews
  Oratorio reviews
Cleveland rock critic Jane Scott may be pushing 70, but she's
  still got the beat. K. Myers. il pors *People Wkly* 27:91–2
  Je 8 '87
Rock's most influential album? [reaction to Sgt. Pepper]
  M. Goldberg. *Roll Stone* p57+ Je 18 '87
Music education *See* Music—Study and teaching

1. The main topic of this section of the *Readers' Guide* is (*a*) Literature
   (*b*) Dictionaries (*c*) Music (*d*) Africa.   1. _____

2. An article on Stevie Wonder can be found in the magazine (*a*) *People
   Weekly* (*b*) *Jet* (*c*) *Essence* (*d*) *Smithsonian*.   2. _____

3. Jermaine Gardner is described as a (*a*) movie star (*b*) critic (*c*) blind
   musician (*d*) Latin American singer.   3. _____

4. A person interested in Latin American music would find infor-
   mation in the magazine (*a*) *Essence* (*b*) *Life* (*c*) *Jet* (*d*) *Smithsonian*. 4. _____

5. K. Hubbard is a writer for (*a*) *Jet* (*b*) *People Weekly* (*c*) the *New Grove
   Dictionary* (*d*) *The New Yorker*.   5. _____

Answers

1. (*c*) Since every topic begins with the word *music*, the major topic is obvious.
2. (*b*) Stevie Wonder is mentioned under the topic *Music and the Blind*, which contains an article about him.
3. (*c*) Jermaine Gardner is the subject of three articles mentioned under the topic *Music and the Blind*. In the first two articles, he is identified within brackets: [J. Gardner]. In the third, his name appears in the title of the article.
4. (*a*) Under the topic *Music, Latin American*, an article by F. Hernandez is listed for the magazine *Essence*.
5. (*b*) Two articles are listed for K. Hubbard. One is under *Music and Literature*. The other is under *Music and the Blind*. Both indicate that K. Hubbard writes for *People Weekly*.

Dictionaries

Dictionaries contain more information than just definitions. They usually indicate an acceptable pronunciation of a word. The key to pronunciation is at the bottom of the dictionary page. Dictionaries indicate the part of speech for the definition that follows. They often give the origin of the word. They may provide synonyms. They may provide a cross reference to enrich the meaning of a word. They may provide a context for the word defined. At least one dictionary, *Webster's Ninth New Collegiate Dictionary*, suggests the date at which the word probably entered the language. The guide words at the top of a dictionary page tell you which words appear on that page.

Examples from excerpt, *Webster's Ninth New Collegiate Dictionary*, page 776:

pronunciation	\\ˈmaȯnt-i-baŋk\\
part of speech	*vt* (transitive verb — *vi* = intransitive verb)
word origin	[mounted policeman]
synonym	CHARLATAN
cross reference	more at MUSKETEER
context	chocolate ~ (mousse)
date of entry into language	13c (13th century)
guide words	**mountain time • movement**

Question 5: How Do You Use a Dictionary?

Study the dictionary excerpt* on page 165 and answer the questions at the end.

---

*By permission. From *Webster's Ninth New Collegiate Dictionary* © 1990 by Merriam-Webster Inc., publisher of the Merriam-Webster® dictionaries.

mountain time *n, often cap M* (1883) : the time of the 7th time zone west of Greenwich that includes the Rocky mountain states of the U.S. — see TIME ZONE illustration
moun·tain·top \'maůnt-ᵊn-,täp\ *n* (1593) : the summit of a mountain
moun·tainy \'maůnt-ᵊn-ē, 'maůnt-nē\ *adj* (1613) **1** : MOUNTAINOUS **2** : of, relating to, or living in mountains
¹moun·te·bank \'maůnt-i-,baŋk\ *n* [It *montimbanco,* fr. *montare* to mount (fr.—assumed—VL) + *in* in, on (fr. L) + *banco, banca* bench — more at BANK] (1586) **1** : a person who sells quack medicines from a platform **2** : a boastful unscrupulous pretender : CHARLATAN — **moun·te·bank·ery** \-,baŋ-k(ə-)rē\ *n*
²mountebank *vt, obs* (1607) : to beguile or transform by trickery ⟨I'll ~ their loves —Shak.⟩ ~ *vi* : to play the mountebank
Mount·ie \'maůnt-ē\ *n* [*mount*ed policeman] (1914) : a member of the Royal Canadian Mounted Police
mount·ing \'maůnt-iŋ\ *n* (1563) : ³MOUNT 2
mourn \'mō(ə)rn, 'mȯ(ə)rn\ *vb* [ME *mournen,* fr. OE *murnan;* akin to OHG *mornēn* to mourn, Gk *mermēra* care — more at MEMORY] *vi* (bef. 12c) **1** : to feel or express grief or sorrow **2** : to show the customary signs of grief for a death; *esp* : to wear mourning **3** : to murmur mournfully — used esp. of doves ~ *vt* **1** : to feel or express grief or sorrow for **2** : to utter mournfully — **mourn·er** *n* — **mourn·ing·ly** \'mōr-niŋ-lē, 'mȯr-\ *adv*
mourn·ful \'mō(ə)rn-fəl, 'mȯ(ə)rn-\ *adj* (15c) **1** : expressing sorrow : SORROWFUL **2** : full of sorrow : SAD **3** : causing sorrow : SADDENING — **mourn·ful·ly** \-fə-lē\ *adv* — **mourn·ful·ness** *n*
mourn·ing \'mōr-niŋ, 'mȯr-\ *n* (13c) **1** : the act of sorrowing **2 a** : an outward sign (as black clothes or an armband) of grief for a person's death ⟨is wearing ~⟩ **b** : a period of time during which signs of grief are shown
mourning cloak *n* (1898) : a blackish brown butterfly (*Nymphalis antiopa*) with a broad yellow border on the wings found in temperate parts of Europe, Asia, and No. America
mourning dove *n* (1833) : a wild dove (*Zenaidura macrourc carolinensis*) of the U.S. with a plaintive call
¹mouse \'maůs\ *n, pl* **mice** \'mīs\ [ME, fr. OE *mūs;* akin to OHG *mūs* mouse, L *mus,* Gk *mys* mouse, muscle] (bef. 12c) **1** : any of numerous small rodents (as of the genus *Mus*) with pointed snout, rather small ears, elongated body, and slender tail **2 a** *slang* : WOMAN **b** : a timid person **3** : a dark-colored swelling caused by a blow; *specif* : BLACK EYE **4** : a small mobile manual device that controls movement of the cursor on a computer display
²mouse \'maůz\ *vb* **moused; mous·ing** *vi* (13c) **1** : to hunt for mice **2** : to search or move stealthily or slowly ~ *vt* **1** *obs* **a** : BITE, GNAW **b** : to toy with roughly **2** : to search for carefully — usu. used with *out*
mouse–ear \'maů-,si(ə)r\ *n* (13c) **1** : a European hawkweed (*Hieracium pilosella*) that has soft hairy leaves and has been introduced into No. America **2** : any of several plants other than mouse-ear that have soft hairy leaves
mouse–ear chickweed *n* (1731) : any of several hairy chickweeds (esp. *Cerastium vulgatum* and *C. viscosum*)
mous·er \'maů-zər\ *n* (15c) : a catcher of mice and rats; *esp* : a cat proficient at mousing
¹mouse·trap \'maů-,strap\ *n* (14c) **1** : a trap for mice **2** : a stratagem that lures one to defeat or destruction **3** : TRAP 2b
²mousetrap *vt* (ca. 1890) : to snare in or as if in a mousetrap
Mous·que·taire \,mü-skə-'ta(ə)r, -'te(ə)r\ *n* [F — more at MUSKETEER] (1705) : a French musketeer; *esp* : one of the royal musketeers of the 17th and 18th centuries conspicuous for their daring and their dandified dress
mous·sa·ka \,mü-sə-'kä\ *n* [NGk *mousakas*] (1931) : a Middle Eastern dish of ground meat (as lamb or beef) and sliced eggplant often topped with a seasoned sauce
mousse \'müs\ *n* [F, lit., froth, fr. LL *mulsa* hydromel; akin to L *mel* honey — more at MELLIFLUOUS] (1892) **1** : a light spongy food usu. containing cream or gelatin **2** : a molded chilled dessert made with sweetened and flavored whipped cream or egg whites and gelatin ⟨chocolate ~⟩
mous·se·line \,müs-(ə-)'lēn\ *n* [F, lit., muslin — more at MUSLIN] (1696) **1** : a fine sheer fabric (as of rayon) that resembles muslin **2 a** : a sauce (as hollandaise) to which whipped cream or beaten egg whites have been added **b** : MOUSSE 1 ⟨salmon ~⟩
mousseline de soie \-də-'swä\ *n, pl* **mousselines de soie** *same*\ [F, lit., silk muslin] (1850) : a silk muslin having a crisp finish
mous·tache \'məs-,tash, (,)məs-'\ *var of* MUSTACHE
mous·ta·chio \(,)məs-\ *var of* MUSTACHIO
Mous·te·ri·an \mü-'stir-ē-ən\ *adj* [F *moustérien,* fr. Le *Moustier,* cave in Dordogne, France] (1890) : of or relating to a middle Paleolithic culture that is characterized by well-made flake tools often considered the work of Neanderthal man
mousy *or* **mous·ey** \'maů-sē, -zē\ *adj* **mous·i·er; -est** (1853) : of, relating to, or resembling a mouse: as **a** : QUIET, STEALTHY **b** : TIMID, RETIRING **c** : grayish brown — **mous·i·ly** \-sə-lē, -zə-\ *adv* — **mous·i·ness** \-sē-nəs, -zē-\ *n*
¹mouth \'maůth\ *n, pl* **mouths** \'maůthz *also* 'maůz, 'maůths; *in synecdochic compounds like "blabbermouths" ths more frequently*\ *often attrib* [ME, fr. OE *mūth;* akin to OHG *mund* mouth, L *mandere* to chew, Gk *masasthai* to chew, *mastax* mouth, jaws] (bef. 12c) **1 a** (1) : the opening through which food passes into the body of an animal (2) : the cavity bounded externally by the lips and internally by the pharynx that encloses in the typical vertebrate the tongue, gums, and teeth **b** : GRIMACE ⟨made a ~⟩ **c** : an individual requiring food ⟨had too many ~s to feed⟩ **2 a** : VOICE, SPEECH ⟨finally gave ~ to her feelings⟩ **b** : MOUTHPIECE 3a **c** (1) : a tendency to excessive talk (2) : saucy or disrespectful language : IMPUDENCE **3** : something that resembles a mouth esp. in affording entrance or exit: as **a** : the place where a stream enters a larger body of water **b** : the surface opening of an underground cavity **c** : the opening of a container **d** : an opening in the side of an organ flue pipe — **mouth·like** \'maůth-,līk\ *adj* — **down in the mouth** : DEJECTED, SULKY
²mouth \'maůth *also* 'maůth\ *vt* (14c) **1 a** : SPEAK, PRONOUNCE **b** : to utter bombastically : DECLAIM **c** : to repeat without comprehension or sincerity ⟨always ~ing platitudes⟩ **d** : to form soundlessly with the lips ⟨the librarian ~ed the word "quiet"⟩ **e** : to utter indistinctly : MUMBLE ⟨~ed his words⟩ **2** : to take into the mouth; *esp* : EAT ~ *vi* **1 a** : to talk pompously : RANT — often used with *off* **b** : to talk insolently or impudently — usu. used with *off* **2** : to move the mouth esp. so as to make faces — **mouth·er** *n*
mouth·breed·er \'maůth-,brēd-ər\ *n* (1927) : any of several fishes that carry their eggs and young in the mouth; *esp* : a No. African percoid fish (*Haplochromes multicolor*) often kept in aquariums
mouthed \'maůthd, 'maůtht\ *adj* (14c) : having a mouth esp. of a specified kind — often used in combination ⟨a soft-*mouthed* fish⟩
mouth·ful \'maůth-,fůl\ *n* (15c) **1 a** : as much as a mouth will hold **b** : the quantity usu. taken into the mouth at one time **2** : a small quantity **3 a** : a very long word or phrase **b** : a comment or a statement rich in meaning or substance
mouth hook *n* (1937) : one of a pair of hooked larval mouthparts of some two-winged flies that function as jaws
mouth organ *n* (1866) : HARMONICA 2
mouth·part \'maůth-,pärt\ *n* (1799) : a structure or appendage near the mouth
mouth·piece \-,pēs\ *n* (1607) **1** : something placed at or forming a mouth **2** : a part (as of an instrument) that goes in the mouth or to which the mouth is applied **3 a** : one that expresses or interprets another's views : SPOKESMAN **b** *slang* : a criminal lawyer
mouth–to–mouth *adj* (1909) : of, relating to, or being a method of artificial respiration in which the rescuer's mouth is placed tightly over the victim's mouth in order to force air into his lungs by blowing forcefully enough every few seconds to inflate them
mouth·wash \'maůth-,wȯsh, -,wäsh\ *n* (1840) : a usu. antiseptic liquid preparation for cleaning the mouth and teeth or freshening the breath
mouthy \'maů-thē, -thē\ *adj* **mouth·i·er; -est** (1589) **1** : excessively talkative : GARRULOUS **2** : marked by or given to bombast
mou·ton \'mü-,tän, mü-'\ *n* [F, sheep, sheepskin, fr. MF, ram — more at MUTTON] (1944) : processed sheepskin that has been sheared and dyed to resemble beaver or seal
¹mov·able *or* **move·able** \'mü-və-bəl\ *adj* (14c) **1** : capable of being moved **2** : changing date from year to year ⟨~ holidays⟩ — **mov·abil·i·ty** \,mü-və-'bil-ət-ē\ *n* — **mov·able·ness** \'mü-və-bəl-nəs\ *n* — **mov·ably** \-blē\ *adv*
²movable *or* **moveable** *n* (14c) : something (as an article of furniture) that can be removed or displaced
¹move \'müv\ *vb* **moved; mov·ing** [ME *moven,* fr. MF *movoir,* fr. L *movēre*] *vi* (13c) **1 a** (1) : to go or pass from one place to another with a continuous motion ⟨*moved* into the shade⟩ (2) : to proceed in a certain direction or toward a certain state or condition ⟨*moving* up the executive ladder⟩ ⟨*moved* into second place in the tournament⟩; *also* : to become transferred during play ⟨checkers ~ along diagonally adjacent squares⟩ (3) : to keep pace ⟨*moving* with the times⟩ **b** : to start away from some point or place : DEPART **c** : to change one's residence or location **2** : to carry on one's life or activities in a specified environment ⟨~s in the best circles⟩ **3** : to change position or posture : STIR ⟨told him to be quiet and not to ~⟩ **4** : to take action : ACT **5 a** : to begin operating or functioning or working in a usual way **b** : to show marked activity ⟨after a brief lull things really began to ~⟩ **c** : to move a piece (as in chess or checkers) during one's turn **6** : to make a formal request, application, or appeal **7** : to change hands by being sold or rented ⟨goods that were *moving* slowly⟩ **8** *of the bowels* : EVACUATE ~ *vt* **1 a** (1) : to change the place or position of (2) : to dislodge or displace from a fixed position : BUDGE **b** : to transfer (as a piece in chess) from one position to another **2 a** (1) : to cause to go or pass from one place to another with a continuous motion ⟨*moved* the flag slowly up and down⟩ (2) : to cause to advance **b** : to cause to operate or function : ACTUATE ⟨this button ~s the whole machine⟩ **c** : to put into activity or rouse up from inactivity **3** : to cause to change position or posture **4** : to prompt or rouse to the doing of something : PERSUADE ⟨the report *moved* the faculty to take action⟩ **5 a** : to stir the emotions, feelings, or passions of ⟨was deeply *moved* by such kindness⟩ **b** : to affect in such a way as to lead to an indicated show of emotion ⟨the story *moved* her to tears⟩ **6 a** *obs* : BEG **b** : to make a formal application to **7** : to propose formally in a deliberative assembly ⟨*moved* that the meeting adjourn⟩ **8** : to cause (the bowels) to void **9** : to cause to change hands through sale or rent
syn MOVE, ACTUATE, DRIVE, IMPEL mean to set or keep in motion. MOVE is very general and implies no more than the fact of changing position; ACTUATE stresses transmission of power so as to work or set in motion; DRIVE implies imparting forward and continuous motion and often stresses the effect rather than the impetus; IMPEL suggests a greater impetus producing more headlong action.
²move *n* (1656) **1 a** : the act of moving a piece (as in chess) **b** : the turn of a player to move **2 a** : a step taken so as to gain an objective : MANEUVER ⟨a ~ to end the dispute⟩ **b** : the action of moving from a motionless position **c** : a change of residence or location — **on the move** **1** : in a state of moving about from place to place ⟨a salesman is constantly *on the move*⟩ **2** : in a state of moving ahead or making progress ⟨said that civilization is always *on the move*⟩
move in *vi* (1898) : to occupy a dwelling or place of work — **move in on** : to make advances or aggressive movements toward
move·less \'müv-ləs\ *adj* (1578) : being without movement : FIXED, IMMOBILE — **move·less·ly** *adv* — **move·less·ness** *n*
move·ment \'müv-mənt\ *n* (14c) **1 a** (1) : the act or process of moving; *esp* : change of place or position or posture (2) : a particular instance or manner of moving **b** (1) : a tactical or strategic shifting of a military unit : MANEUVER (2) : the advance of a military unit **c** : ACTION, ACTIVITY — usu. used in pl. **2 a** : TENDENCY, TREND ⟨detected a ~ toward fairer pricing⟩ **b** : a series of organized activities working toward an objective; *also* : an organized effort to promote or attain an end ⟨the civil rights ~⟩ **3** : the moving parts of a mechanism that transmit a definite motion **4 a** : MOTION 7 **b** : the rhythmic character or quality of a musical composition **c** : a distinct structural unit or division having its own key, rhythmic structure, and themes and forming part of an extended musical composition **d** : particular rhythmic flow of language : CADENCE **5 a** : the quality (as in a painting or sculpture) of representing or suggesting motion **b** : the quality in literature of having a quickly moving plot or an abundance of inci-

1. *Mouse-ear* is defined as (*a*) an animal (*b*) a cloth (*c*) a plant (*d*) a kind of person.   1. _____

2. When the word *mouse* means "search or move stealthily," it is used as (*a*) *n* (*b*) *adj* (*c*) *adv* (*d*) *vi*.   2. _____

3. The word *muscle* is related to the word (*a*) *mourn* (*b*) *mousse* (*c*) *mustache* (*d*) *mouse*.   3. _____

4. *Sad* is provided as a synonym of (*a*) *mourn* (*b*) *mournful* (*c*) *mourning* (*d*) *mousetrap*.   4. _____

5. If you wish to find out more about the word *mousse*, look up (*a*) *mellifluous* (*b*) *mouse* (*c*) *moussaka* (*d*) *mousseline*.   5. _____

6. *Mousseline* is a (*a*) cloth (*b*) dessert (*c*) hair spray (*d*) hair style.   6. _____

7. *Mousetrap* entered the language in the (*a*) 12th century (*b*) 13th century (*c*) 14th century (*d*) 15th century.   7. _____

8. You would expect to find all the following words on page 776 EXCEPT (*a*) *mountaintop* (*b*) *mouth* (*c*) *movable* (*d*) *much*.   8. _____

Answers

1. (*c*) The definition specifically identifies mouse-ear as "a hawkweed" or "any of several plants."
2. (*d*) The label *vi* is listed right after the entry itself, indicating that in the definitions following, *mouse* is used as an intransitive verb.
3. (*d*) The explanation of *mouse's* origin includes a reference to the Greek (Gk) *mys mouse, muscle.*
4. (*b*) *Sad* is listed as a synonym for *mournful*, along with *sorrowful*.
5. (*a*) *More at MELLIFLUOUS* appears after the word *mousse*.
6. (*a*) *Mousseline* is defined as a "fine, sheer fabric."
7. (*c*) The explanation *14c* after *mousetrap* indicates that the word entered the language in the 14th century.
8. (*d*) *Much* is not included within the guide words *mountain time—movement*.

Maps

You will undoubtedly own a car someday and plan trips to other cities, scenic areas, or theme parks like Walt Disney World. Do you know how to read a ***road map***?

On Your Own 1: Studying a Map

Study the following road map and answer the questions at the end.

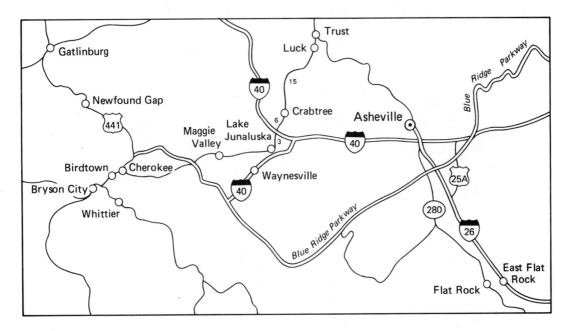

1. If you wanted to travel from Asheville to East Flat Rock, you would take the route numbered (*a*) 26 (*b*) 40 (*c*) 25A (*d*) 280.   1. _____

2. The distance between Crabtree and Lake Junaluska is (*a*) 3 miles (*b*) 6 miles (*c*) 9 miles (*d*) not given.   2. _____

3. A characteristic of the Blue Ridge Parkway is that (*a*) it is very short (*b*) it flows in a very straight line (*c*) it avoids towns and cities (*d*) it goes through both Waynesville and Maggie Valley.   3. _____

4. The shortest route between Gatlinburg and Cherokee passes through (*a*) Newfound Gap (*b*) Bryson City (*c*) Whittier (*d*) Birdtown.   4. _____

5. Trust and Luck are (*a*) mountains (*b*) towns (*c*) lakes (*d*) museums.   5. _____

Recipes

Cookbooks are among the most popular books published every year. Everyone is interested in cooking—or at least in the results of cooking. Following a *recipe* is not too difficult, but there is always one danger: You may omit one important step and ruin your project! How well can you read a recipe?

On Your Own 2: Studying a Recipe

Study the recipe on page 168 and answer the questions at the end.

Toffee Butter Cookies

Ingredients

1 cup butter	**1 teaspoon vanilla**
1 cup brown sugar	**2 cups sifted flour**
1 egg	**8 plain milk chocolate bars**

½ cup chopped nuts (your choice)

Procedure

Whip the butter and brown sugar until they are fluffy. Mix the egg and vanilla together and add to the butter and sugar. Then add the 2 cups of sifted flour to the above and mix thoroughly. Spread mixture on a 9 × 13 cookie pan. Don't put the batter too near the edge. Bake for 15 minutes in a 350-degree oven.

Take the cookie pan from the oven and set it on a surface that will not scorch. Break up the chocolate bars and place pieces all over the cookie dough. When they start to melt, spread the chocolate evenly over the baked cookie batter. Sprinkle nuts over the top of the chocolate. Let cool and cut into desired sizes for cookies.

1. Of the following steps, the one that comes before the others is (*a*) sprinkling the nuts (*b*) adding the chocolate (*c*) baking for 15 minutes (*d*) whipping the butter and brown sugar.   1. _____

2. The milk chocolate is added (*a*) right after the batter is spread on the cookie pan (*b*) before the vanilla is added (*c*) after the nuts have been added (*d*) while the baked batter is still hot.   2. _____

3. When the cookie pan comes out of the oven, (*a*) the cookies have still not been separated (*b*) the brown sugar must still be added (*c*) only half the flour has been used (*d*) the butter and brown sugar are still fluffy.   3. _____

4. When the flour is added to the mixture, it should be (*a*) partly baked (*b*) sifted (*c*) filled with nuts (*d*) heated.   4. _____

Charts

Information is often presented in graphic form. ***Charts*** compress a great deal of information in a small space. Can you read and understand a chart?

On Your Own 3: Analyzing a Chart

A major problem of all modern societies is the disposal of garbage and other solid wastes. The problem can be presented in the form of a chart. Study the following chart and answer the questions at the end.

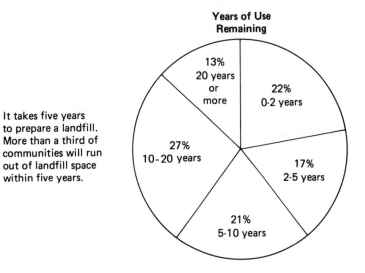

THE PROBLEM OF LANDFILLS

Years of Use Remaining

13% 20 years or more

22% 0-2 years

It takes five years to prepare a landfill. More than a third of communities will run out of landfill space within five years.

27% 10-20 years

17% 2-5 years

21% 5-10 years

1. The statement that ''more than a third of communities will run out of landfill space within five years'' is found by adding together the percentages (*a*) 13% and 22% (*b*) 17% and 27% (*c*) 22% and 17% (*d*) 13% and 21%.   1. _____

2. The percentage of landfills with a life of 10 to 20 years is (*a*) 13% (*b*) 17% (*c*) 21% (*d*) 27%.   2. _____

3. From the statistics presented, you may infer that (*a*) communities are planning adequately for the disposal of solid wastes (*b*) the landfill situation is inadequate for long-term needs (*c*) new landfills are being created at the rate of several each year (*d*) the collection of solid wastes is not a problem.   3. _____

Statistics

What is the highest mountain in the continental United States? Who won the Pulitzer Prize for Poetry in 1979? What two teams played in the 1987 Super Bowl? How many passenger cars did the United States export last year? Which state produces more corn, Illinois or Iowa? To find answers to questions like these, you'll have to consult lists of *statistics* as reported in various almanacs.

On Your Own 4: Analyzing Statistics

Study the following statistics* about principal rivers of the world and answer the questions at the end. *Confluence* means a flowing together.

Principal Rivers of the World
(For other U.S. rivers, see Index)

River	Source	Outflow	Approx. length miles	km
Nile	Tributaries of Lake Victoria, Africa	Mediterranean Sea	4,180	6,690
Amazon	Glacier-fed lakes, Peru	Atlantic Ocean	3,912	6,296
Mississippi-Missouri-Red Rock	Source of Red Rock, Montana	Gulf of Mexico	3,880	6,240
Yangtze Kiang	Tibetan plateau, China	China Sea	3,602	5,797
Ob	Altai Mts., U.S.S.R.	Gulf of Ob	3,459	5,567
Yellow (Huang Ho)	Eastern part of Kunlan Mts., west China	Gulf of Chihli	2,900	4,667
Yenisei	Tannu-Ola Mts., western Tuva, U.S.S.R.	Arctic Ocean	2,800	4,506
Paraná	Confluence of Paranaiba and Grande rivers	Rio de la Plata	2,795	4,498
Irtish	Altai Mts., U.S.S.R.	Ob River	2,758	4,438
Congo	Confluence of Lualaba and Luapula rivers, Zaire	Atlantic Ocean	2,716	4,371
Amur	Confluence of Shilka (U.S.S.R.) and Argun (Manchuria) rivers	Tatar Strait	2,704	4,352
Lena	Baikal Mts., U.S.S.R.	Arctic Ocean	2,652	4,268
Mackenzie	Head of Finlay River, British Columbia, Canada	Beaufort Sea (Arctic Ocean)	2,635	4,241
Niger	Guinea	Gulf of Guinea	2,600	4,184
Mekong	Tibetan highlands	South China Sea	2,500	4,023
Mississippi	Lake Itasca, Minnesota	Gulf of Mexico	2,348	3,779
Missouri	Confluence of Jefferson, Gallatin, and Madison rivers, Montana	Mississippi River	2,315	3,726
Volga	Valdai plateau, U.S.S.R.	Caspian Sea	2,291	3,687

* From THE 1988 INFORMATION PLEASE ALMANAC edited by Otto Johnson. Copyright © 1987 by Houghton Mifflin Company. Reprinted by permission of Houghton Mifflin Company.

1. The rivers are arranged according to their (*a*) alphabetic order (*b*) length (*c*) source (*d*) outflow. 1. _____

2. The longest river in the U.S.S.R. is the (*a*) Ob (*b*) Yenisei (*c*) Irtish (*d*) Amur. 2. _____

3. The river that flows into the Rio de la Plata is the (*a*) Nile (*b*) Volga (*c*) Missouri (*d*) Paraná. 3. _____

4. Among the following, the shortest river is the (*a*) Congo (*b*) Nile (*c*) Mississippi (*d*) Volga. 4. _____

5. The approximate length of the Ob River (in miles) is (*a*) 4,180 (*b*) 3,459 (*c*) 2,600 (*d*) 2,291. 5. _____

6. The river whose source is in Peru is the (*a*) Nile (*b*) Amur (*c*) Amazon (*d*) Missouri. 6. _____

7. Another name for the Yellow River is the (*a*) Ob (*b*) Huang Ho (*c*) Lena (*d*) Irtish. 7. _____

8. The number of rivers that flow into a strait is (*a*) 1 (*b*) 2 (*c*) 3 (*d*) 4. 8. _____

Want Ads

Many people find jobs by reading the "Help Wanted" section of the daily newspaper. Some are disappointed, however, because they fail to read carefully before they apply. Can you read a *want ad* accurately?

On Your Own 5: Studying a Want Ad

Study the following want ad and answer the questions at the end.

NOW HIRING

Busy Seafood Restaurant now hiring a line cook, waiter/waitress, part-time hostess/host, and part-time salad person. Also secretary, temporary, for two months. Experience in typing and filing essential. Apply 2–4 P.M., Tuesdays and Thursdays only: Seascape Restaurant, Shore Road and Bahama Drive.

1. A part-time job is open for a (*a*) line cook (*b*) cashier (*c*) secretary (*d*) salad person. 1. _____

2. The only job that specifies that experience is necessary is for a (*a*) cook (*b*) secretary (*c*) salad person (*d*) hostess/host. 2. _____

3. Wages or salaries have not been mentioned, probably because (*a*) different jobs earn different pay (*b*) waiters and waitresses earn tips (*c*) a host or hostess requires more skill than a secretary (*d*) the owners always pay more than minimum wage. 3. _____

4. A suitable time for applying for any of the jobs would be (*a*) all day Monday, after the weekend (*b*) Friday morning (*c*) 3:00 P.M. on Thursday (*d*) 2:30 P.M. on Wednesday. 4. _____

Job Applications

Some employers require written *job applications*. Neatness, accuracy, and completeness in filling out an application are essential. Read a job application carefully before you start to fill it out.

On Your Own 6: Studying a Job Application Form

The following form is a portion of an application for a bank job. Study the excerpt and answer the questions at the end.

EDUCATION AND/OR TRAINING

	Name & Location	Major/Minor	From	To	Type Degree Received
High School					
Business or Technical					
College or University					
Graduate School					

Additional Business Courses _____

Typing Speed _____   Shorthand Speed _____   Right Handed/ Left Handed _____   Other Skills _____

EMPLOYMENT INTEREST

Position(s) Applied For _____

Areas of Career Interest _____

Date Available _____   Location Preference _____

Are you willing to: Work Part Time   Yes ☐   No ☐   Travel   Yes ☐   No ☐
Work at Night   Yes ☐   No ☐   Relocate   Yes ☐   No ☐
Work on a Temporary Basis   Yes ☐   No ☐
Work on an On-Call Basis   Yes ☐   No ☐

PREVIOUS EMPLOYMENT

(Begin with current or last employment. Please complete even if you have submitted a résumé.)

Company Name _____   Date From _____ To _____   Phone (___) _____
Area

Address _____   Present or Last Supervisor _____
(Street)   (City)   (State)   (Zip)

Reason for Leaving _____   May We Contact?   Yes ☐   No ☐

Positions Held/Last Salary	Duties/Dates

1. All the following information is requested EXCEPT (*a*) previous job information (*b*) schooling (*c*) willingness to travel (*d*) condition of health.   1. _____

2. The request for information about additional business courses is probably included to (*a*) help the bank fit the job to the applicant (*b*) eliminate anyone who doesn't have a business course (*c*) see whether the applicant has friends in another bank (*d*) satisfy the curiosity of the personnel officer.   2. _____

3. The bank is probably interested in learning an applicant's reason for leaving a previous job so that it can (*a*) provide a perfect job for the applicant (*b*) reject a possibly troublesome applicant (*c*) learn something about competitors (*d*) make a substantial reduction in the salary offered.   3. _____

4. Previous jobs are to be listed starting with your (*a*) first job (*b*) favorite job (*c*) most recent job (*d*) best paying job.   4. _____

Where to Look for Information

For success in school and later, you need to know which reference books to use, where to find them, and how to use them when you find them. It is a good idea to browse through the reference section of your school or public library. Familiarize yourself with dictionaries, almanacs, and encyclopedias. You'll find them extremely helpful.

Bonus: Reviewing Information Sources

Read the following passage and answer the questions at the end.

> As an intelligent citizen, what should you know about reference books? Of course, you should own a good dictionary and should know how to use the large, unabridged dictionaries. In addition to traditional dictionaries, there are many specialized dictionaries, like the *Dictionary of American Biography* and *Webster's Biographical Dictionary*.
>
> You should also be able to use an almanac, or book of facts. Two of the most popular are the *World Almanac and Book of Facts* and the *Information Please Almanac*. Here you will find up-to-date information about every country in the world, statistics on industrial production, and a history of space exploration, among many other things.
>
> Encyclopedias provide in-depth material only touched upon in almanacs and dictionaries. You will find extensive articles on thousands of subjects alpha-

betically arranged. Cross-references and indexes provide even more help in finding just the information you are seeking. The *World Book Encyclopedia* is intended for young people. The *Encyclopedia Britannica* is written at a more adult level and goes into greater depth in many areas. Other encyclopedias include *Collier's Encyclopedia*, *Encyclopedia Americana*, and the truly remarkable one-volume *New Columbia Encyclopedia*.

If you are trying to locate an African nation like Zaire, use the maps in an atlas. There are many fine atlases available, like the *Rand McNally International World Atlas* and the *New York Times Atlas of the World*. Some atlases include the term *gazetteer* in the title, like the *Columbia-Lippincott Gazetteer of the World*. Gazetteers, along with many atlases, include a dictionary of geographical names.

There are many other sources of information. Among the various directories available is the telephone directory, a most important source of information about people, organizations, commercial establishments, and industry. You should know how to use the classified directory, often called the *Yellow Pages*, to find the service or store you want.

Periodicals are also important resources. The daily newspaper is a major source of information, much of it not available on the shorter television reports. Magazines provide follow-up on newspaper stories and go into greater depth. Encyclopedias, for all their special qualities, cannot be as up-to-date as newspapers and magazines. Encyclopedias should be used for background material; newspapers and magazines, for current information.

Many people have a glancing, superficial knowledge of current events and their background. To go beneath the surface and add depth to what you know, become familiar with all the reference material easily available.

KNOW THESE WORDS

unabridged: not shortened
gazetteer: geographical dictionary
periodicals: newspapers and magazines
superficial: on the surface only

1. Which of the following titles best summarizes the content of the passage?

    (*a*) Encyclopedias: The Key to Knowledge
    (*b*) All about Words and Their Origins
    (*c*) Major Reference Books and Other Sources
    (*d*) The Well-Informed Citizen   1. _____

2. Write the letter of the sentence that best expresses the main idea.

    (*a*) Many people have a glancing, superficial knowledge of current events and their background.
    (*b*) You will find extensive articles on thousands of subjects alphabetically arranged.
    (*c*) Encyclopedias provide in-depth material only touched upon in almanacs and dictionaries.
    (*d*) To go beneath the surface and add depth to what you know, become familiar with all the reference material easily available.   2. _____

3. As used in paragraph 3, *extensive* means (*a*) intensive (*b*) far-reaching (*c*) interesting (*d*) well-written.   3. _____

4. All the following reference books are mentioned EXCEPT (*a*) *New World Dictionary* (*b*) *Information Please Almanac* (*c*) *World Book Encyclopedia* (*d*) *New York Times Atlas of the World*.   4. _____

5. To find the latest figures on the U.S. cotton crop, you would probably consult (*a*) the *Rand McNally International World Atlas* (*b*) *Webster's Biographical Dictionary* (*c*) the *World Almanac and Book of Facts* (*d*) the *Encyclopedia Britannica*.   5. _____

6. Which of the following is an opinion?

    (*a*) Space exploration is mentioned in almanacs.
    (*b*) The classified directory is often called the *Yellow Pages*.
    (*c*) Encyclopedias use cross-references and indexes.
    (*d*) For general use, the *World Book Encyclopedia* is better than the *New Columbia Encyclopedia*.   6. _____

7. From the passage, we may infer that (*a*) gazetteers always include a geographical dictionary (*b*) the unabridged dictionary is better than a desk dictionary for everyday use (*c*) the *Information Please Almanac* is more up-to-date than the *World Almanac and Book of Facts* (*d*) atlases always include a geographical dictionary.   7. _____

8. The key term that distinguishes newspapers and magazines from encyclopedias is (*a*) industrial (*b*) up-to-date (*c*) adult (*d*) unabridged.   8. _____

9. Which of the following sentences contains figurative language?

   (a) As an intelligent citizen, what should you know about refer-
       ence books?
   (b) Of course, you should own a good dictionary.
   (c) Encyclopedias provide in-depth material only touched upon
       in almanacs and dictionaries.
   (d) Among the various directories available is the telephone
       directory, a most important source of information about
       people, organizations, commercial establishments, and
       industry.   9. _____

10. As used in the last paragraph, the figurative expression *glancing*
    means (a) shallow (b) profound (c) uninterested (d) calm.   10. _____

11. The author's purpose in writing this passage was to
    (a) inform (b) entertain (c) arouse (d) pass the time.   11. _____

12. The tone of the passage is (a) indifferent (b) inspirational
    (c) argumentative (d) matter-of-fact.   12. _____

19. Thinking Clearly

Groucho Marx once said that he'd never join a club that would accept him as a member. Groucho was, of course, being funny, but the thought processes of some people display a similar confusion. Clear thinking supports reading skills and plays a major role in competent reading. Can you avoid the typical pitfalls of thinking?

Question 1: How Well Can You Practice Clear Thinking?

Point out the possible error in thinking in each of the following statements.

1. The Joneses have a 42-foot recreation vehicle. We should get one, too.

   _____

   _____

2. So you don't believe my uncle once swam the English Channel. Well, here's his picture.

   _____

   _____

3. Sue Martin would make an excellent student-council president. She's so sweet.

   _____

   _____

4. I had a touch of the flu last week. I wore a copper bracelet and I felt better. The bracelet is a surprisingly good cure for the flu.

   _____

   _____

5. I have a lot of studying to do, but I need relaxation; so I think I'll go to the movies. It will probably do me a lot more good than studying.

   _____

   _____

Answers

1. Your family's situation may be different from the Joneses'. They may be wealthier. Mr. Jones may be retired, better able to use such a vehicle. The rest of your family may not prefer a vacation with a recreation vehicle.
2. A picture, of course, doesn't prove anything. It may not even be the right picture!
3. The office of president of the student council requires more qualities than sweetness.

4. This confuses sequence with cause and effect. Just because something happens *after* something else doesn't prove it occurred *because* of it.
5. This is rationalization, giving self-serving reasons for justifying a possibly irrational action.

Spotting Self-Contradiction

Some self-contradictory statements, like the one attributed to Groucho Marx, are meant to be funny. A second group consists of those that reveal a confused mind. Sam Goldwyn, famous Hollywood producer, is reported to have said, "It's an impossible situation but it has possibilities."

A third group consists of those intended to deceive. A political candidate proclaims, "I promise to cut taxes, decrease the deficit, and retain all current programs at full strength." The critical voter asks, "How?" Contradictions like these are sometimes more difficult to challenge. They often are separated by other sentences, concealing some obvious contradictions.

Question 2: Can You Spot Examples of Self-Contradiction?

Point out the contradictions in each of the following. What does each statement probably mean?

1. That restaurant has become so popular nobody goes there any more.

   _____

   _____

2. That oral agreement isn't worth the paper it's printed on.

   _____

   _____

3. An alibi is being someplace where you are not.

   _____

   _____

4. He's an executive who proves to be smarter than anyone else by hiring others who are smarter than he.

   _____

   _____

5. If you want good advice, listen to a silent man.

   _____

   _____

6. A woman rushed up to a train platform and asked, ''Has the next train gone by yet?''

_____

_____

7. A tourist at an archaeological site exclaimed, ''Where can you find a modern building that has lasted as long as these ancient ones?''

_____

_____

8. A hunter said, ''I didn't see that deer until he was out of sight.''

_____

_____

9. A restaurant patron complained, ''If they weren't so crowded here all the time, they'd do a lot more business.''

_____

_____

10. Some music is so loud that if Beethoven were alive, he'd turn over in his grave.

_____

_____

Answers

1. It cannot be popular if ''nobody goes there any more.'' The speaker probably means that his or her group doesn't go there any more.
2. If an agreement is verbal, it isn't printed on paper. The speaker probably means that the verbal agreement is worthless.
3. Being and not being some place at the same time is a contradiction. The speaker probably means, ''An alibi is trying to prove you are someplace where you are not.''
4. He can't be smarter if others are smarter. It is sufficient to say he is smart.
5. A silent man can't give advice. The speaker probably means ''a man who doesn't waste words.''
6. The ''next'' train cannot already have gone. The speaker may mean, ''Have I just missed a train? Is there another coming?''
7. Modern buildings cannot match ancient buildings for durability, since they haven't had time to prove themselves. The tourist probably means, ''Modern buildings will not survive as long as the ancient ones.''
8. If the deer was ''out of sight,'' he couldn't be seen. The hunter probably means he caught just a glimpse of the deer when he was almost out of sight.
9. The restaurant is doing a lot of business. The speaker probably means . . . ''I'd be a lot happier.''
10. He couldn't be alive and turn over in his grave. The speaker probably means, ''. . . he'd disapprove.''

Identifying the Correct Cause

Which of the following seems a more reasonable statement?

I failed the test because I didn't study.

I failed the test because I broke a mirror after breakfast.

Cause and effect probably acted in the first sentence but not in the second. Any relationship between failing a test and breaking a mirror seems farfetched.

Most events have many causes. That test failure may also be blamed on fatigue, illness, worry over a family situation. You may tend to simplify, settling on the first cause that occurs to you. Sometimes apparent cause and effect may in fact be mere coincidence.

Superstition sets up unscientific cases of cause and effect. Seeing a black cat has nothing to do with hitting your finger with a hammer later that day. Faulty explanations of bad luck abound: getting out of bed wrong foot first; putting on the left shoe before the right shoe; walking under a ladder; being a member of 13 at dinner. Some persons try positive means to avoid bad luck. Some athletes have lucky charms to keep them from getting into batting slumps.

"These work!" the athletes will insist. Of course, if the athlete believes that the charm works, he or she is more likely to perform well. Such improved performance, however, does not indicate a direct causal connection between the charm and the performance.

On Your Own 1: Studying Mistaking the Cause

Four of the following show muddled thinking. Identify the one that shows clear thinking and suggest other causes for the four faulty ones.

1. I left my good-luck ring at home and slipped on an icy patch in the road.

    _____

    _____

2. Russ Wilson came in first in his age group in the New York Marathon. The months of advance preparation and conditioning paid off.

    _____

    _____

3. Terry made a combined score of 1220 on the College Boards. Genevieve, on the other hand, did better, achieving a score of 1398. Genevieve is obviously much smarter than Terry.

    _____

    _____

4. I should never have taken my driver's-license test on Friday the 13th. I failed. I know I'd have passed on another day.

_____

_____

5. After I spilled the salt this morning, everything went wrong. I missed the school bus, failed a test, lost my wallet, and then missed the bus home.

_____

_____

Understanding Rationalizations

"Don't make excuses. Make good."

This old quotation zeroes in on one of the commonest errors in thinking: self-deception. We like to consider ourselves reasonable people. Sometimes when we want to do something unwise, we invent reasons to justify our actions. If we want two extra desserts, for example, we may convince ourselves we need the extra calories for studying. Such self-deception, also called *rationalization*, may quiet our consciences, but it obscures the truth.

On Your Own 2: Studying Rationalization

Show that the reasoning in four of the following is faulty because of self-deception. Identify the one that shows clear thinking.

1. I made a winning point, but a prejudiced tennis official called the ball out.

_____

_____

2. I promised Dad I'd clip the hedge, but there are some clouds. It may rain. I'll go down to the lake for a swim.

_____

_____

3. I won't tell Dad I didn't clip the hedge. I don't want to worry him in any way.

_____

_____

4. I need some extra money for the ski outing. I think I'll get an after-school job.

_____

_____

5. I'm a poor speller. All the members of my family are poor spellers.

_____

_____

Avoiding Jumping to Conclusions

''All Doberman pinschers are vicious. Never trust one.''

Though some dogs of that breed are vicious, not all are. There are many gentle, loving Dobermans. Perhaps the speaker had an unfortunate experience with a particular dog, but the generalization is not fair. *All* is a dangerous word.

Generalizations are useful. You have learned that gardenias have a lovely odor, that smaller cars tend to get better gas mileage than larger ones, that the flower impatiens thrives better in part shade than full sun. You have, in your mind, hundreds of helpful generalizations based upon experience, but you must keep alert. Keep in mind the following dangers.

1. Generalizations may be based upon faulty thinking, like mistaking the cause.

2. Generalizations may be based on too few samples or experiences, like the generalization about Doberman pinschers.

3. Generalizations nearly always have exceptions.

4. Life moves along and changes. Don't hold onto outdated generalizations.

5. Though generalizations are convenient and even necessary, the world is composed of individual persons and things. Generalizations help us act. But be on guard against absolute words like *all, every, always, never,* and *nobody.* Instead, use qualifying words like *some, frequently, most, many, occasionally,* or *few.*

On Your Own 3: Studying Faulty Generalizations

Show how each of the following generalizations may be unsound.

1. Tammy has had two errors on her phone bill. Those monthly statements are always unreliable.

_____

_____

2. I enjoyed Agatha Christie's *Death on the Nile.* I'm sure I'll enjoy all detective stories.

_____

_____

3. Democrats (or Republicans) are always showing their ineptness for governing.

_____

_____

4. I've seen some rude behavior by tennis players on TV. Tennis players are not so nice as golfers.

_____

_____

5. It rained last year on our vacation. It always rains when we leave for our holiday destination.

_____

_____

Analyzing Misleading Comparisons

In families with two or more children, the younger members usually pester their parents about privileges. These young people fail to see why they can't be allowed to do what the older children are allowed to do. The essential differences in age and maturity are conveniently overlooked. Argument by *comparison* or *analogy*, as this kind of thinking is sometimes called, assumes that because two persons or things are alike in one respect, they'll be alike in all. True, the children are all members of the same family, but the similarities may end there.

Argument by comparison is sound only if the points of similarity are numerous and significant. If a school by a river has a rowing team, you may lobby for such a team if your school is roughly comparable with equal access to the water. If your school is far from any body of water, the comparison breaks down.

On Your Own 4: Studying Misleading Comparisons

Four of the following may be using questionable arguments. Show why the compared situations in these four may not be sufficiently similar to justify the conclusion. Identify the one that shows clear thinking.

1. My cousin Toby is being sent to an expensive camp for the entire summer. I don't see why I am not being sent also.

_____

_____

2. Sarah, who enjoys nature writing as much as I do, has recommended the books of Rachel Carson. I think I'll try her *Under the Sea Wind*.

_____

_____

3. The soils of San Antonio are influenced by the limestone underneath the topsoil. Crepe myrtle does well there. I'm sure azaleas and rhododendrons will also do well.

_____

_____

4. If eight glasses of water a day are better than one, then eight multiple vitamin pills a day would be better than one.

_____

_____

5. Sharon looks good in black. I'll have to get a black dress.

_____

_____

Bonus: Reviewing Clear Thinking

Eight of the following demonstrate thinking that may be muddled. Identify those that show clear thinking. For the others, tell why the thinking is faulty.

1. All overweight people are jolly.

_____

_____

2. Since the desert is unbearably hot at midday in July, we're planning to cross it at night.

_____

_____

3. Be sincere—whether you mean it or not.

_____

_____

4. I believe everything happens in threes. I cut my finger, lost my key ring, and I'm just waiting for the third disaster.

_____

_____

5. I think I'll break my appointment with the dentist. My toothache will probably go away in time.

_____

_____

6. Corinne and I don't enjoy violence in a movie. She warned me away from _Blood Sports_. I think I'll skip it.

_____

_____

7. Ralph Amner, an English musician, once said to his godson, ''I hope I may live to see thee preach my funeral sermon.''

   _____

   _____

8. If I want the rains to come, I wash my car.

   _____

   _____

9. The stream at our mountain cabin has been tested and is pure enough to drink. This stream, at the foot of Mt. Pisgah, is probably also good enough to drink.

   _____

   _____

10. If you save something, then you'll have something when you have nothing.

   _____

   _____

20. Understanding Literary Types

Fiction and Nonfiction

In the library, books are generally divided into fiction and nonfiction. For purposes of classification, fiction includes short stories and novels. Nonfiction includes everything else. The dictionary defines *fiction* as ''something invented by the imagination . . . an invented story.'' The distinction is tricky. Plays are ''invented by the imagination,'' but they are classified with nonfiction. In talking about fiction and nonfiction, use the library classifications, but keep in mind that some nonfiction is as creatively invented as a novel or a short story. Classifications sometimes overlap. Years ago, Truman Capote wrote what he called *a nonfiction novel*, a factual reporting using the techniques of the novel. Others have also blended fiction and nonfiction. Somerset Maugham was fascinated by the life of the artist Paul Gauguin. He based the novel *The Moon and Sixpence* on Gauguin's life, but he named his character *Charles Strickland*. A work of fiction in which actual people are presented under fictitious names is called a *roman à clef—a novel with a key*.

Though biography and the novel are distinct forms, there are many hybrids, using the elements of both. In such blends, though the major facts are correct, there is much invention of dialogue and minor situations. Such books are called *biographical novels* or, sometimes, *novelized* (or *fictionalized*) *biographies*.

Like biographical novels, historical novels are also a blend, but of history and fiction. In Charles Dickens' novel *A Tale of Two Cities*, three fictitious characters lead their lives among the historical perils of the French Revolution.

Practice 1: Reviewing Fiction and Nonfiction

Answer each question *true* or *false*. Base your answers on the preceding information.

1. According to library classifications, Shakespeare's *Hamlet* would
   be placed with fiction.   1. _____

2. In the dictionary sense, a play may be as fictional as a novel.   2. _____

3. There is often no clear distinction between a novel and a biography. 3. _____

4. The French word for *key* is *roman*.   4. _____

5. Writers who give a picture of a person's life never introduce
   dialogue into their books unless they, the writers, were present.   5. _____

Answers

1. False.   Plays are classified as nonfiction.
2. True.   Plays invent incidents, plots, dialogue just as novels do.

3. True.   Some books take on the characteristics of both.
4. False.   The French word for *key* is *clef*. *Roman* is clearly related to the English word *romance*.
5. False.   Writers are free to do what they like, invent dialogue if it suits their purposes.

The Novel and the Short Story

Clearly, the novel and the short story belong to the same literary family. Both tell a story through characters who act or are acted upon. The novel, however, is a long prose narrative usually weaving many plot incidents together to form a connected story. Though it is often inspired by actual events, it is essentially fictional.

The short story, by contrast, is characterized by far greater compression than the novel. Somerset Maugham defined the short story as ''a piece of fiction that has unity of impression, that can be read at a single sitting and is moving, exciting or amusing.'' It frequently strives for a single effect. The most common range of the short story is between 5,000 and 7,500 words. The most common range of the novel is between 60,000 and 200,000 words.

Both the short story and the novel often depend heavily upon plot. For many works of fiction, the old humorous summary of plot isn't too far wrong: ''Boy meets girl. Boy loses girl. Boy wins girl.'' Basically, plot involves a situation, an opening that is complicated by an unexpected event. In Walter D. Edmonds' short story ''Death of Red Peril,'' the opening situation discusses the author's father and his interest in caterpillar racing. The complication is a caterpillar race in which Red Peril, the racing caterpillar, will be entered. Conflict develops when a competitor takes unfair advantage of Red Peril's fear of butter. The development proceeds with plans for another crucial race to demonstrate the racing skills of Red Peril. The climax comes when Red Peril is fouled in the critical race. The bittersweet outcome has Red Peril winning, but at a price. There, in brief, are the elements of plot.

You will notice that many television sitcoms (situation comedies) use the tested formula. At the opening, all is calm (situation). The father of the family is quietly reading. One of the children comes in with a problem (complication). There is disagreement about how to handle the problem (conflict). The program explores some of the elements of the problem (development). A sudden, unexpected move is made by one of the characters (climax). The problem is solved and quiet returns (outcome).

The Play

Though classified as nonfiction, the play has much in common with the novel and the short story. The full-length play resembles the novel. The one-act play resembles the short story. Though a play is entirely in dialogue and meant to be performed, it stimulates the same interests as the novel and short story.

The play has fostered many offshoots. The musical comedy, the operetta, and the opera are plays with music. They usually include a typical plot, recognizable characters, and a suitable setting. A play may not only be seen on the stage but also read for enjoyment like the novel and the short story.

Practice 2: Reviewing the Novel, the Short Story, and the Play

Answer the following questions. Base your answers on the preceding explanations.

1. ''Death of Red Peril'' is a (a) science-fiction story (b) play (c) short story (d) novel.   1. _____

2. Television programs are mentioned to (a) demonstrate a simple plot outline (b) demonstrate an inferiority to the average short story (c) criticize lack of imagination in television (d) add some humor to the presentation.   2. _____

3. Which of the following sequences is illustrated in the text?

    (a) situation, conflict, complication, climax, development, outcome
    (b) situation, complication, conflict, outcome, development, climax
    (c) situation, development, complication, conflict, climax, outcome
    (d) situation, complication, conflict, development, climax, outcome   3. _____

4. The summary ''Boy meets girl. Boy loses girl. Boy wins girl'' is mentioned in a way that is (a) sneering (b) mildly approving (c) disapproving (d) wildly enthusiastic.   4. _____

5. All the following are mentioned as offshoots of plays EXCEPT the (a) short story (b) opera (c) musical comedy (d) operetta.   5. _____

Answers

1. *c*   2. *a*   3. *d*   4. *b*   5. *a*

The Article and the Essay

Two types that are often difficult to distinguish are the article and the essay. Together, they comprise a major block of reading in periodicals. Articles are especially prevalent in magazines that seek to make us more aware of the world we live in. They tend to be factual and impersonal. They may describe the situation in Northern Ireland, tell about the greenhouse effect, plead for laws to protect the dolphin, or praise one of the presidential candidates. They deal with science, ecology, politics, finance, economics, and literature. They attack government waste, inadequate housing, poor health care, reckless supervision of nuclear plants. In short, *any* topic is suitable for development as an article.

How does the essay differ from the article? It is much more personal. It tends to use the pronoun *I*. A formal essay tends to be serious, dignified and informative, but it is still more personal than an article. An informal essay is often light and humorous. James Thurber, Robert Benchley, and S.J. Perelman are great names from the past. Current humorous essayists include Erma Bombeck, Art Buchwald, and Lewis Grizzard.

Suppose the topic to write about is the VCR. How might an article and an essay treat the subject? An article would probably be quite thoughtful, perhaps outlining the history of the VCR, seriously considering the impact the VCR has had on entertainment, and emphasizing our dependence upon the Japanese for our VCR sets. An essay, by contrast, might detail the writer's frustrations trying to operate the machine. The possibilities for blunders are numerous, and a humorous report on the writer's experiences could be entertaining.

The Biography and the Autobiography

The Greek root *bio* means *life* and *graph* means *write* (page 23). A biography is thus "a life written down," a history of a person's life. It is more than a factual outline, however. It frequently attempts to interpret a person's motives. A conscientious biography tries to restrict itself to objective evidence and factual materials, but the author's bias is inevitable. The writer must select details from a tremendous amount of material. The very selection inevitably leaves out something else. There have been numerous biographies of Charles Dickens, for example. One biography strives to show that Charles Dickens was a frustrated actor. Another pays much more attention to Dickens's childhood experiences to explain his later actions. New biographies of the same person keep appearing, suggesting that the last word can never be said in summing up a person's life.

Well, if an outsider has some problems in summing up a person's life, wouldn't a biographical subject be the best person to recount his or her life? After all, who knows someone better than himself or herself? The answer isn't clear-cut.

The root *auto* means *self*. Combining *self* with *a life written down* gives us *autobiography*, a person's attempt to tell his or her own life story. Like the biography, the autobiography inevitably omits and selects to provide a point of view. Being human, autobiographers often prefer to omit certain unflattering insights and details. Often they forget. Besides, even the most honest writer doesn't understand everything he or she does or has done. Thus, even the best biography or autobiography is necessarily incomplete.

There are other forms of biographical and autobiographical writings. Collections of anecdotes often reveal many facets of a subject. Diaries, memoirs, and journals can record life while it is recent and easily remembered. Letters reveal a great deal about both correspondents.

Poetry

Poetry is even more difficult to pin down than some of the other literary types. *Webster's New Collegiate Dictionary* defines poetry as "writing that formulates a concentrated imaginative awareness of experience in language chosen and arranged to create a specific emotional response through meaning, sound, and rhythm."

Just when we think we have captured a definition, something comes along to change our minds. We might say, "Poetry rhymes." But blank verse doesn't rhyme. Or we may say, "Poetry has a fixed rhythm." But free verse has no fixed rhythm. Or we may say, "Poetry uses figurative language." But beautiful poetry can exist without figurative language. One of the most beautiful poetic forms, the simple 17-syllable haiku, uses straightforward *literal* language to create an effect.

Some people label poetry by the effect it has on them. If they feel the little hairs on the back of the neck standing up, it's poetry!

Often a distinction is made between poetry and verse. Some critics say that Carl Sandburg, Robert Frost, and John Keats created poetry, while Ogden Nash, W.S. Gilbert (of Gilbert and Sullivan), and Dorothy Parker created verse. Greeting cards print myriad verses every year. Perhaps, after all, labels are unimportant. Are you moved by a selection? Perhaps then for you it's poetry.

On Your Own: Reviewing Literary Types

Answer the following questions. Base your answers on the preceding explanations.

1. The topic "How I Learned to Operate My Electric Can Opener" would probably be for a(n) (*a*) short story (*b*) essay (*c*) biography (*d*) memoir.   1. _____

2. All the following essayists were mentioned EXCEPT (*a*) S.J. Perelman (*b*) Art Buchwald (*c*) Russell Baker (*d*) Robert Benchley   2. _____

3. It is impossible for a biography or autobiography to be (*a*) consistently readable (*b*) funny (*c*) accurate (*d*) complete.   3. _____

4. All the following were mentioned as poets EXCEPT (*a*) John Keats (*b*) Lord Byron (*c*) Carl Sandburg (*d*) Robert Frost.   4. _____

5. The journal is listed as being related to (*a*) the autobiography (*b*) free verse (*c*) the article (*d*) the poem.   5. _____

Bonus: Studying Literary Types

Read the following selection and answer the questions at the end.

> The novel is usually divided into different types. Often a library will have special shelves for one or more of the types. Fans seek each kind—for example, mystery, science fiction, the western, adventure, and romance.
>
> The mystery is a perennial favorite. It is, itself, divided into recognizable types. There is the detective story, a narrative of pure detection. A crime is committed. The detective, usually a gifted amateur, unravels the crime, examining each clue as presented. The reader is invited to solve the crime along with the

detective. Of course, the clever author tries to trick the reader by inserting false clues, misleading motives, red herrings. At the end, though, the reader admits, "The author played fair. I should have guessed." Except for the crime, violence is usually played down.

Another type of mystery is the hard-boiled tale involving a private detective, or "private eye." The detective is often down on his luck, eager to find a case that will pay his bills. The puzzle element is missing. Violence is frequent and graphic.

Science fiction also is divided into different types. One type is the philosophical narrative that uses science fiction to consider humanity's fate in the face of advancing technology. Then there are interplanetary adventures involving civilizations that have solved the limitations of space travel as we know it. Extremely popular are the bug-eyed-monsters (BEMs!) who land in spaceships, come from the interior of the earth, rise from dark lagoons, or are created in the laboratory by evil or incompetent scientists.

The western has its own traditions. Favorite themes recur. A single lawman faces an evil gang. Settlers are at odds with cattlemen over the open range. Water rights find a small group of ranchers or farmers against a powerful combination of villains. There are many such themes set against the overpowering scenery of the American West.

Adventure stories take readers to exotic lands. The James Bond novels, and the movies based on them, are excellent examples. Bond is trapped in impossible situations with no hope of escape, but he manages to get away somehow. Books like these are often called pure "escapism," but such reading has a place in any reader's schedule.

Romance stories emphasize man-woman relationships, often in historical settings. The leading characters are basically admirable. The man is handsome. The woman is beautiful. There are obstacles to the romance, sometimes the character traits of the characters themselves, but love triumphs.

Further divisions can be made: psychological novels, tales of growing up, spy stories. There is something for every reader. The library carries incredible riches, yet many Americans never sample the wealth.

KNOW THIS WORD

exotic: foreign

1. A major idea of the passage is that (*a*) westerns make better reading than mysteries (*b*) some literary types have shelves of their own (*c*) escapism is to be avoided (*d*) there is reading for everyone's taste.   1. _____

2. The James Bond novels are suggested as examples of (*a*) science fiction (*b*) adventure (*c*) romance (*d*) westerns.   2. _____

3. As used in paragraph 2, *perennial* means (*a*) unexpected (*b*) consistent (*c*) occasional (*d*) scary.   3. _____

4. All the following are mentioned as origins of bug-eyed monsters EXCEPT (*a*) lagoons (*b*) laboratories (*c*) volcanoes (*d*) spaceships.   4. _____

5. The puzzle element is most frequently found in the (*a*) detective story (*b*) western (*c*) romance (*d*) adventure story.   5. _____

6. Which of the following is an opinion?

   (*a*) Escapism is not necessarily harmful.
   (*b*) Water rights are a source of contention in some westerns.
   (*c*) Detective stories usually involve a crime.
   (*d*) The library often has separate shelves for types of fiction. 6. _____

7. We may infer that romance stories (*a*) are more interesting than westerns (*b*) sometimes have tragic endings (*c*) combine the qualities of both westerns and adventure stories (*d*) do not necessarily reflect real life.   7. _____

8. The best example of figurative language is (*a*) ''each clue'' (*b*) ''impossible situations'' (*c*) ''red herrings'' (*d*) ''humanity's fate.''   8. _____

9. The author's basic purpose in writing this passage was to (*a*) amuse (*b*) arouse (*c*) inform (*d*) reassure.   9. _____

10. The tone of the passage is (*a*) straightforward (*b*) argumentative (*c*) understated (*d*) hurried.   10. _____

PART II
Multiple-Choice Tests

In tests A–E, write the letter of the correct answer for each numbered item. (*Note:* The italicized numbers in parentheses refer to text pages where you can find help in answering the questions.)

Test A

(3)   1. All the following reading skills are mentioned in the first chapter of this text EXCEPT

      A. making inferences
      B. finding details
      C. getting the main idea
      D. using statistics   1. _____

(2)   2. Which of the following statements is false?

      A. A handy desk dictionary is a major tool in reading.
      B. Context solves all meaning problems in reading.
      C. The dictionary is a basic tool for checking spelling.
      D. Guessing at word meanings through context should be combined with using the dictionary.   2. _____

(4)   3. One of the worst obstacles to effective reading habits is

      A. a distracting setting
      B. eating while reading
      C. reading material that is not challenging enough
      D. reading in direct sunlight   3. _____

(4)   4. The reading skill *skimming* may best be compared with

      A. crawling
      B. sitting
      C. running
      D. speaking   4. _____

(7)   5. The British writer Charles Dickens had the ability to

      A. build suspense
      B. create beautiful poetry
      C. write powerful political plays
      D. defeat opponents in debate   5. _____

(8)   6. The word *defend* contains

  A. a suffix and a root
  B. a prefix and a root
  C. a prefix, a suffix, and a root
  D. just a root   6. _____

(8)   7. Most common words have been derived from

  A. Latin
  B. Greek
  C. Anglo-Saxon
  D. French   7. _____

(10) 8. The language mentioned as having entered English at many different times is

  A. German
  B. Latin
  C. Spanish
  D. American Indian   8. _____

(27) 9. All the following statements about context are true EXCEPT

  A. The context of a word is the setting in which it appears.
  B. Context is a major help in guessing at the meanings of unfamiliar words.
  C. The entire sentence is often a help in determining the meaning of a new word.
  D. Context is a major help in determining the correct spelling of a word.   9. _____

(34) 10. The main idea of a reading selection is

  A. always stated in the opening sentence
  B. impossible to determine without at least three readings
  C. usually summed up in a short sentence
  D. supported by the details in the selection   10. _____

Test B

(40) 11. To find the best title, a reader must also

  A. get the main idea
  B. be able to write extremely well
  C. pay special attention to the middle of the selection
  D. separate fact from opinion   11. _____

(44)   12. A reader can usually answer a question on details by

      A. drawing an inference
      B. pointing to a statement in the reading passage
      C. paying special attention to synonyms and antonyms
      D. learning how to make a generalization   12. _____

(55)   13. Which of the following statements about inferences is true?

      A. Inferences are helpful but must be checked for accuracy.
      B. Nearly all inferences are unreliable.
      C. People who make decisions based on inferences are doomed to disappointment.
      D. Most people do not draw inferences.   13. _____

(55)   14. Another way of explaining *drawing inferences* is

      A. finding the topic sentence
      B. looking for misstatements of fact
      C. reading between the lines
      D. skimming a reading passage   14. _____

(64)   15. Which of the following statements about synonyms is true?

      A. Pairs of synonyms have exactly the same meanings.
      B. Pairs of synonyms have nearly the same meanings.
      C. Synonyms do not serve as clues in drawing inferences.
      D. Synonyms are usually equally common or familiar.   15. _____

(73)   16. Which of the following pairs of words are antonyms?

      A. vigorous—ample
      B. commonplace—friendly
      C. unrelenting—sturdy
      D. spendthrift—miser   16. _____

(88)   17. Which of the following groups of words contains a general word that includes the others?

      A. diamond, ruby, sapphire, opal
      B. courthouse, mansion, log cabin, building
      C. elm, maple, oak, hickory
      D. Omaha, Duluth, Orlando, Seattle   17. _____

(94)   18. Which of the following pairs of sentences shows the sequence cause-to-effect?

    A. The children burst out laughing. The clown was being pulled along by a tiny dog.
    B. The chimney bricks had fallen to the ground. The chimney had been struck by lightning.
    C. Pete Sampras joyfully threw his arms in the air. He had just won the U.S. Open tennis tournament.
    D. The pine tree became infested with bark beetles. It started to die.   18. _____

(101)   19. Sequence refers to

    A. a new edition of a book
    B. a television miniseries
    C. the order of events
    D. figurative language   19. _____

(108)   20. Another expression for *figurative language* is

    A. *colloquial speech*
    B. *literal English*
    C. *figures of speech*
    D. *Standard English*   20. _____

Test C

(109)   21. The most common example of figurative language is

    A. metaphor
    B. personification
    C. simile
    D. hyperbole   21. _____

(119)   22. An opinion differs from a fact in that

    A. it cannot be as easily checked
    B. it is almost certain to be false
    C. it is usually expressed in a loud voice
    D. it is rarely introduced into television debates   22. _____

(119)   23. Which of the following is more likely to be used in a statement of fact than in an expression of opinion?

    A. *overrated*
    B. *foolhardy*
    C. *ninety*
    D. *out-of-date*   23. _____

(129) 24. Which of the following statements about propaganda is UNTRUE?

A. Propaganda is often used by political candidates
B. Propaganda is a subtle appeal used in advertising
C. Propaganda is sometimes emotional
D. Propaganda is always evil   24. _____

(129) 25. The appeal of the bandwagon technique in propaganda is

A. a person's desire to belong
B. everyone's secret wish to be deceived
C. the skillful use of rhythm and rhyme
D. stimulation of a sense of humor   25. _____

(130) 26. Two propaganda devices that may be said to be opposed are

A. bandwagon and testimonial
B. name-calling and scientific slant
C. plain folks and snob appeal
D. stereotypes and glittering generalities   26. _____

(137) 27. Frequent use of negative words like *cluttered, sloppy*, and *slipshod* characterize

A. the author's assumptions
B. the author's intention
C. the author's lack of skill
D. the author's lack of interest   27. _____

(139) 28. Though all the following may play a role, the most important purpose in advertising may be linked to

A. the composition to explain
B. the narrative composition
C. the descriptive composition
D. the composition to persuade   28. _____

(140) 29. An author's assumptions

A. are false
B. need critical analysis
C. rarely play a part in writing
D. are immediately apparent   29. _____

(150) 30. Predicting outcomes in a book or movie may be confirmed by

A. a sequel
B. rereading the book or seeing the movie again
C. inspired guessing
D. agreement with a friend's guess   30. _____

Test D

(158–163) 31. Of the following, the one that is NOT listed alphabetically is

A. the index
B. the card catalog
C. the *Readers' Guide*
D. the table of contents   31. _____

(158–160) 32. Which of the following statements about the index is UNTRUE?

A. It lists specific subjects in the book.
B. The first word of each reference is capitalized.
C. It is less detailed than the table of contents.
D. More than one subject may be referred to on a specific page.   32. _____

(160) 33. The card catalog may be called a kind of

A. table of contents
B. encyclopedia
C. index
D. dictionary   33. _____

(162) 34. The *Readers' Guide* is basically an index to

A. biographical literature
B. poetry anthologies
C. detective fiction
D. magazines   34. _____

(164) 35. The dictionary tends to include all the following EXCEPT

A. biographical sketches
B. word origins
C. parts of speech
D. pronunciation   35. _____

(164) 36. The words at the top of a dictionary page

A. emphasize the spelling of difficult words
B. are guides to words on that page
C. provide cross-references to other pages
D. provide a key to illustrations on that page   36. _____

(166–   37. A typical road map contains all the following infor-
167)   mation EXCEPT

    A. mileages between points
    B. route numbers
    C. parkway routes
    D. populations of cities   37. _____

(167)   38. In following a recipe, a cook should

    A. proceed in order
    B. change quantities to experiment
    C. avoid all fats
    D. never use eggs   38. _____

(169)   39. A major reason for using a chart is that

    A. a picture may be worth many words
    B. charts are more accurate than tables of information
    C. everyone can understand a chart
    D. a chart is hard to falsify   39. _____

(170)   40. A good source to check the accuracy of statistics is

    A. a dictionary
    B. the Sunday newspaper
    C. a television quiz show
    D. an almanac   40. _____

Test E

(174)   41. The best source for maps is

    A. a Sunday newspaper
    B. an atlas
    C. a dictionary
    D. the *Readers' Guide*   41. _____

(180)   42. In thinking, reliance upon superstition is an example of

    A. misleading comparisons
    B. jumping to conclusions
    C. mistaking the cause
    D. faulty generalization   42. _____

(181)   43. Making excuses for what one wants to do anyway is
       called

    A. testimonial
    B. name-calling
    C. misleading comparisons
    D. rationalization   43. _____

(186) 44. In the library, a work that is classified as nonfiction is

    A. a historical novel
    B. a biographical novel
    C. a play
    D. a short story   44. _____

(187) 45. A long narrative work of prose fiction is called a

    A. play
    B. biography
    C. short story
    D. novel   45. _____

(187) 46. Television sitcoms (situation comedies) tend to use

    A. highly complex characters
    B. a tested formula
    C. fresh and unfamiliar routines
    D. real-life stories   46. _____

(188–189) 47. The essay is different from the article in that it tends to be more

    A. factual
    B. serious
    C. personal
    D. statistical   47. _____

(189) 48. Both the biography and the autobiography must

    A. select and omit materials
    B. give up the pretense of being reliable
    C. provide a complete, definitive picture of a person
    D. tell only the highlights of a person's life   48. _____

(190) 49. The expression that is often contrasted with *figurative language* is

    A. *body language*
    B. *gestures*
    C. *free verse*
    D. *literal language*   49. _____

(191) 50. Science fiction is often used to

    A. raise important questions about humanity's place and responsibilities
    B. trace historical events through a fictional narrative
    C. glorify great men and women in history
    D. introduce poetry into fiction   50. _____

PART III
Reading Practice Tests

Reading Practice Test 1

Reading Practice Test 1 consists of seven passages (**A** to **G**), together with the questions based upon them.

A. Read the following passage and answer the questions at the end.

A man on a subway car at rush hour discovered a daddy-longlegs tiptoeing up his sleeve. He didn't want it to be harmed, so he covered it with his hat. The insect darted into the interior of the hat, and the man put the hat on his head. He knew that while the daddy-longlegs may not be handsome, it is a fascinating and completely harmless insect.

A daddy-longlegs moves in an unusual way. If you watch one, you will find its movements quite curious. Its legs are like tall, bent stilts, as thin as threads. They look as if they should get tangled, but they all move in perfect harmony.

Although its legs are long, the daddy-longlegs' body is small. It bobs up and down as its legs move. The insect is so light it can dash across water without sinking. Its touch on your skin is so gentle you can scarcely feel it. The daddy-longlegs is well named. If you had such legs in proportion to your body, you would be 40 feet tall!

The insect uses its longest pair of legs to check its surroundings. The daddy-longlegs is constantly checking for food. It prefers plant lice, but it will eat other tiny insects, as well as decaying vegetable matter.

If you pick up a daddy-longlegs by one of its legs, it will struggle wildly. But then it will scurry off, free. You will have a twitching leg in your hand. But don't worry. Although these delicate legs break off easily, new ones always grow back.

1. Write the letter of the statement that best expresses the main idea of the passage.

   (a) The daddy-longlegs is small but very agile.
   (b) Insects are among the most adaptable of all creatures.
   (c) The daddy-longlegs is a fascinating creature to study.
   (d) Though it looks dangerous, the daddy-longlegs is harmless.   1. _____

2. A person built in proportion to a daddy-longlegs would (a) be 40 feet tall (b) grow extra legs (c) never go hungry (d) look quite handsome.   2. _____

3. The diet of the daddy-longlegs can best be described as (a) entirely vegetarian (b) slightly harmful (c) unwholesome (d) varied.   3. _____

4. The purpose of the man on the subway was to (a) amuse his fellow passengers (b) protect the daddy-longlegs (c) take the daddy-longlegs home to his children (d) write an article for a newspaper.   4. _____

5. The author describes the daddy-longlegs (a) affectionately (b) inaccurately (c) excitedly (d) distastefully.   5. _____

6. Which of the following sentences contains a figurative expression?

   (a) He didn't want it to be harmed, so he covered it with his hat.
   (b) The insect darted into the interior of the hat, and the man put the hat on his head.
   (c) Its legs are like tall, bent stilts, as thin as threads.
   (d) But don't worry. Although these delicate legs break off easily, new ones always grow back.   6. _____

7. Which of the following is an opinion?

   (a) A man on a subway car at rush hour discovered a daddy-longlegs tiptoeing up his sleeve.
   (b) It bobs up and down as its legs move.
   (c) The daddy-longlegs is well named.
   (d) It can dash across water without sinking.   7. _____

B. Read the following passage and answer the questions at the end.

Various animals help human beings to survive. Some of these animals are almost unknown, but others are familiar. Everyone knows that bees work hard to make honey. Many people know that bacteria help in cheese making and in fermenting. The plowhorse, camel, and sheepdog are well known, but there are other animal helpers that few people have heard about.

Because animals know by instinct that they have to provide food for the winter months, they hoard food. Many primitive people learned to find and use what these animals hoard. The Eskimos, for example, used to collect roots and tubers from storage chambers that had been dug out by the tunnel vole, a small, mouselike animal. The storage chambers, or caches, were close to the surface of the ground, not far from a vole's grass-lined nest.

Before the first snowfall, the Eskimos would jab the ground with pointed sticks. When the stick went in easily, they knew they had found a cache. One such treasure chamber often provided a peck or more of crisp, fresh roots. The Eskimos ate these roots during the long winter, along with fish and meat, their other winter foods.

A small creature called the bean mouse was important to the Indians of the Missouri River Valley. The bean mice, like the voles, dug storage chambers in which they put beans and wild vegetables. Lewis and Clark, the famous explorers, mentioned a dinner of wild artichokes provided by the Indians. The Indians had gotten their artichokes from the bean mice.

The Indians looked upon these tiny creatures as their friends. Some Indians thought that a one-way "borrowing" from the mice was not right. Women of the Dakota nation would carry a bag of corn with them when they went searching for the mice's underground stores. When the women removed beans, they replaced them with the same amount of corn. By making such an exchange, they felt they were being fair to the mice.

Other animals besides voles and bean mice supplied food. Muskrat caches yielded certain kinds of bulbs. Wood-rat caches gave the Navajos piñon seeds. Honey ants supplied a nectar considered a delicacy by Indians of the American Southwest.

8. Which of the following titles best summarizes the content of the passage?

   (*a*) How the Indians Found Artichokes
   (*b*) All About Animal Ingenuity
   (*c*) How Animals Have Helped People
   (*d*) A True Story About Eskimos and Indians   8. _____

9. In the part they played, the little creatures might be labeled (*a*) hunters (*b*) gatherers (*c*) anglers (*d*) surveyors.   9. _____

10. As used in paragraphs 2 and 3, *cache* means (*a*) hiding place (*b*) hole in the ice (*c*) root (*d*) surprise.   10. _____

11. *Borrowing*, in the fifth paragraph, is put in quotation marks because the borrowing was really (*a*) a temporary loan (*b*) an act of kindness (*c*) a plan to increase the mouse population (*d*) stealing.   11. _____

12. All the following are mentioned as taken from small animals EXCEPT (*a*) roots (*b*) artichokes (*c*) seeds (*d*) corn.   12. _____

13. The author probably considers the information he provides as (*a*) boring (*b*) unimportant (*c*) surprising (*d*) shocking.   13. _____

C. Read the following passage and answer the questions at the end.

When Geraldine Ferraro ran for Vice President of the United States in 1984, she was hailed as a pioneer in the women's rights movement. Exactly one hundred years earlier, however, Belva Ann Lockwood had run for President of the United States. Her party was the National Equal Rights Party. She faced criticism and even ridicule, but she ran again in 1888. At that time, women could not vote, but she won the votes of several thousand American men.

Belva Ann Lockwood spent her life crusading for women's rights. She was born in Royalton, New York, and began teaching school at the age of 15. She received $3 a week, less than half the salary paid to male teachers. When she protested, she was told, "You cannot help yourself, for it is the way of the world." This so angered her that she vowed to devote her life to furthering women's rights.

Between her first teaching assignment and her death at the age of 87, Mrs. Lockwood fought for her cause. After graduating from Geneseo College in upstate New York, she became a school principal. She was paid $400 a year, but the annual salary of her male assistants was much higher.

She went to law school, where the members of her graduating class objected to being graduated with a woman. She was denied her diploma, and had to appeal to President Ulysses S. Grant to get it. In 1874, a court of claims refused to hear a case because she was a woman. She struggled for years to overcome such bias. She finally succeeded.

Her achievements as an attorney were many. She gained passage of a law requiring equal pay for women employees of the federal government. She handled more than 7,000 pension cases. She won a $5 million settlement for the Cherokee Indians against the government. She backed uniform marriage and divorce laws, equal property rights for women, education for all, and world peace.

She did not win all her battles, but when she died in 1917, she had helped bring about many gains. A number of states had already given women the right to vote. In 1920, the 19th Amendment made women's suffrage the law throughout the nation. To honor the memory of Mrs. Lockwood, the U.S. Postal Service in 1986 issued a postage stamp bearing her portrait.

14. Write the letter of the statement that best expresses the main idea of the passage.

   (a) Belva Ann Lockwood ran for President of the United States in 1884.
   (b) Up to 1984, only one woman had ever run for President of the United States.
   (c) Belva Ann Lockwood was a pioneer in the struggle for women's rights.
   (d) The U.S. Postal Service issued a stamp in honor of Belva Ann Lockwood.   14. _____

15. In paragraph 2, the "way of the world" can best be described as (a) really not too common (b) well thought out (c) open-minded (d) unfair.   15. _____

16. Mrs. Lockwood received $3 a week as a (*a*) lawyer (*b*) teacher (*c*) school principal (*d*) student.   16. _____

17. If Mrs. Lockwood had not appealed to President Ulysses S. Grant, she would probably (*a*) have lost her job as school principal (*b*) not have run for President (*c*) have lost the case for the Cherokee Indians (*d*) not have received her diploma.   17. _____

18. Women were given the right to vote anywhere in the United States (*a*) when the Constitution was adopted (*b*) shortly after the birth of Belva Ann Lockwood (*c*) in 1874 (*d*) three years after Belva Ann Lockwood's death.   18. _____

19. As used in paragraph 4, *bias* means (*a*) unfairness (*b*) lack of interest (*c*) enthusiasm (*d*) ingenuity.   19. _____

20. The author's purpose in writing this passage was to (*a*) retell a familiar story (*b*) pay tribute (*c*) criticize men as a group (*d*) explore the meaning of education.   20. _____

D. Read the following passage and answer the questions at the end.

The names of American wildflowers sometimes rival the beauty of the flowers themselves. Who can forget the name *forget-me-not*? Who can help but see the flames dancing in a *fireweed*? These are only two wildflowers among the dozens whose names are as vivid as their colors.

Some of the flower names come from articles of dress. *Dutchman's-breeches, monkshood,* and *lady's slipper* are just three of the items of clothing in this colorful wardrobe of flowers. A *bluebonnet* also belongs in the floral closet.

Then there are names that deal with parts of the body, such as *lady's-thumb, five-fingers,* and *black-eyed Susans.* A deep-pink flower with heart-shaped blossoms is called a *bleeding heart,* just as you might expect. Perhaps all of these could be reflected in a *Venus's-looking-glass.* Not to be forgotten either are the flower names that come from animals and birds. The *cattail, catchfly, bee-blossom, horsemint, lizard's tail, toadflax,* and *wake-robin* are just a few of the names with roots in the animal kingdom.

Many names include objects or people—or both in the same name. *Indian paintbrush, jack-in-the-pulpit,* and *Queen Anne's lace* are among the poetic names that combine a person and an object. Some names, such as *buttercup* and *sunflower,* include only objects.

If you look carefully at the plants bearing these names, you will usually see why the name was applied. A *foxglove* actually looks like a tiny glove that could fit the paw of a fox. A *bluebell* looks exactly like a small bell colored blue. These names and many others are appropriate for the flowers that bear them.

Some of the origins of flower names are not so obvious. To understand the name, you may have to know the history of the word. A *daisy*, for instance, is a "day's eye" in Old English. An *aster* is a "star," a *chrysanthemum* is a "gold flower," and a *heliotrope* is a "sun turner" in Latin and Greek.

These are just a few of the names that cause a person talking about wildflowers to sound poetic. The lovely flowers are matched by the equally delightful names.

21. Which of the following titles best summarizes the content of the passage?

    (*a*) The Poetry of Flower Names
    (*b*) The Beauty of Wildflowers
    (*c*) The Excitement of Language Study
    (*d*) Names from Birds and Animals   21. _____

22. All the following wildflowers are named EXCEPT (*a*) bluebell (*b*) buttercup (*c*) cattail (*d*) organ-pipe cactus.   22. _____

23. "Perhaps all of these could be reflected in a *Venus's-looking-glass*" is intended as (*a*) a touch of humor (*b*) a serious analysis (*c*) unimportant (*d*) a statement of literal truth.   23. _____

24. The "floral closet" in paragraph 2 is (*a*) decorated with many kinds of wallpaper (*b*) not a real closet at all (*c*) a carpenter's nightmare (*d*) constructed principally of oak and maple.   24. _____

25. The figurative expression "roots in the animal kingdom" in paragraph 3 deals with (*a*) gardening (*b*) animal study (*c*) word origins (*d*) biology.   25. _____

26. The author considers the name *foxglove* (*a*) exaggerated (*b*) appropriate (*c*) strange (*d*) repetitious.   26. _____

27. The tone of this passage is (*a*) dull (*b*) argumentative (*c*) enthusiastic (*d*) uncertain.   27. _____

E. Read the following passage and answer the questions at the end.

For nearly half a century, from the 1830's to 1880, the United States Patent Office had a strict rule. It required that a small model of each invention accompany the patent application. These models began to pile up at an alarming rate, and space became a problem. Thousands of models had to be kept somewhere. But where?

Even after 1880, when the model requirement was dropped, the models kept pouring in. By 1895, the Patent Office owned 155,000 of these miniatures. Many of them were put on display as tourist attractions. A large number of the models disappeared over time, although groups of them occasionally turn up at special exhibitions. A few years ago, 500 of them were shown at the Cooper-Hewitt Museum in New York City.

The models tell a fascinating story of American inventiveness. They provide a miniature history of American life as reflected in the material comforts enjoyed by Americans. They give some indication of the difficulties and concerns our ancestors had. One model demonstrates a bedbug trap with a braided mattress from which the pests could easily be dislodged each morning. Another model presents a mattress to be used as a life preserver on a sinking ship. Still another model shows how to lessen the shock of recoil from a naval gun. Even Abraham Lincoln applied for a patent. His device consisted of air chambers to be attached to steamboats. When these air chambers were lowered, they lifted boats off sandbars.

Many inventions related to home life. A Minnesotan invented an early form of the modern egg carton. Another inventor concocted a device for cleaning and renovating feathers, which were often used in women's clothing. Clothespin models abound, as inventor after inventor tried to improve the basic design. One kitchen cabinet had cutaway sides to deprive pests of hiding places. A mechanical creeping doll, operated by clockwork, anticipated the walking dolls of today.

> The ingenuity of the inventors is shown in the construction of the models themselves. Every patent model had to fit into a 12-inch cube. This size restriction held whether the invention was a new mousetrap or an elaborate fire-protection device. Thus, many inventors had to miniaturize their inventions before the applications could be considered.
>
> At first, the patent model requirement seemed like a good idea, but the sheer volume of patent applications eventually made the requirement impractical. Today, only a drawing and a written description have to accompany a patent application.

28. Write the letter of the statement that best expresses the main idea of the passage.

    (*a*) Models submitted to the U.S. Patent Office provide a history of American ingenuity.

    (*b*) The U.S. Patent Office no longer requires working models of patents applied for.

    (*c*) The U.S. Patent Office is an overworked branch of the national government.

    (*d*) The Cooper-Hewitt Museum once ran a display of models submitted to the U.S. Patent Office.   28. _____

29. Models submitted along with patents (*a*) had to be made of wood (*b*) were full-size models (*c*) had to fit into a 12-inch cube (*d*) are displayed in the Smithsonian Institution.   29. _____

30. The passage suggests that (*a*) Abraham Lincoln's idea was impractical (*b*) insect pests have long been a problem (*c*) most of the models didn't work (*d*) most patents helped the farmer more than the factory worker.   30. _____

31. From paragraph 5, we may infer that the patent application of an inventor who submitted a two-foot-long model would be (*a*) processed quickly (*b*) processed slowly (*c*) accepted (*d*) rejected.   31. _____

32. As used in paragraph 3, *recoil* means (*a*) kickback (*b*) noise (*c*) bright flash (*d*) failure.   32. _____

33. As used in paragraph 4, *concocted* means (*a*) imitated (*b*) cooked (*c*) rejected (*d*) put together.   33. _____

34. Which of the following contains a figurative expression?

   (*a*) Thousands of models had to be kept somewhere.
   (*b*) Even after 1880, when the model requirement was dropped, the models kept pouring in.
   (*c*) A large number of the models disappeared over time.
   (*d*) A Minnesotan invented an early form of the modern egg carton.   34. _____

35. The author's purpose is to (*a*) criticize the methods of the U.S. Patent Office (*b*) study the origins of the U.S. Patent Office (*c*) provide information (*d*) encourage young inventors to try their luck.   35. _____

F. Read the following passage and answer the questions at the end.

When you wear cap and gown at your high school graduation, you will be following a custom that is many centuries old. Although high school graduates have worn caps and gowns only since 1908, the use of caps and gowns in colleges and universities goes back to medieval times. These garments had their origin in the common style of dress in the late Middle Ages and Renaissance.

Nearly all gowns are made of black cloth. Some doctoral gowns use other colors, but the vast majority are black. Different degrees, schools, and areas of study are indicated by either the shape of the sleeves or the color on the hoods of the gowns.

The gowns for high school graduates have short, full sleeves. For the bachelor's degree in college, the gowns have pointed sleeves that extend halfway to the hem of the garment. The gowns for the master's degree have oblong sleeves with a long, narrow pouch cut out of the cloth. The gowns for various doctors' degrees have full bell-shaped sleeves with three bars of black velvet. The sleeves thus provide important clues to the degree being conferred.

Colors on the hoods tell something more about the candidate. The colors on a doctor's hood show the subject of the candidate's study and the school from which he or she is graduating. In the United States, if the hood's velvet facing is green, the degree is in medicine. Doctorates in philosophy call for dark blue. Orange indicates engineering, yellow means science, and so on. The color of the hood's inner lining identifies the school (such as School of Business or School of Agriculture).

The cap began to appear in the 16th century. At Scottish universities, it was called the *John Knox cap*. The familiar term *mortarboard* can be traced back only to 1854. Up to the present day, there has been no agreement—in fact, there have been many disagreements—about what to do with the tassel on the cap. Some people have said that tradition requires the tassel to be worn on the right side of the cap as candidates begin the ceremonies. The tassel is then moved to the left side when the degree is actually conferred. American college officials met in 1895 and again in 1932 partly to settle how the tassel should be worn. Their conclusion both times was that the right-to-left procedure had ''no warrant in precedent or in common sense.''

Sometimes restrictions have had to be placed on caps and gowns. In 1314 at the University of Toulouse, academic gowns and hoods had to be regulated. Students were spending great sums of money to make these garments beautiful. Competition had become so keen that education was affected. Tailors were getting rich producing ever more elegant gowns, while some impoverished scholars were leaving school in despair. The university set a price limit for gowns, thereby establishing a necessary early dress code.

36. Which of the following titles best summarizes the content of the passage?

    (a) What Academic Gowns Mean
    (b) The Meaning of the Cap and Tassel
    (c) The Story of Caps and Gowns
    (d) The History of College Graduations   36. _____

37. The introduction of caps and gowns for high school graduations can be traced back to (a) 1314 (b) 1895 (c) 1908 (d) 1932.   37. _____

38. When the university officials set a price limit for gowns, they were acting (a) hastily (b) thoughtlessly (c) wisely (d) strangely.   38. _____

39. The color orange on a gown indicates (a) science (b) medicine (c) philosophy (d) engineering.   39. _____

40. A person wearing a gown that had bell-shaped sleeves with three bars of black velvet would be getting a (a) high school diploma (b) bachelor's degree (c) master's degree (d) doctor's degree.   40. _____

41. For most of those wearing it, the gown is probably a source of (a) pride for an achievement (b) irritation at a useless expense (c) amusement at the display (d) bitter disappointment.   41. _____

42. As used in paragraph 5, *precedent* means (*a*) common law
(*b*) previous custom (*c*) effective action (*d*) controlled expense. 42. _____

43. As used in paragraph 6, *impoverished* means (*a*) uncooperative
(*b*) poor (*c*) outstanding (*d*) consenting. 43. _____

G. Read the following passage and answer the questions at the end.

According to some experts, the game of chess was in existence long before the earliest archaeological finds. The origins are lost in legend and myth, surrounded by fairy tales and the power of magic. In all probability, chess began in the Orient, most likely in India. Early Persian and Arabic writings contain evidence for this theory of the origin of the game.

Chess spread to the West by way of Persia, along with the *Arabian Nights*. The influence of the Orient can be seen in the terms of chess. *Rook*, *check*, and *checkmate*, for example, all have Oriental roots. The word *check* comes from the word *shah*, for "king." On the chessboard, when the king (shah) is put in danger, he is *mated*, which can mean either "dead" or "helpless." The game is over when the king is checkmated. *Checkmate* means that the king is trapped, unable to escape.

A thousand years ago, the Persian poet Firdausi described the line of battle between two armies. The armies consisted of chess pieces. In Firdausi's vivid description, which follows, the modern name for each chess piece is put in parentheses.

"Ready for battle, the king stood in the center. On one side was the counsellor (queen). Close to the king on both sides were two elephants (bishops), casting a shadow as dark as indigo about the throne. Two camels (knights) were placed next to the elephants, and two men of fast intent were mounted on them. Next to the camels were two horses with their riders (rooks), ready to fight on the day of battle. As warriors, these two Rukhs (rooks) at the ends of the line of battle raised their empty hands to their lips as if to drink their enemies' blood. In front moved the foot soldiers (pawns) who were to come to the assistance of the others in the battle."

Firdausi tells about a foot soldier who fought desperately through the battle line to the very side of the opposing king. This brave soldier was raised to the rank of counsellor. Nowadays we say that such a pawn is "queened."

We also learn that when the king is surrounded on all sides, with his army destroyed, he dies. That is to say, he is checkmated.

The description of the "battle" sounds very much like a modern chess game on a 64-square board. Though the game has had many modifications and variations, it is still a war game in which opposing armies attack and attempt to destroy the "enemy." But in this kind of war, the combat is mental, and the results are not fatal.

44. Which of the following titles best summarizes the content of the passage?

  (a) The Meaning of *Checkmate*
  (b) An Exciting and Challenging Board Game
  (c) The Naming of the Chess Pieces
  (d) Chess: An Ancient Substitute for Battle   44. _____

45. Firdausi was a (a) chess master (b) king of Persia (c) poet (d) warrior.   45. _____

46. A pawn that reaches the last row on the chessboard is said to be (a) trapped (b) queened (c) mated (d) captured.   46. _____

47. The major goal of a chess player is to (a) checkmate the king (b) capture the queen (c) surround both knights and bishops (d) capture all the opponents' pieces.   47. _____

48. The lengthy quotation (paragraph 4) is included to (a) show the similarity between chess and battle (b) explain how the knights got their name (c) add a light touch to the passage (d) suggest the origin of the word *chess*.   48. _____

49. Which of the following contains the best example of figurative language?

  (a) In all probability, chess began in the Orient.
  (b) According to some experts, the game of chess was in existence long before the earliest archaeological finds.
  (c) The word *check* comes from the word *shah*, for "king."
  (d) It is still a war game in which opposing armies attack and attempt to destroy the "enemy."   49. _____

50. The attitude of the author toward chess is one of (a) polite indifference (b) vigorous opposition (c) informed interest (d) unrestrained enthusiasm.   50. _____

END OF READING PRACTICE TEST 1

Reading Practice Test 2

Reading Practice Test 2 consists of seven passages (**A** to **G**), together with the questions based upon them.

A. Read the following passage and answer the questions at the end.

What urge prompts nearly everyone to collect something? Stamps, coins, matchboxes, spoons, antiques—all these have their supporters. One of the most interesting collecting areas is that of baseball cards. These pictures of major-league baseball players are a big business. Sold by one company with chewing gum and by others without any other product, they have fascinated collectors for generations.

Some of the older cards bring high prices. A Mickey Mantle card from 1951, for example, may bring a thousand dollars or more, depending on its condition. The physical condition and appearance of a card make a difference in price. Worn corners, creases, tears, and pinholes can drastically reduce a card's value. For this reason, many collectors keep their cards in protective vinyl sheets or in specially designed boxes.

Older cards, like those for Roberto Clemente and Willie Mays, are fairly stable in value. The cards of more recent players fluctuate in value as the baseball fortunes of the stars go up and down. A player in his first, or rookie, year may become an overnight sensation. His card may rise dramatically in value. But if he has a bad second year, the value of his card may drop equally dramatically. On the other hand, if a player is inducted into the Baseball Hall of Fame, the value of his card is secure.

Who are these baseball-card collectors? They seem to fall into two major groups—young people and those in their thirties and forties. Young people enjoy the excitement of the chase—and they can start collecting new cards for relatively little money. The second group is attracted by nostalgia, as they think back to their youth. Collectors in the second group have more money than those in the first. They are able to bid up the value of cards of old-timers like Hank Aaron and Roger Maris.

Card values are unpredictable. In 1977, one store-keeper sold cards of three rookies for the same price. Ten years later, the cards for Mark Fidrych and Gary Templeton were worth much less than the original purchase price, but the card for Dale Murphy had become a collector's item. Location is another factor in price. The card for a Cincinnati player will be worth more in Cincinnati than in Oakland.

Some collectors worry that the baseball-card bubble may burst. Like other fads, it may drop in popularity. But there will always be a hard-core group of collectors who cherish an Ernie Banks card from 1954.

1. Which of the following titles best summarizes the content of the passage?

   (a) Collecting Baseball Cards
   (b) An Excellent Investment
   (c) A Hobby for Everyone at Any Age
   (d) How Hobbies Bring Relaxation   1. _____

2. All the following are mentioned as collectible items EXCEPT
   (a) antiques (b) spoons (c) coins (d) books.   2. _____

3. The most valuable card mentioned was that for (a) Hank Aaron (b) Roberto Clemente (c) Mickey Mantle (d) Roger Maris.   3. _____

4. The date associated with Ernie Banks is (a) 1951 (b) 1954 (c) 1977 (d) not given.   4. _____

5. From the report in paragraph 5, we may infer that (a) Gary Templeton became a superstar (b) Cincinnati card collectors are wealthy (c) even a star's popularity seldom lasts longer than a year (d) Dale Murphy has had a successful career.   5. _____

6. As used in paragraph 3, *fluctuate* means (a) increase in value (b) decrease in value (c) go up and down in value (d) stay the same.   6. _____

7. As used in paragraph 4, *nostalgia* means (a) yearning for past times (b) greed for easy money (c) changing fashion (d) the challenge of the chase.   7. _____

8. The author of this passage (a) thinks collectors are fools (b) shows a lively interest in card collecting (c) fails to mention the dangers of collecting baseball cards (d) probably has a complete set of all baseball cards printed since 1951.   8. _____

B. Read the following passage and answer the questions at the end.

One of the world's great success stories is the popularity surge of the microwave oven. Just a few short years ago, the microwave was a curiosity. "Who needs an extra oven?" was the usual reaction to any sales promoting the microwave. But the microwave is truly a remarkable appliance. Suddenly, sales took off.

In 1980, only 19% of all U.S. households had microwave ovens. Seven years later, the percentage of microwave owners had jumped to nearly 50%. What was once considered a luxury had suddenly become a necessity. Why?

Consider these disadvantages. Sometimes food seems to heat unevenly in a microwave. A dish that has been frozen may be hot on the inside, cold on the outside. Or it may have hot and cold sections side by side. Pie crusts may be soggy. Foods may look unappetizing. Complicated cooking tasks may be beyond the capacity of the microwave. True gourmet cooking is very difficult. Why bother with a microwave?

There are many important advantages when owners learn how to use microwaves efficiently. There is nothing better for heating leftovers than a microwave. Meat can be quickly defrosted in a microwave and then cooked by other means, if necessary. Commercially prepared foods especially designed for the microwave can be brought to the table in minutes. For many busy people, this advantage alone makes the microwave a much-appreciated appliance.

Few foods cook equally well in both conventional and microwave ovens. The old familiar oven uses dry heat to cook from the outside. The microwave generates heat through electromagnetic energy that stirs up water molecules. Since it acts almost like a steamer, foods that respond to steaming do especially well in the microwave. Vegetables, for example, which contain much water, are ideal for microwave cooking.

The growing popularity of the microwave has stimulated interest in food prepared especially for the microwave. "Shelf-stable" meals, which can survive long periods without refrigeration, are especially well suited for the microwave. Large food processors are spending fortunes on research for these convenience foods.

> The microwave is the perfect oven for modern times. Working people welcome the speed and convenience of foods prepared for the microwave. And they don't spend precious time later cleaning greasy pans and pots with burnt food. The microwave is here to stay.

9. Write the letter of the statement that best expresses the main idea of the passage.

   (*a*) Microwave ovens are important appliances in modern kitchens.
   (*b*) Microwave ovens are significantly better than conventional ones.
   (*c*) Microwave ovens use only foods specially designed for them.
   (*d*) Microwave ovens have advantages and disadvantages.   9. _____

10. Microwave ovens generate heat by (*a*) natural gas (*b*) electromagnetic energy (*c*) external steam pressure (*d*) the evaporation of water.   10. _____

11. The microwave is especially well suited for (*a*) pie crusts (*b*) desserts (*c*) pancakes (*d*) vegetables.   11. _____

12. One of the most important advantages of the microwave can be summarized in the word (*a*) *economy* (*b*) *space* (*c*) *convenience* (*d*) *durability*.   12. _____

13. Which of the following statements contains the best example of figurative language?

    (*a*) There are disadvantages.
    (*b*) Suddenly, sales took off.
    (*c*) Old-fashioned ovens use dry heat to cook from the outside.
    (*d*) Few foods cook equally well in both conventional and microwave ovens.   13. _____

14. Which of the following is an opinion?

    (*a*) The microwave is a remarkable appliance.
    (*b*) Meat can quickly be defrosted in a microwave.
    (*c*) Large food processors are spending money on research for convenience foods.
    (*d*) A dish that has been frozen may be hot on the inside, cold on the outside.   14. _____

C. Read the following passage and answer the questions at the end.

Fifty million and more years ago, dinosaurs ruled the land. Tyrannosaurus rex and his huge relatives dominated the landscape. These giant "lizards" capture the imagination of all who see the huge skeletons assembled in museums throughout the world. Movies especially enjoy showing human hunters being attacked by one of the meat-eating carnivores—even though dinosaurs disappeared long before there were any human beings to fear them.

Yet all people, with a little imagination, can see a living dinosaur. The alligator, a modern "dinosaur" of the reptile family, suggests how the long-extinct creatures looked and acted. The alligator of the Southeastern United States is truly a fascinating creature from the past.

The American alligator, though worthy of respect, is not as viciously aggressive as the crocodile of Africa and Asia. In the United States, the number of deaths from alligators is low. Alligators do seek to eat a wide variety of foods: fish, turtles, water birds, raccoons, snakes, and possums. They occasionally also take calves, hogs, young deer, and even careless household pets. When one Florida gator was killed, its stomach held a dog tag with this poignant message: "My name is Blackie. Leave me alone and I'll go home."

Once an alligator reaches adulthood, it has little trouble surviving—if it can elude a human hunter. But baby alligators are extremely vulnerable. Though they grow a foot a year for the first five years, this growing period is threatened by herons, snakes, turtles, raccoons, even other gators.

Once on the endangered-species list, alligators have recovered and now exist in substantial numbers. They wander about at will, sometimes blocking busy roadways, resting on golf courses, and even enjoying private swimming pools. Then officials must arrange to trap and remove the intruders. These alligator experts go about their task very warily, for the alligator's jaws may crunch with a pressure of 1200 pounds per square inch. Oddly enough, though, the alligator's ability to open its jaws is limited. A person of ordinary strength (and extraordinary nerve) can hold the jaws closed with one hand.

One of the oddest things about an alligator is the determination of its sex. During the first two or three weeks of an alligator's life, the temperature determines whether the alligator is to be a male or a female. At an average reading of 86 degrees Fahrenheit, all the alligators will be female. At 93 and above, all the young will be males. Temperatures between 86 and 93 produce a mixture of males and females.

Though a human adult is too large for an alligator to swallow, young children should be carefully protected. For the most part, the alligator minds its business and concentrates on its varied nonhuman diet. Still, the experts recommend extreme care in the presence of this living fossil.

15. Which of the following titles best summarizes the content of the passage?

   (a) How Dinosaurs Became Alligators
   (b) Masters of Their Environment
   (c) The Fascinating American Alligator
   (d) How Alligators Differ from Crocodiles   15. _____

16. All the following are mentioned as part of an alligator's diet EXCEPT (a) deer (b) goat (c) opossum (d) water bird.   16. _____

17. Which of the following describes a scene that would be impossible now or in the past?

   (a) An alligator attacks and eats a calf.
   (b) A young male alligator survives in 95-degree temperatures.
   (c) A human family is attacked by a dinosaur.
   (d) A Tyrannosaurus rex attacks another dinosaur.   17. _____

18. In paragraph 2, *dinosaur* is in quotation marks because (a) much has been written about dinosaurs (b) alligators merely resemble dinosaurs (c) alligators are indeed dinosaurs (d) the author of the passage wished to show a knowledge of natural history.   18. _____

19. We may assume that only a small percentage of baby alligators (a) survive to adulthood (b) are eaten by other creatures (c) become females (d) become males.   19. _____

20. As used in paragraph 3, *poignant* means (a) informative (b) complicated (c) confusing (d) sad.   20. _____

21. As used in paragraph 4, *vulnerable* means (a) aggressive (b) tame (c) interesting to observe (d) easily hurt.   21. _____

D. Read the following passage and answer the questions at the end.

Once upon a time, purchasers paid for merchandise with cash or a check. Then along came the credit card, allowing them to defer payment and to take out a loan for the amount, if they wished. The idea took hold, and the number of credit cards increased rapidly, actually doubling in a short six-year period between 1980 and 1986. During that same period, the population of the United States increased only 6%. Within another year, there were more than 800 million credit cards in circulation.

Growth goes merrily on. Though thousands of American consumers are trying to reduce their credit-card debts, they are tempted to take out more credit cards as the enticing offers arrive in the mails. There is a major disadvantage in having credit-card debt. At one time, the interest paid on consumer debts could be deducted in full for income-tax purposes. But a new tax-reform bill gradually eliminated those deductions, making borrowing more expensive than ever. Some consumers tried to reduce their debts accordingly, but others disregarded the expense and went on borrowing.

Of course, if bills are paid in full each month, there are no interest charges. For those who pay in full, there are two advantages: the convenience of not having to carry a great deal of cash and the use of money for a period without paying interest. An appliance may be bought on the first of the month, but the bill may not have to be paid until a month later. This period, called the "float," is not only interest free. It also preserves the purchaser's own interest during that period, for money need not be withdrawn from the bank until the credit-card statement comes through.

Why do issuers of credit cards permit this generous situation? Even if bills are paid promptly, the issuer has another source of income: a percentage charged to the store for every purchase made. Why do stores want credit cards if they have to pay a percentage on every purchase? Credit cards increase store sales. People are more willing to buy something if they don't have to pay cash on the spot. Buying a refrigerator, for example, is "painless." The money doesn't have to be supplied at once. Stores are paid by the credit-card issuer—minus a percentage, of course. Collecting the money becomes the problem of the issuer. The second advantage for the credit-card issuer is collecting interest on any unpaid balance. Then regular monthly payments are necessary because a great many consumers do *not* pay their bills in full each month.

Credit-card issuers prefer card holders in the 35-to-54 age group. Though families in that age group represent only 35% of all households, they are responsible for 47% of all credit-card debt. Many of these families are raising children—always an expensive burden. The issuers welcome ''revolvers,'' people who always make a payment each month but never pay off their debts as they buy more and more things.

Credit cards can be a marvelous convenience in a great many ways, but they can be an attractive danger to those who cannot curtail their spending. Credit-card debt can be compared with carrying a 60-pound backpack up a mountain trail. Credit cards should be used wisely.

22. Write the letter of the statement that best expresses the main idea of the selection.

    (*a*) Credit cards have attractive advantages and some possibly serious disadvantages.
    (*b*) People in the 35–54 age group hold the most debt.
    (*c*) Credit cards are a recent addition to people's purchasing power.
    (*d*) Consumers have many credit agencies to choose from.   22. _____

23. The period during which the United States population gained 6% was for a span of (*a*) a year (*b*) six years (*c*) twenty years (*d*) time not actually specified.   23. _____

24. The ''float'' (*a*) is a monthly statement (*b*) is the price paid for a stock (*c*) saves interest (*d*) is not used in credit cards.   24. _____

25. In paragraph 4, *painless* is in quotation marks because (*a*) refrigerators are always bought on time (*b*) payment is put off till later (*c*) salespersons are especially keen on selling refrigerators (*d*) some credit cards do not require a fee.   25. _____

26. In paragraph 1, *defer* means (*a*) demand (*b*) overlook (*c*) put off (*d*) make a record of.   26. _____

27. In paragraph 2, *enticing* means (*a*) frequently arriving (*b*) unreliable (*c*) ingenious (*d*) tempting.   27. _____

28. In the final paragraph, *curtail* means (a) reduce (b) analyze
    (c) enjoy (d) increase.   28. _____

29. In the next-to-the-last sentence, the author suggests that credit-
    card debt perhaps should be (a) encouraged (b) studied
    (c) reduced (d) increased.   29. _____

E. Read the following passage and answer the questions at the end.

Our alphabet is a genuine miracle that people take for granted. Many languages have no written form at all. Of the languages that do, not all of them have an alphabet. The alphabet is a great invention, though, because it allows so much flexibility. There is no question that languages with alphabets have advantages over languages that do not.

When the cave dweller drew a picture of an animal on the cave wall, the picture had meaning. It communicated something. This use of pictures to carry a message is an early form of pictographic writing. Originally, a picture of the sun looked like the sun, but, as time went on, the pictures became more stylized. They began to look less like realistic pictures and more like some form of writing. Among modern written languages, Chinese is basically pictographic. All those exotic-looking symbols in Chinese came originally from pictures.

Pictographic systems have an advantage where the spoken languages vary widely, as in China. The forms of spoken Chinese differ from one part of the country to another. These speakers can all understand the same writing, however, since the pictographs mean the same thing to all readers. The differences in sound do not affect reading or writing.

To express more than simple thoughts, pictographic writing can become inadequate. For that reason, pictographic languages usually develop ideograms. If pictographs are "written pictures," then ideograms are "written ideas." Ideograms are often formed from pictographs. The Chinese, for example, combine the symbols for *sun* and *moon* to mean *light*.

International traffic signals are pictographic or ideographic. They are universal, even though languages differ. When an American driving in Europe sees a certain symbol, he says to himself, "Hospital." An

Italian seeing the same symbol says, "Ospedale." The German sees it and says, "Krankenhaus." A French person sees it and says, "Hôpital." The words do not sound alike, but the symbol is recognizably the same.

The great advantages of an alphabet come from its relative simplicity. The Chinese use more than 50,000 separate symbols in their writing system. We use 26 letters. Those 26 letters will form any of the hundreds of thousands of words in the language. Of course, you must learn how these 26 letters are put together to form words, but all words use the same ingredients.

Typewriters can be simple and compact with a 26-letter alphabet. With Chinese pictographs and ideographs, however, a small, simple typewriter is impossible. Think, too, how hard it would be to find words in a dictionary without the advantage of alphabetical order. All in all, the invention of the alphabet was a landmark event in the history of language.

30. Which of the following titles best summarizes the content of the passage?

    (*a*) Pictographs: The Origin of Writing
    (*b*) The Alphabet: A True Miracle
    (*c*) The Differences Between Ideograms and Alphabets
    (*d*) Chinese and English: A Contrast   30. _____

31. The word for *hospital* is presented in each of the following languages EXCEPT (*a*) French (*b*) Italian (*c*) German (*d*) Chinese.   31. _____

32. In their ability to construct complicated words, the letters of the alphabet can be compared with (*a*) pictographs (*b*) building blocks (*c*) sun symbols (*d*) traffic signals.   32. _____

33. The earliest form of writing was probably (*a*) pictographic (*b*) ideographic (*c*) alphabetic (*d*) phonetic.   33. _____

34. When the Chinese combined the symbols for *sun* and *moon* to mean *light*, the result was both ideographic and (*a*) humorous (*b*) literal (*c*) ineffective (*d*) figurative.   34. _____

35. Which of the following is an opinion?

    (*a*) Our alphabet is a genuine miracle that people take for granted.
    (*b*) Many languages have no written form at all.
    (*c*) It communicated something.
    (*d*) Of course, you must learn how these 26 letters are put together to form words.   35. _____

36. The author's attitude toward the alphabet is one of (*a*) polite indifference (*b*) moderate interest (*c*) great respect (*d*) slight disapproval.   36. _____

F. Read the following passage and answer the questions at the end.

Collecting Roman coins is an exciting hobby, for the coins are still available and are of great interest historically. Although prices have risen in the past few years, many bronze coins from ancient Rome are still within the reach of the average collector. The reason is simple: they exist in substantial numbers.

Some of the most plentiful coins come from the reigns of lesser-known emperors. Times were often hard under those emperors, and coinage was debased. Gold and silver were not available in sufficient quantity, so cheaper metals were used. A great many coins were minted to pay the salaries of Roman soldiers. These cheaper coins, buried centuries ago for safekeeping, still turn up now and then in the countries that were once part of the Roman Empire.

Roman coins are a lesson in history. The coins usually have a bust of the emperor on the front, or obverse, of the coin. The reverse of the coin may show conquests, architectural achievements, or purely symbolic features. Every emperor proudly advertised his own successes.

In periods when several men shared power, the coins reflect that fact, carrying the image of each of the leaders. The coinage indicates clearly when the Empire was divided into eastern and western halves. In 364, Valens ruled the eastern half and Valentinian I the western half. The eastern half continued to exist for a thousand years after the western half fell. Coinage tells that story, too.

There is another special feature of Roman coins that sets them apart from the coinage of most other nations. The portraits of the emperors are realistic, with all the warts in place. Many emperors were brutal, hard-living men who destroyed everything and everyone who stood in their way. The coins show these tough, often homely men just as they were, no attempt having been made to have them look heroic.

There were exceptions, of course. Not all the emperors were coarse and unattractive. Marcus Aurelius was a rather handsome man, and the coins show it. His portraits are realistic, though, not glorified. The coins portray Marcus Aurelius at various stages in his life: as a beardless young man, a bearded middle-aged man, and an older man.

Roman coinage has another distinctive feature. Women who were not themselves leaders are pictured on coins. Wives and mothers of the powerful emperors, for example, appear occasionally. Modern students of fashion find these coins especially interesting, for they reflect the changing tastes and styles of that era, especially changing hairdos. Like other Roman coins, they are fascinating bits of history and excellent reflections of character.

37. Write the letter of the statement that best expresses the main idea of the passage.

   (a) The lesser-known Roman emperors minted many coins.
   (b) Some Roman coins are relatively inexpensive.
   (c) Roman soldiers were often paid in cheaper, less valuable coins.
   (d) Roman coins provide lessons in both history and art.   37. _____

38. The most readily available Roman coins were minted in (a) iron (b) bronze (c) silver (d) gold.   38. _____

39. The year 364 is mentioned because (a) Rome had been overrun (b) Rome changed from an empire to a republic (c) there were two emperors (d) Marcus Aurelius was the outstanding emperor.   39. _____

40. The likenesses of emperors on coins suggest that the emperors (a) were not vain (b) were generous rulers (c) were influenced by their wives (d) insisted upon idealized portraits.   40. _____

41. As used in paragraph 1, *substantial* means (*a*) limited (*b*) uncontrolled (*c*) large (*d*) varying.   41. _____

42. As used in paragraph 2, *debased* means (*a*) increased (*b*) reduced (*c*) lowered in quality (*d*) slightly improved.   42. _____

43. The author's attitude toward the emperor Marcus Aurelius is (*a*) doubtful (*b*) hostile (*c*) unusual (*d*) favorable.   43. _____

G. Read the following passage and answer the questions at the end.

A profound truth about language is contained in the statement that ''words by themselves have no meanings.'' People sometimes overlook that truth. They tend to mistake the word for the thing itself. They imagine that there is one ''right'' word for a given idea, action, or object.

But words mean only what people agree they should mean, and no more. The word *snake* may cause shudders even if the creature is absent, but it is only a word. The word *steak* may cause mouths to water, but the word is not the thing. People are responding to certain sounds or to a few ink spots on a page, not the actual object that is a snake or a steak.

If a small child calls her highchair a *chy*, is *chy* a word? Three other questions will help to provide an answer. Does *chy* play a role in the life of the child? Does *chy* stand for a particular object in the child's environment? Do the child's parents understand what is meant by *chy*? Since the answer to all three questions is ''Yes,'' *chy* qualifies as a word. However, it is a word of very limited use. It will not appear in any dictionary, in any magazine or newspaper, or in any news report. In a practical sense, *chy* does not function as the kind of word we mean when we say *word*. It is a genuine word, but one that very few people use.

Older children sometimes make up special words to communicate with their friends. Just as the small child created *chy* to mean ''highchair,'' older children invent words for certain objects or ideas. They then send messages in a kind of code. These children have coined new words that perform all the functions that words should perform. Of course, outsiders are confused when confronted by these words. They don't know the code— just as you probably don't know the code when faced with the language of the Finns or the Watusi.

Language is a contract. Words mean only what people agree they should mean. Travelers abroad soon find out that the contract they are familiar with—the English language—is not in force in many countries of the world. English, for example, is not the principal language of Hungary. Hungarians have a different contract, one that is understandable to even a small Hungarian child but a mystery to most American tourists.

The contractual nature of language is apparent in matters of usage. "It don't mean nothing" conveys meaning, but the English contract prefers "It doesn't mean anything." The majority of literate people have decided that certain ways of using English words are preferable to other ways. This general agreement about English usage is another part of the language contract.

44. Write the letter of the statement that best expresses the main idea of the passage.

   (a) Children often develop special languages all their own.
   (b) Language is basically a contract accepted by users of a language.
   (c) A Hungarian child understands a language that baffles American adults.
   (d) Language is a mysterious creation, a miracle of communication.   44. _____

45. The passage suggests that *chy* (a) appears in slang dictionaries (b) is actually a word (c) is taken from the Watusi language (d) is as generally useful a word as *steak*.   45. _____

46. Children invent codes to (a) speak faster (b) write more easily (c) keep secrets (d) annoy their closest friends.   46. _____

47. The article suggests that (a) there is no *right* word for an object (b) the word for *steak* is actually better than the word for *snake* (c) young children communicate very poorly (d) Hungarian children have a great deal of trouble learning their language. 47. _____

48. In paragraph 4, *confronted* means (a) tricked (b) puzzled (c) faced (d) angered.   48. _____

49. Which of the following is an example of figurative language?

    (a) The word is not the thing.
    (b) Do the child's parents understand what is meant by *chy*?
    (c) Hungarians have a different contract.
    (d) English, for example, is not the principal language of Hungary.   49. _____

50. The author of the passage assumes that the reader (a) has learned at least one foreign language (b) has some interest in the subject of language (c) realizes that words do have meanings in themselves (d) is a teacher of English.   50. _____

END OF READING PRACTICE TEST 2

Reading Practice Test 3

Reading Practice Test 3 consists of seven passages (**A** to **G**), together with the questions based upon them.

A. Read the following passage and answer the questions at the end.

One of the most picturesque scenes on a sheep or goat ranch is that of a dog herding and protecting the animals. From ancient times, dogs have been trained to work with domestic animals to keep them from harm. In Texas, a new guardian has been pressed into service—the donkey.

When Perry Bushong of Mountain Home, Texas, paid good money for ten donkeys, his friends laughed and said he had made a big mistake. Perry sent the donkeys out to guard his Rambouillet sheep and Angora goats. The donkeys turned out to be effective guardians, and the other ranchers were impressed. They started buying donkeys for their own herds. The price of donkeys doubled, as each rancher tried to obtain this new kind of protector.

Why are donkeys so good at their job? For one thing, they don't like coyotes at all, and coyotes are the most dangerous predators to sheep and goats. According to Eddie Tom, who raises donkeys, "You get them riled, they'll throw their ears back, start kicking with their front feet, and throw a fit. I've seen one of those jennies go after a coyote like she wanted to kill it." The donkey's loud cry, or bray, also frightens the coyotes.

The donkeys, like sheepdogs, must be trained for their job. Only female donkeys, or jennies, can be used, because the males can be just too mean. The young donkeys are raised with the herd of sheep or goats. After a while, a donkey seems to think it *is* a sheep or goat. It will graze, feed, and sleep with the herd. Most important, it will protect them as it would its own young.

The year before trying out the guard donkeys, Perry Bushong lost about 250 sheep and goats to coyotes. Losses as serious as that could easily bankrupt a rancher. Since using the donkeys, he has lost almost no animals. Other ranchers have had the same results. A herd of sheep may look more romantic with a faithful sheepdog in the picture, but those donkeys seem to be doing the job very well.

1. Write the letter of the statement that best expresses the main idea of the passage.

   (a) Donkeys can be effective guardians of sheep and goat herds.
   (b) Female donkeys are better at guard duty than male donkeys.
   (c) Coyotes are the principal enemy of sheep herders.
   (d) Strange and unlikely ideas usually work.   1. _____

2. All the following animals were named EXCEPT (a) sheep (b) dogs (c) coyotes (d) wolves.   2. _____

3. *Mountain Home* is the name of a (a) dude ranch (b) large house (c) Texas river (d) town.   3. _____

4. Perry Bushong's friends laughed at him because he (a) disagreed with Eddie Tom (b) tried a wholly new idea (c) used male donkeys for guard duty (d) raises donkeys as well as sheep and goats.   4. _____

5. As used in paragraph 3, *predators* means (a) sheepdogs (b) male donkeys with a vicious temper (c) animals who prey on others (d) a special variety of Angora goat.   5. _____

6. The passage suggests that a jenny is (a) unpopular with sheep and goats (b) more than a match for a coyote (c) less manageable than a male donkey (d) not a favorite of Perry Bushong.   6. _____

7. The attitude of the author toward donkeys is one of (a) faint disapproval (b) lack of interest (c) affection (d) excessive enthusiasm.   7. _____

   B. Read the following passage and answer the questions at the end.

   Young people know Benjamin Franklin as one of the nation's Founding Fathers. He helped draft the Declaration of Independence. A thoughtful philosopher, Franklin coined the idea in "We hold these truths to be self-evident." But there was much more to him than the familiar textbook biography reveals.

   Benjamin Franklin was a problem-solver. He liked to take large, sometimes fuzzy, scientific theories and turn them to practical use. Everyone knows Franklin's famous experiment with a kite and electricity, but few people know that he used electricity to roast turkeys. He invented the lightning rod that protects modern houses. He designed the Franklin stove, which even today is a model of wood-burning efficiency. These inventions show just one aspect of Franklin's wide-ranging interests.

His curiosity about nature prompted him to study weather. He predicted storms. He studied eclipses, waterspouts, thunderstorms, and the northern lights. He was fascinated by the wandering Gulf Stream and was the first person to try to map its winding course. In his spare time, he studied fossils, marsh gas, smallpox, and sunspots. He was interested in hot air balloons and in reforming English spelling. His interests were extremely varied.

Franklin began his own printing firm in Philadelphia when he was 22. He wrote and published *Poor Richard's Almanack*. In this book, he included many sayings that are still quoted today: "Remember that time is money." "Experience keeps a dear school, but fools will learn in no other." "When the well's dry, we know the worth of water." The *Almanack* sold 10,000 copies a year at a time when Philadelphia's population was only 20,000

Franklin was concerned with virtue and morality, too. In his *Autobiography*, he described a plan for making himself perfect. He listed the virtues that he hoped to achieve and then explained how he went about working on each one in turn. He never attained perfection, of course, but in many ways he came closer to it than most people do.

8. Which of the following titles best summarizes the content of the passage?

   (a) How a Genius Gets His Ideas
   (b) A Student of Science, Weather, and Many Other Subjects
   (c) Benjamin Franklin: Man of Many Interests and Achievements
   (d) The Real Story of the Declaration of Independence   8. _____

9. *Poor Richard's Almanack* is the name of a (a) ballad of the Revolutionary War (b) Franklin's autobiography (c) successful book (d) forerunner of the Declaration of Independence.   9. _____

10. All the following were mentioned as inventions by Franklin EXCEPT a (a) stove (b) lightning rod (c) turkey roaster (d) magnifying glass.   10. _____

11. The author feels that Franklin's present reputation (a) doesn't do him justice (b) is less than it was a hundred years ago (c) should depend only on his contributions to the Declaration of Independence (d) rests on the *Autobiography*.   11. _____

12. "We hold these truths to be self-evident" comes from (*a*) *Poor Richard's Almanack* (*b*) Franklin's *Autobiography* (*c*) the Declaration of Independence (*d*) the Constitution of the United States.   12. _____

13. In the last paragraph, *attained* means (*a*) imitated (*b*) reached (*c*) sought (*d*) described.   13. _____

14. "When the well's dry, we know the worth of water" really means that (*a*) we can make the most of any drought (*b*) irrigation canals can be used to grow crops (*c*) we seldom really learn from experience (*d*) we appreciate something most when it is lost.   14. _____

C. Read the following passage and answer the questions at the end.

Certain plants and animals can survive under what seem like impossible conditions. Blind fish flourish at ocean depths that are perennially dark and cold. Bacteria live at temperatures of 600°F or higher in places where heat from the earth's interior leaks through. One of the most remarkable achievements that we can observe directly is the ability of plants and animals to survive in the desert.

In Death Valley, temperatures of 134°F in the shade have been officially recorded. Yet lizards live there, along with 600 species of plants, 30 species of mammals, and even fish. While the days are brutally hot, the nights are quite cold. Temperatures can plunge by as much as 50°F.

Plants called *xerophytes* are perfectly adapted to the extremely dry conditions. These plants have survived by developing techniques for coping with their environment. Like all living things, they must have water, and they get it in several ways.

The mesquite and the prickly pear pick up moisture in opposite ways. The mesquite sends its roots down as deep as 60 feet to tap the water table. The prickly pear, on the other hand, spreads its roots wide. These roots are shallow but they pick up whatever moisture is available at ground level. The paloverde saves water by shedding leaves in times of extreme drought. The creosote bush discourages competition by killing other plants that grow too close. The barrel cactus makes sure of a water supply by storing water in the plant itself. The saguaro cactus stores so much water it can survive years of drought. But even the saguaro will die sooner or later if there is no rain. All these plants, although well adjusted to their environment, must eventually get water.

Even if the parent plants die, there are always seeds to keep the species alive. Since the desert is so harsh, thousands of seeds must be released to produce one plant. To germinate, seeds must have exactly the right conditions. They can lie dormant for months, even years, until a little water stimulates the spark of life.

15. Write the letter of the statement that best expresses the main idea of the passage.

   (a) Death Valley is a living museum, where many kinds of animals exist side by side.
   (b) Days in the desert can be scorching, but nights can be cold.
   (c) Bacteria survive in the depths of the ocean and in the blazing desert heat.
   (d) Plants and animals can survive in the desert, one of the most inhospitable places on earth.   15. _____

16. The number of plant species in Death Valley is listed as (a) 30 (b) 50 (c) 134 (d) 600.   16. _____

17. The prickly pear survives by (a) sending its roots down 60 feet (b) shedding leaves in times of drought (c) spreading its roots wide (d) killing other plants that grow too close.   17. _____

18. At great ocean depths, fish are blind because (a) their surroundings are so dark (b) a chemical in the water destroys their eyesight (c) the water is so cold (d) the pressure is so great.   18. _____

19. We can guess that the word *xerophyte* comes from two Greek roots that mean (a) ''water shed'' (b) ''dry plant'' (c) ''steam bath'' (d) ''hot night.''   19. _____

20. Of the following expressions, the one that is figurative is (a) *dry conditions* (b) *blind fish* (c) *barrel cactus* (d) *quite cold.*   20. _____

21. For the average reader, the information presented is (a) dull (b) surprising (c) trivial (d) misleading.   21. _____

D. Read the following passage and answer the questions at the end.

Mountain folk in the Appalachian region have always been thrifty. They practiced recycling long before it became fashionable in the rest of the country. Mountaineers put everything to use for as long as possible. Worn-out shoes, for example, became door hinges. Old buckets became stools or were cut into strips for chimney flashing.

During the first half of this century, the mountain folk used newspapers for wallpaper. The paper was not only decorative but practical. It doubled as insulation and sealed the small cracks in the walls. There were general rules for pasting up newspapers on walls; it was not a haphazard process. Within those rules, people showed great individuality. Outsiders might consider the designs jumbled, but actually the application of the printed pages was quite orderly.

Before starting to paper, the mountaineers made a thin paste of flour and boiling water. They made the paste thin enough to spread evenly and thick enough to stay in place. Since mice love the taste of flour, red pepper and rat poison were sometimes added to the paste. The paste was given a pleasant aroma by the addition of sweet anise and arrowroot. Thus, the papering gave the room a fresh new smell as well as a new look.

Sometimes there was not enough of one kind of paper to go around. Then two or more kinds were used, but they were chosen according to a system. For instance, if there was not enough newsprint to cover four walls, the paperer might select catalog pages for one wall. But the two types of paper would not be mixed on the same wall.

Magazine paper was much prized. It was heavier, more durable, and more resistant to fading than newsprint. An old *Saturday Evening Post*, with its many illustrations, was a treasure. Pictures of flowers, Christmas scenes, and favorite landscapes were given prominent places. Pictures of food might be placed in the kitchen. Recipes were pasted near the stove. This separation of pictures was especially noticeable when pages from Sears or Montgomery Ward catalogs were used. Pictures of toys were pasted in boys' rooms, while pictures of dresses and furniture were pasted in girls' rooms.

This custom seems quaint to many people today, but it suited the mountain people. Everything was recycled, and newspapers and magazines were no exception. The readily available paper provided excellent wall covering at little expense. Moreover, the printing on the paper was probably as interesting as the designs on costly wallpaper would have been.

Some paperers preferred newspapers without illustrations to give a uniform effect. Others sought pictures of various kinds. The Sunday funny papers were popular in families with children. Comic strips would be applied at eye level so that the children could read them easily. Since newsprint fades rapidly, the walls had to be repapered quite frequently. Children liked that, because it gave them new cartoons to look at.

22. Which of the following titles best summarizes the content of the passage?

    (a) Unusual Customs of Mountain Folk in the Appalachian Region
    (b) The *Saturday Evening Post:* A Treasure for Decorating
    (c) How the Mountaineers Used Newspapers and Magazines for Wallpaper
    (d) Waste Not: Want Not   22. _____

23. Red pepper was added to flour paste to (a) make the room fragrant (b) help the paper stick better (c) make the paper peelable later on (d) discourage mice.   23. _____

24. The mountain people made door hinges out of (a) old buckets (b) shoes (c) stools (d) newspapers.   24. _____

25. The paper was applied to the walls (a) casually (b) hastily (c) thoughtfully (d) unwillingly.   25. _____

26. The recycling actions of the mountain folk would be especially applauded by modern (a) environmentalists (b) museum attendants (c) newspaper editors (d) newspaper publishers.   26. _____

27. Two words that can be applied to the use of newspaper as wallpaper are (a) *decorative* and *practical* (b) *inexpensive* and *unattractive* (c) *colorful* but *impractical* (d) *ingenious* but *foolish*.   27. _____

28. Which of the following is an opinion?

    (*a*) They practiced recycling long before it became fashionable in the rest of the country.
    (*b*) During the first half of this century, the mountain folk used newspapers for wallpaper.
    (*c*) Sometimes there was not enough of one kind of paper to go around.
    (*d*) Moreover, the printing on the paper was probably as interesting as the designs of costly wallpaper would have been.   28. _____

29. The author assumes that readers (*a*) have some interest in the customs of regional America (*b*) have an extensive experience in arts and crafts (*c*) look down upon the poor efforts of mountaineers to decorate their homes (*d*) will seek to learn from this how to decorate their own homes.   29. _____

E. Read the following passage and answer the questions at the end.

Why did glass mugs that were produced several hundred years ago have bumps on the outside? Couldn't the glassmakers of the time do any better? As a matter of fact, they could, and the bumps were put there for a purpose. People used to eat meat with their fingers. Holding a glass mug with greasy fingers is anything but easy. To prevent greasy fingers from slipping, glassmakers added the bumps.

That is just one of the things a person learns from a visit to the Corning Museum of Glass in Corning, New York. In the museum are more than 2,400 drinking vessels. In addition, there are glass lamps, tables, and even a glass musical instrument. Many of the objects are very valuable. One of the most precious of these pieces is a glass replica of the head of an Egyptian pharaoh made about 3,000 years ago. Even though it is only about an inch and a half high, it is superbly cast, elegant, and one of the many highlights of a visit to the museum.

A number of the treasures feature birds. A Bohemian goblet pictures a phoenix-like creature above a city of Silesia. Another goblet, this one from England, shows a golden bird displayed against a blue and red crest. On a Venetian bottle, several birds with spectacular plumage sit amid images of strawberries and spring flowers. All of this glassware is beautifully designed and exquisitely cut.

The museum is the second largest glass museum in the world. Only the Museum of Applied Arts in Prague has a larger collection. Yet this storehouse of treasures was almost destroyed beyond repair. Corning is situated on the Chemung River, a tributary of the Susquehanna. In 1972, Hurricane Agnes caused disastrous floods in the region. The rampaging Chemung tore through the museum, wrecking display cases and damaging many of the glass objects. A number of treasures were shattered and never reassembled. Five hundred other items had to be pieced together from fragments embedded in mud.

Specialists from all over the world hastened to the scene to offer their assistance. Authorities worried that since a flood had happened once, it could happen again. A new museum building was constructed 13 feet above the flood plain instead of five feet, as before. The glass treasures are now in a safer, less vulnerable home.

30. Which of the following titles best summarizes the content of the passage?

    (*a*) A History of Glass
    (*b*) The Corning Glass Museum
    (*c*) The Art of Glassblowing
    (*d*) A New Home for the Corning Glass Museum   30. _____

31. A goblet with a golden bird pictured comes from (*a*) Silesia (*b*) Egypt (*c*) Prague (*d*) England.   31. _____

32. The Chemung River (*a*) is in Silesia (*b*) was spared by Hurricane Agnes (*c*) runs into the Susquehanna (*d*) is actually just a brook.   32. _____

33. All the following are mentioned as included in the Corning Museum EXCEPT (*a*) tables (*b*) lamps (*c*) drinking vessels (*d*) dishes.   33. _____

34. The bumps on glass mugs were (*a*) useful (*b*) decorative (*c*) colored (*d*) imperfections in the glass.   34. _____

35. In the future, experts think that (*a*) no other museum will be as well attended as the Corning (*b*) glassblowing will never be as good as in the past (*c*) experts will refuse to come from around the world to help (*d*) the river will not rise 13 feet.   35. _____

36. Which of the following is an opinion?

    (*a*) People used to eat meat with their fingers.
    (*b*) Even though it is only about an inch and a half high, it is superbly cast, elegant.
    (*c*) Corning is situated on the Chemung River.
    (*d*) A number of treasures were shattered and never reassembled.

                                                                    36. _____

F. Read the following passage and answer the questions at the end.

American history is filled with fascinating stories that never get into standard textbooks. One of the most unusual is that of the Indian Stream Republic, a tiny ''nation'' that existed from 1832 to 1835 but is all but forgotten now. The area is today part of northern New Hampshire, but for three years long ago it struggled to remain independent.

How did this republic come into existence? The answer lies in the problem of defining a boundary between Canada and the United States. The Treaty of Paris, signed at the end of the American Revolution, attempted to draw an accurate line between the United States and Canada, but in some places the boundary remained vague. One of those places was at the ''northwesternmost head of the Connecticut River.'' As writer Edward Park says, ''In all that maze of boggy ponds and rain-rushing brooks, who could say for certain which was the topmost trickle of the mighty Connecticut?'' Canada claimed one boundary. New Hampshire claimed another.

At the time of the treaty, no white inhabitants lived in the area between the two boundaries. But beginning about 1800, land speculators started to move in. Farmers began to settle there. By 1824, there were 58 families living in the region. Were they Canadians or Americans?

The fact is, the families felt that they were being mistreated by both countries. New Hampshire was levying taxes. Canada had drafted two boys into its army. On July 9, 1832, the annoyed citizens established the republic of the united ''inhabitants of the Indian Stream Territory.'' They even drew up a constitution.

Neither Canada nor the United States recognized the tiny nation. A number of incidents and minor skirmishes occurred, but the little republic never had much hope of prevailing. New Hampshire sent in a regiment of militia to establish its claim to the region. In 1842, the matter was finally settled by treaty, and the disputed territory was given to New Hampshire. The Indian Stream Republic was incorporated as the New Hampshire town of Pittsburg.

37. Write the letter of the statement that best expresses the main idea of the passage.

   (a) The United States and Canada once had a border dispute.
   (b) Northern New Hampshire is a land of many ponds and brooks.
   (c) The Indian Stream Republic had a brief but fascinating history.
   (d) The Indian Stream Republic is now part of the United States.   37. _____

38. The border dispute arose because (a) the origin of the Connecticut River is unclear (b) the inhabitants tried to keep out all newcomers (c) the Treaty of Paris was unfair (d) New Hampshire was unreasonable.   38. _____

39. Edward Park is a (a) farmer (b) soldier (c) inhabitant of the Indian Stream Republic (d) writer.   39. _____

40. The inhabitants of the Indian Stream Republic favored (a) annexation to Canada (b) annexation to the United States (c) independence (d) close ties with England.   40. _____

41. The date for the establishment of the Indian Stream Republic is (a) 1800 (b) 1824 (c) 1832 (d) 1842.   41. _____

42. As used in the last paragraph, *skirmishes* means (a) disagreements (b) small fights (c) pitched battles (d) get-togethers.   42. _____

43. The tone of the passage is (a) disturbed (b) calm (c) amused (d) excitable.   43. _____

G. Read the following passage and answer the questions at the end.

One of the world's greatest painters was ''lost'' for almost 200 years. Jan Vermeer van Delft is today ranked among the finest artists of the remarkable Dutch Renaissance in the 17th century, but his fame came late. For a long time, his works were confused with those of his contemporaries, painters who had outstanding talent but lacked the towering genius of Vermeer. Pieter de Hooch, Gabriel Metsu, and Gerard Ter Borch were tremendously skilled painters, but Vermeer's work stands above that of even these gifted artists.

What do we know about the life of this forgotten genius? Not as much as we would like to know. He was born on October 31, 1632, in Delft. He married before he was 21. Originally, he had no idea of supporting his family by painting. He moved his wife into his parents' house and helped to run his father's tavern. During this period, he began to deal in the art of other painters. He bought and sold paintings rather than creating them. Soon his father died, and Vermeer closed down the tavern, but he kept the art trade going.

Within a few years, Vermeer himself began painting seriously. For 19 years, from 1653 to 1672, he painted pictures that are bright and luminous, capturing a ray of sunlight on a delicate tapestry, revealing the textures of many kinds of fabrics. Fewer than 30 of these great paintings survive, but they have established his reputation as one of the great Old Masters.

How did he acquire his skill? With whom did he study? We don't know. As a child, he may have been sent as an apprentice to the Delft painter Leonaert Bramer. If he did not learn his craft from Bramer, he may at least have gained from him an appreciation of the great masters. Vermeer owned a number of fine canvases by other painters, some of which appear in his interior scenes as part of the background. Carel Fabritius may also have influenced Vermeer, but no one knows for sure. Like most other assertions about this 17th-century genius, it is only a guess.

> Vermeer's life was too short. In 1672, France declared war and invaded the Netherlands. Nonessential business came to a standstill. This cut off Vermeer's income, but with 13 people to support, he still had major expenses. He began to exchange his own paintings for food at the local stores. These marvelous paintings survived, but Vermeer did not. He died in 1675 at the age of 43.

44. Write the letter of the statement that best expresses the main idea of the passage.

    (a) Dutch painters of the 17th century were tremendously gifted artists.
    (b) Jan Vermeer at one time was an important dealer in the works of other painters.
    (c) An artist often has a remarkably varied career, though a short one.
    (d) Jan Vermeer belongs in the top rank of Dutch Renaissance artists.   44. _____

45. When Vermeer began dealing in the works of other artists, he was (a) already an active artist himself (b) a tavern keeper (c) a close friend of Gabriel Metsu (d) a soldier in the army of the Netherlands.   45. _____

46. The surviving paintings of Vermeer are (a) in dozens of museums around the world (b) mostly outdoor scenes (c) few in number (d) not favored by certain critics.   46. _____

47. All the following Dutch painters are mentioned EXCEPT (a) Fabritius (b) Rembrandt (c) Metsu (d) Bramer.   47. _____

48. From paragraphs 2 and 3, we can infer that Vermeer began painting at the age of (a) 19 (b) 21 (c) 30 (d) 43.   48. _____

49. Old Masters are (a) outstanding painters of the past (b) artists especially skilled in painting house interiors (c) the teachers of great artists (d) past dealers who have recognized the genius of great artists.   49. _____

50. Each of the following contains a figurative expression EXCEPT (a) towering genius (b) born on October 31, 1632 (c) came to a standstill (d) cut off Vermeer's income.   50. _____

END OF READING PRACTICE TEST 3

Reading Practice Test 4

Reading Practice Test 4 consists of seven passages (**A** to **G**), together with the questions based upon them.

A. Read the following passage and answer the questions at the end.

Once upon a time, amusement parks were fairly simple in design and conservative in the rides offered. There was always a roller coaster to tempt the stout-hearted. Then there was a carousel for the children or less daring adults. There were also a number of other rides that spun around, dipped and twisted, providing a variety of motion sensations. There was always a Ferris wheel, towering above the other attractions. This is still the description of state and county fairs.

Then, along came Disneyland, with its introduction of themes: Adventureland, Tomorrowland, Fantasyland, and Frontierland. Thus began the age of popular theme parks. Sea World, Frontier Village, Six Flags Over Georgia, Six Flags Over Texas, and Kings Dominion—these theme parks flourished, and a new concept took hold.

There were still other changes to come. Amusement parks entered the age of technology, the application of science for practical purposes. World's fairs, like those in Knoxville, New Orleans, and Seattle, provided glimpses into the future. Walt Disney's Epcot, next to Walt Disney World in Florida, provided an ever-changing examination of technological advances, along with visits to many nations in miniature. But perhaps the most dramatic and thrilling uses of technology were demonstrated in amusement rides around the country.

Thrill rides became the major attraction of these parks. Roller coasters were still popular, of course, though park owners tried to make them even more scary. Variations on the roller coaster dared visitors to be sent at breakneck speed into dangerous curves and breathtaking loop-the-loops. Kings Island, near Cincinnati, billed its four-million-dollar Vortex as the first roller coaster with six upside-down turns. Typhoon Lagoon, another Disney creation, planned a 50-acre water-entertainment village. It boasted a 95-foot mountain with nine water slides, a 2.5-acre wave-making lagoon, and a saltwater snorkeling pool.

There was more to come. Visitors demanded even more sophisticated entertainment. In 1987, Disneyland in California opened its Star Tours attraction. On the 4½-minute ride, passengers take a simulated space voyage, using an ingenious flight simulator like those used to train jumbo-jet pilots. The machine twists and turns to avoid meteorites and laser cannon blasts in a "Star Wars" experience. Passengers really feel as if they are flying.

What next? Many officials predict that the next wave of attractions will be "interactive rides." On these rides, guests will press buttons or levers to choose the experience they are seeking. Because these will, in effect, be creating many different possibilities, guests will be eager for repeat rides.

Amusement parks have come a long way from the mild roller coaster and gentle merry-go-round, but the central purpose is still the same: to provide visitors entertainment, thrills, and out-of-the-ordinary experiences. Who knows what the amusement park will look like twenty-five years from now!

1. Which of the following titles best summarizes the content of the passage?

   (a) How Disneyland Got Started
   (b) The Changing American Amusement Park
   (c) The Influence of the County Fair on Amusement Parks
   (d) How Disneyland Changed Amusement Parks   1. _____

2. All the following are mentioned as a part of state and county fairs EXCEPT (a) carousel (b) roller coaster (c) Ferris wheel (d) loop-the-loop.   2. _____

3. The word that includes the three other words is (a) *Tomorrowland* (b) *Fantasyland* (c) *Disneyland* (d) *Frontierland*.   3. _____

4. The Walt Disney organization owns (a) Sea World (b) Typhoon Lagoon (c) Kings Dominion (d) Six Flags Over Georgia.   4. _____

5. A ride on the Vortex is probably (a) thrilling (b) wet (c) mild (d) too short.   5. _____

6. "Interactive rides" (a) give people choices (b) were introduced by Kings Island (c) are becoming out-of-date (d) are common in state fairs.   6. _____

7. An example of figurative language is the expression (*a*) *simple in design* (*b*) *practical purposes* (*c*) *breakneck speed* (*d*) *wave-making lagoon*.

7. _____

8. The author's attitude toward amusement parks is one of (*a*) active concern (*b*) casual indifference (*c*) keen interest (*d*) mild disapproval.

8. _____

B. Read the following passage and answer the questions at the end.

Every weekend in suburban America, optimistic homeowners are holding garage sales. Instead of throwing out old furniture, utensils, and all kinds of odds and ends, these weekend salespersons are selling unwanted objects at a small fraction of their original cost. Happy browsers examine the merchandise, socialize with the sellers, and often go home with a treasure all their own.

According to students of garage sales, these increasingly popular events originated in the 1960s as more and more Americans moved to suburbia. Since that time, the sales have become big business. In 1984, the number of garage sales outnumbered births and deaths combined. By 1987, garage sales generated two billion dollars in annual revenue. Sellers needn't own garages. There are lawn sales, yard sales, and other variations of the original.

There are many identifiable appeals that draw buyers to the sales. First and foremost is the treasure-hunt possibility. Who knows what wonderful relics of the past may find their way to garage sales? Professional buyers recognize this possibility and often arrive at garage sales before anyone else—to pick over the items being offered. Many a fine antique has been discovered in a garage.

Second, there is the possibility of getting a bargain, finding a needed item and paying a tiny fraction of its usual retail price. Young couples starting out in life together can furnish their homes with used-but-sound pieces that have outlived their usefulness elsewhere. Dishes, utensils, pots and pans, chairs and tables—these find a second life in many a newlywed's home.

Third, there are the bored, who find garage sales a welcome diversion on a dull weekend. They may not be interested in buying anything, but their presence stimulates others to buy. They enjoy the animated conversation that often follows a question about a piece being offered.

Fourth, there are the scholars, who study garage sales as keenly as if they were religious rites of a primitive tribe. These researchers insist that garage sales tell us a great deal about ourselves, about our buying habits, about the fads and fancies that come and go in American life. They enjoy garage sales as a slice of life and an insight into history.

Whatever the motivation, garage sales grow more popular each year. They act like a marketplace in an old European town. They also provide a gathering place for neighbors who rarely see each other throughout the rest of the year. They can even help a community become more closely knit. The garage sale is a useful merchandising idea.

9. Write the letter of the statement that best expresses the main idea of the passage.

   (a) Garage sales are being studied by researchers and social historians.
   (b) Professional buyers comb garage sales for values overlooked by the sellers.
   (c) Garage sales have come to take an important place in American life.
   (d) Garage sales really deal with junk, not expensive items.   9. _____

10. All the following are mentioned as attending a garage sale EXCEPT (a) professional buyers (b) bargain hunters (c) scholars (d) manufacturers.   10. _____

11. For most items in a garage sale, the major sales appeal is (a) price (b) durability of object (c) rarity (d) novelty.   11. _____

12. As used in paragraph 5, *diversion* means (a) purchase (b) pastime (c) mild argument (d) trip.   12. _____

13. The passage implies that (a) by far, the major appeal of the garage sale is the possibility of finding a valuable antique (b) most items in a garage sale are not valuable (c) scholars are the most enthusiastic purchasers at a garage sale (d) buyers at a garage sale do not get their money's worth.   13. _____

14. Which of the following is an example of figurative language?

    (*a*) Homeowners are selling these unwanted objects at a small fraction of their original cost.
    (*b*) Many a fine antique has been discovered in a garage.
    (*c*) There is the possibility of getting a bargain.
    (*d*) They enjoy garage sales as a slice of life.   14. _____

15. Which of the following is an opinion?

    (*a*) In 1984, the number of garage sales outnumbered births and deaths combined.
    (*b*) Sellers needn't own garages.
    (*c*) These find a second life in many a newlywed's home.
    (*d*) The garage sale is a useful merchandising idea.   15. _____

C. Read the following passage and answer the questions at the end.

> Driving through the Blue Ridge Mountains of Virginia and North Carolina, tourists often see a melancholy sight. In a field overrun with weeds and small trees, there will be a lonely chimney. The house that once depended upon the chimney for warmth has long since disappeared. The chimney, perhaps along with a lilac bush, is the only evidence that a farmhouse or mountain cabin once stood there.
>
> With the arrival of oil, gas, and electrical heat, the chimney nearly disappeared from residential buildings, except for the popular fireplace used as an occasional supplement to the heating system. The serious oil shortages of the 1970s brought back woodburning stoves to many houses. With those stoves came chimneys.
>
> The smoking chimney is often criticized as a visible symbol of air pollution. Yet the chimney is not the cause. It is actually a device for reducing surface air pollution. The pollution itself comes from the factories, mills, and utility plants that help make our civilization possible. Smokestacks, which are merely tall chimneys, remove smoke and gases that pollute those living or working at ground level and disperse the offenders into the upper atmosphere. Devices for removing many pollutants before they are loosed into the atmosphere provide some hope for the future. But the chimneys are not the villains.

In earliest days, chimneys did not exist. A hole in the roof or slats in the wall were intended to keep indoor atmosphere bearable. Then someone invented the chimney to remove smoke from the room while allowing for radiant heat to warm the inhabitants. The excavation of the ancient city of Mari on the Euphrates River uncovered a palace with chimneys nearly 4,000 years old. The idea of the chimney may have been brought to Europe from the East by traders more than 1,200 years ago. The idea took hold, though only the wealthy and powerful at first had chimneys. In the 11th century, King Olaf III of Norway installed corner fireplaces with chimneys in the royal residence.

Many of these old chimneys have long since disappeared. The oldest chimneys still standing are in a 12th-century abbey where Henry II of England, his wife, Eleanor of Aquitaine, and their son Richard the Lion-Hearted are buried. Paintings from 15th-century Europe show that by then chimneys had become commonplace. Chimney building had become an art, with secrets closely guarded from one generation of chimney builders to the next. A poorly designed chimney will not draw properly, nor will it heat the room in which the fireplace is located.

There are sad footnotes to the chimney story. Inevitably, soot accumulated. From time to time, chimneys had to be cleaned. The flues were often small, no wider than the length of two bricks. Many young children in England were hired as chimney sweeps. These "climbing boys," as they were called, were supposed to be no younger than eight years of age. Often they were no more than four. They were forced to climb up the chimney, crying and complaining. Sometimes they were prodded from below by pins stuck into their bare feet. They spent their lives in black dirt and generally died young from cancer or lung disease. It was not until 1875 that these cruelties were banned by Parliament.

Cleaning up the atmosphere by installing antipollution devices on chimneys is a long and expensive task. But something must be done to decrease the acid rain that forms from industrial pollutants. The chimney is a part of this polluting process, but it is not the cause.

16. Which of the following titles best summarizes the content of the passage?

    (a) The Abuse of Children
    (b) A History and a Defense of Chimneys
    (c) Chimneys: An Ancient Device
    (d) The Problems of Pollution in Modern Society   16. _____

17. The earliest chimneys in Europe were built for (a) Henry II of England (b) Richard the Lion-Hearted (c) Olaf III of Norway (d) Eleanor of Aquitaine.   17. _____

18. Which of the following is NOT a true statement?

    (a) Smokestacks are tall chimneys.
    (b) ''Climbing boys'' are chimney sweeps.
    (c) Acid rain forms from industrial pollutants.
    (d) Children younger than eight did not serve as climbing boys.   18. _____

19. The hole in the roof as a smoke outlet (a) disappeared soon after the founding of the city of Mari (b) was never satisfactory (c) occurs in many cabins in the Blue Ridge Mountains (d) was never generally used.   19. _____

20. As used in paragraph 3, *disperse* means (a) scatter (b) identify (c) conceal (d) concentrate.   20. _____

21. Which of the following is an example of figurative language?

    (a) But the chimneys are not the villains.
    (b) In earliest days, chimneys did not exist.
    (c) Inevitably, soot accumulated.
    (d) They were forced to climb up the chimney, crying and complaining.   21. _____

22. The author's purpose is to (a) have readers look at chimneys in a different way (b) mention ways in which pollution may be overcome (c) show his own insight and wisdom (d) hold up chimneys as a work of art.   22. _____

23. The author's attitude toward the use of ''climbing boys'' is one of (a) intelligent interest (b) keen disapproval (c) unconcealed curiosity (d) mild puzzlement.   23. _____

D. Read the following passage and answer the questions at the end.

Two knights circle each other warily. Swords are brandished. First one rushes in, then the other, hoping to catch the opponent off guard. At last there is an opening. As the opponent rushes in with his mace to finish the combat, the waiting combatant twists his sword upward to blunt the attacking mace. Then he strikes a final blow to the opponent's head, "decapitating" him. But the defeated warrior lifts the visor of his helmet and puts his arm around the man who has just "slain" him. It's all make-believe.

The herald cries out, "Victor by Death—Lord Geoffrey Maynard of York." Then he adds, "The King announces court will be held in the Great Hall in 20 minutes." The brightly clothed spectators begin the walk toward the hall.

What is going on here? Why are all these modern people dressed like characters from the Middle Ages? What was that combat all about? This is a field day for a special group calling themselves the Society for Creative Anachronism. *Anachronism* is a misplacing of events in time. Just as an automobile would be an anachronism at the court of Charlemagne, so knights are an anachronism in the present. This society has members around the world, all of whom try to relive the life that existed between the fall of Rome and 1600 A.D.

Why do they bother? They like a change. Everyday life can get to seem humdrum. Events tend to be cut-and-dried, predictable. A 9–5 job may leave workers daydreaming of a more colorful time. True, the glamorous days of the past were often times of ignorance, discomfort, cruelty, pestilence, and violent death. Members of the society, however, prefer to emphasize the brighter side: the color, the pageantry, the code of honor, and the romance. For a while, they can live in a splendid fantasy world, where all men are gallant, all women beautiful, and everyone immortal.

For the society, the world is divided into various kingdoms, each with its own king and queen. Most of the state of Florida, for example, is designated the Kingdom of Trimaris. Trimaris holds its own feast days, with simulated combat. Titles are earned in various ways. Coats of arms are issued when the king honors a member by creating him or her a lord or lady. Coats of arms may be earned for deeds of service to the society.

As "Lord Lance" Nystrom, a herald of the society, explains, "Everything members do is voluntary. People who work in the kitchen at feasts stand a pretty good chance of receiving a title."

Members carry the fantasy into areas other than costuming. They get into the spirit by eating authentic medieval-period foods. They collect anything connected with the medieval period.

The king is chosen by combat, but the fighting is safe. Instead of steel weapons, rattan is used. A blow to a limb is considered an amputation, and a blow to the head, decapitation. The latter event ends the combat, as does a blow to any other part of the body except the limbs. The king rules for six months and then is replaced by another.

Members of the Society for Creative Anachronism may be playing at make-believe like children, but they are having fun and are harming no one. Perhaps all sports and activities should be equally harmless.

24. Write the letter of the statement that best expresses the main idea of the passage.

   (a) Adults sometimes live out their daydreams just as children do.
   (b) Knights sometimes do battle even in the peaceful fields of Florida.
   (c) Even nowadays it is possible to earn a coat of arms.
   (d) The Society for Creative Anachronism helps members relive the past.   24. _____

25. In paragraph 1, *decapitating* and *slain* are in quotation marks because (a) the words don't mean what they usually mean (b) members make fun of the knights in combat (c) the words are taken from a well-known song about medieval warfare (d) members are forbidden to use these words during a combat.   25. _____

26. An example of an anachronism would be (a) swords at the time of Julius Caesar (b) a theater at the time of William Shakespeare (c) a television set in an old silent movie (d) a spaceship during the presidency of Jimmy Carter.   26. _____

27. As used in paragraph 1, *warily* means (a) cautiously (b) angrily (c) rapidly (d) repeatedly.   27. _____

28. As used in paragraph 5, *simulated* means (*a*) deadly (*b*) pretended (*c*) absurd (*d*) repeated.   28. _____

29. Nystrom suggests that members will earn titles if they (*a*) are wealthy (*b*) do research (*c*) bring in new members (*d*) work unselfishly.   29. _____

30. The attitude of the author toward the Society for Creative Anachronism is (*a*) critical (*b*) scornful (*c*) unbelieving (*d*) sympathetic.   30. _____

E. Read the following passage and answer the questions at the end.

Great European cathedrals have been standing for 800 years or more. The Parthenon has been standing for nearly 2,500 years, even though it was partially destroyed in wartime. The Pyramids have been standing for 5,000 years. These structures were built to endure.

But there is one kind of art or architecture that lasts only a short time. It may take the form of a beautiful cathedral, a splendid castle, a heroic statue, or a miniature city—but it is destined to be destroyed soon after completion. This fleeting creation is built of sand.

At the seashore, children have an irresistible impulse to play in the sand. Just below high water, the sand is wet and plastic. It is easy to mold into various forms. At low tide, the young sculptors begin, working rapidly to complete their structures before the incoming tide destroys everything. The impermanence of the sand sculpture fascinates young people. Watching the rising waters eat away at the foundations, observing the proud turrets as they topple into an incoming wave—these bring *oohs* and *ahs*. There is jubilation, but there is some sadness, too, as the sand castle collapses, its transient shape dissolving.

This children's pastime has attracted adult artists for decades, but the first mammoth sand sculpture is fairly recent. Constructed in 1969, it was a monumental 90-ton sand castle that dominated Moonlight Beach in Southern California. It proved so popular that sand sculpture became increasingly sought after, almost a big business for a few artists. Companies with names like Sand Sculptors International and Sandtastic provide resort hotels, conventions, advertisers, and others with professional sand magic. Some of the sand structures they build are so colossal that the available beach sand is insufficient. In these cases, loads of sand are trucked in.

Painters use oil, ink, acrylic, gouache, and their creations survive. Sand artists use an entirely different material, and their creations are quickly destroyed. Why create something that is fated to wash away in the tide? Sand sculptors consider the short life of a sand castle to be an important part of its appeal. Says one, "There is something to be said for watching the tide roll in and clean your canvas." This is truly ephemeral art.

31. Which of the following titles best summarizes the content of the passage?

    (*a*) Tide: The Destructive Agent
    (*b*) A New Kind of Art
    (*c*) Sculptures in the Sand
    (*d*) A Beach Hobby   31. _____

32. Sand sculptures on a large scale began (*a*) 5,000 years ago (*b*) 2,500 years ago (*c*) in 1969 (*d*) within the past ten years.   32. _____

33. The Parthenon and the Pyramids were mentioned because they are (*a*) tall (*b*) hard to reach (*c*) made of marble (*d*) very old.   33. _____

34. As used in paragraph 3, *jubilation* means (*a*) rejoicing (*b*) disagreement (*c*) sadness (*d*) upset.   34. _____

35. As used in paragraph 3, *transient* means (*a*) bulky (*b*) fleeting (*c*) sturdy (*d*) irregular.   35. _____

36. As used in paragraph 5, *ephemeral* means (*a*) long-lasting (*b*) memorable (*c*) original (*d*) temporary.   36. _____

37. The beautiful cathedral in paragraph 2 (*a*) is made of sand (*b*) stands near Moonlight Beach in Southern California (*c*) is part of a 90-ton structure (*d*) took years to complete.   37. _____

F. Read the following passage and answer the questions at the end.

Of the world's most honored plays, perhaps the best known is Shakespeare's *Hamlet*. There are many reasons for its preeminence. First of all, it is exciting theater. The plot is a rousing one, with plenty of action at key moments. Hamlet may seem at times a creature destroyed by hesitation, but in the course of the play he courageously faces a ghost, traps a king through a trick, accidentally slays a courtier, duels with an old friend, and ultimately kills the king, his stepfather. He himself becomes the victim of treachery, dying by a poisoned sword. There is enough excitement on the stage to satisfy even an unsophisticated spectator.

Second, the settings are varied and intriguing. The lonely, ghost-haunted battlements of Elsinore Castle are contrasted with the brightly lit rooms within the castle. The tense opening scene sets the stage for the tragedy to come, but there are many bright spots and much humor amid the sadness.

Finally, the characters are complex and elusive. The king is a murderer; yet he is genuinely in love with his queen, for whom he commits the murder. The queen dotes on her son Hamlet, though at times she seems more interested in her own pleasures. Polonius, loyal adviser to the king, is a garrulous old man much given to long-winded speeches. His son Laertes is a hothead, a man whose sword is too ready to speak for him. His daughter Ophelia is pretty and obedient, but not very intelligent. The warrior Fortinbras, a foil to the thoughtful Hamlet, is in love with battle and glory. Hamlet's good friend Horatio may be the soundest person in the play, noted for his bravery and his loyalty to Hamlet, but he is an observer, not a participant.

The most interesting and complicated character is of course Hamlet. Many questions arise about him. Is he a man of action, or a man fatally reluctant to act? When the pressures become great, is he actually mad, or does he only feign madness? Does he really love Ophelia? If so, why does he treat her so shabbily? Why does he go off docilely to England when the king sends him? Why doesn't he show more remorse after killing Polonius? There are as many explanations as there are critics.

> Hamlet contains contradictions, because that is the nature of human beings. Hamlet is indecisive, but he is also a man of action. His motives are generally lofty, but sometimes they seem wholly selfish. He is compassionate and cruel in turn. Though basically gentle, he is also ruthless. These contradictions make Hamlet human. There are no final answers, because life has no final answers.

38. Write the letter of the statement that best expresses the main idea of the passage.

    (a) As a play, *Hamlet* reflects the sadness, the complexity, and the inconsistencies of life.
    (b) In *Hamlet*, Shakespeare shows us the problems that arise when people are false.
    (c) The character of Hamlet is one of the most generous and noble in all of literature.
    (d) The gloomy castle of Elsinore is a fit setting for the tragic events in the tale of Hamlet.   38. _____

39. The person identified as a hothead is (a) Horatio (b) Polonius (c) the king (d) Laertes.   39. _____

40. The passage devotes a paragraph to each of the following EXCEPT (a) character (b) language (c) setting (d) plot.   40. _____

41. The passage mentions many questions associated with *Hamlet* and then (a) explains why Hamlet acted as he did (b) leaves them unanswered (c) suggests that Horatio, of all the characters, knows the answers (d) tells why the queen acted as she did.   41. _____

42. As used in paragraph 1, *preeminence* means (a) inferiority (b) contradiction (c) superiority (d) interesting plot.   42. _____

43. As used in paragraph 3, *dotes on* means (a) constantly checks up on (b) pays excessive attention to (c) makes excuses for (d) fails to understand.   43. _____

44. As used in paragraph 3, *garrulous* means (a) loyal (b) observant (c) shrewd (d) talkative.   44. _____

G. Read the following passage and answer the questions at the end.

Mathematicians have always been fascinated by the concept of infinity. Most people think of infinity as "a very large number." That is incorrect. The largest number anyone can think of is no closer to infinity than the number *one*. To a mathematician, the ideas of "very large" and "infinite" are quite different. No number, however great, will ever reach infinity, because infinity, by definition, is boundless and endless. A person cannot "count to infinity."

There are numbers so large that it is hard to comprehend them. But they are still numbers. For instance, how many atoms of oxygen are there in an average thimble? A mathematician might represent the number by writing 1 followed by 27 zeros. That is a very large number, to be sure, but it is tiny when compared with the total number of atoms in the universe. How many drops of water flow over Niagara Falls in a century? The number of drops is about the same as the number of electrons that pass through the filament of an ordinary 50-watt bulb in one minute. The number is huge, but, being a number, it is not infinite.

When dealing with very large numbers, mathematicians use exponents, which indicate numbers multiplied by themselves the number of times shown. This device eliminates writing a lot of extremely long numbers. According to one scientist, raising 10 to the 79th power would include all the electrons in the entire universe. That is a very large number, but it is not as large as a googol. What, you may ask, is a googol?

The mathematician Edward Kasner wanted to coin a word to express 10 to the 100th power. He asked his 9-year-old nephew to suggest one. The boy thought for a moment and said, "Googol." The word has since been adopted by serious mathematicians and scientists everywhere. It is in all standard dictionaries.

Some time later, the same boy suggested a word for a still larger number. When a googol is multiplied by itself googol times, the result is a *googolplex*. How large is a googolplex? If you wanted to write the number, you would not have enough space to write it even if you traveled on a direct line to the farthest star in the farthest nebula, writing zeros all the way.

Now, that's a large number, but it still isn't infinity.

45. Which of the following titles best summarizes the content of the passage?

    (a) The Fascination of Very Large Numbers
    (b) How the Word for a Very Large Number Was Coined
    (c) The Long Road to Infinity
    (d) How Infinity Differs from Large Numbers   45. _____

46. The word for the number 10 to the 100th power is (a) *infinity* (b) *googol* (c) *googolplex* (d) none of these.   46. _____

47. One followed by 27 zeros expresses the number of (a) drops of water flowing over Niagara Falls in a century (b) atoms in the entire universe (c) electrons that pass through a 50-watt bulb filament in a minute (d) atoms of oxygen in an average thimble.   47. _____

48. Which of the following statements is NOT true?

    (a) A child invented a scientific name.
    (b) Infinity is not a number.
    (c) A googol is larger than a googolplex.
    (d) Most people think of infinity as ''a very large number.''   48. _____

49. The comparison of water over Niagara Falls and electrons in a light bulb can be described as (a) commonplace (b) inaccurate (c) dramatic (d) little understood.   49. _____

50. The tone of the passage is (a) light and straightforward (b) breathless and sensational (c) somewhat sarcastic (d) one-sided and argumentative.   50. _____

END OF READING PRACTICE TEST 4

Index